PHOTOGRAPHERS
OF THE THIRD REICH

PHOTOGRAPHERS OF THE THIRD REICH

IMAGES FROM THE WEHRMACHT

PAUL GARSON

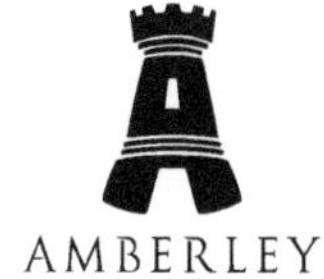

AMBERLEY

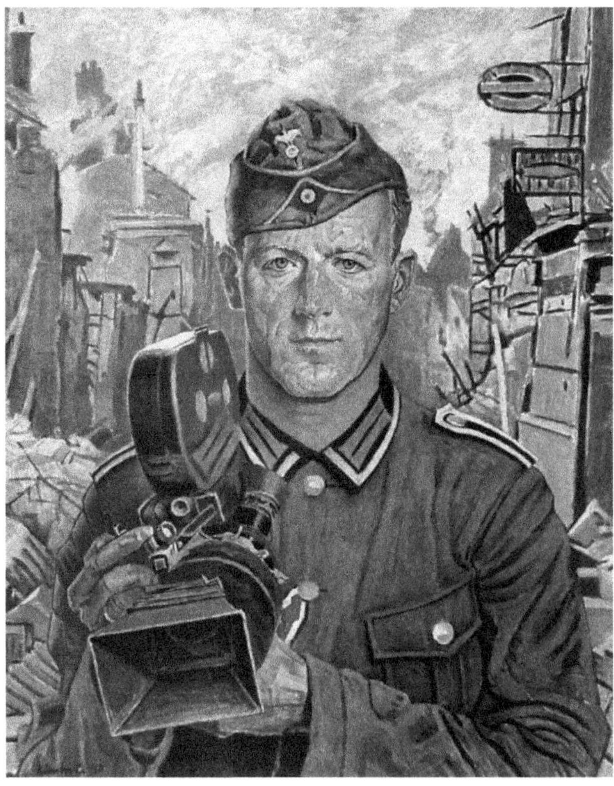

The original portrait of a German general's personal filmographer was painted with the rubble of France as the scenic background, dating it to 1940. It was reproduced on large format art paper and offered for sale to the German public.

First published 2019

Amberley Publishing
The Hill, Stroud
Gloucestershire, GL5 4EP

www.amberley-books.com

British Library Cataloguing in Publication Data.
A catalogue record for this book is available from the British Library.

ISBN 978 1 4456 8718 6 (print)
ISBN 978 1 4456 8719 3 (ebook)

Typesetting by Aura Technology and Software Services, India.
Printed in the UK.

Contents

Introduction

Of the millions of German soldiers who went to war, many brought their personal cameras to chronicle their *Dienstzeit,* or military service, often via meticulously prepared photo albums, as individual 'snapshots' and as custom processed photo postcards sent to family and friends.

No other group of combatants has documented a war in such quantities of images in an era before television, the video camera and satellite link-ups. The range of cameras included the established 127 and 120 photographic film formats, the new developments in 35 mm still cameras and even 8 mm and 16 mm cine cameras. At times the *soldaten* aimed them with the same accuracy as their Mauser rifles and Krupp cannon. In turn, the photos reflect upon the photo-takers, a mirrored view of a mindset clouded by a fatal arrogance, the eye of the beholder blinded by a cruel and rapacious ideology.

Most of the original photographs seen in the following were taken by German amateur cameramen and camerawomen, others commercially reproduced via the vast propaganda machine that in great part foisted the impression of the invincibility of Nazi Germany. That impression, ultimately proved false, still lingers and enthralls. For twelve years, the light went out of the world, and it took millions of hands to bring on the darkness. Many of those hands held weapons and pressed triggers, but many also pressed the shutter buttons of their cameras to record a moment in their lives that happened to have been part and parcel of the Third Reich.

All photos, illustrations, cameras, artwork and artifacts seen in the following pages are from the author's personal collections acquired over several years from sources in Germany, Austria, Argentina, Spain, the US, Britain, Canada, Poland, Estonia, Hungary, Latvia, Lithuania, Russia, Ukraine, Norway, Belgium, Holland, the Netherlands, Italy, Greece, Turkey, Mexico and Israel. Some of the photos were marked with handwritten notations: most unreadable, some decipherable as to date and place, some with inscriptions to family and friends and some with terse cryptic commentary, but in great part anonymous as to the individuals seen and unseen, including the person behind the camera.

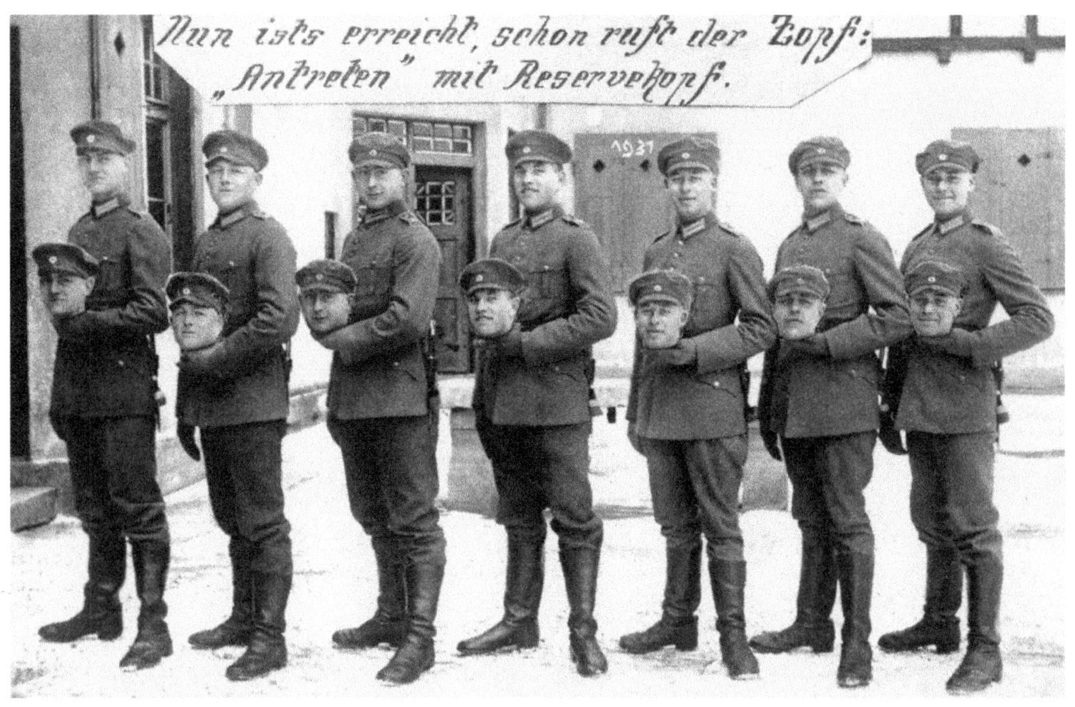

Korps und Kopf

The 'trick' photograph was a popular format for German soldiers looking for a souvenir postcard to send to family and friends. This example's caption relates to attracting recruits to the Reserve Corps in 1931, two years prior to the ascension to power of the Nazi Party. The image could be seen as presaging the barbarity that would engulf Europe or as a graphic metaphor for how the German people would 'lose their heads' over the mesmerizing rantings of Adolf Hitler.

Opposite: Cameras in Action

'Without motor-cars, sound films and wireless, no victory of National Socialism.'

Adolf Hitler

A still image from a newsreel captures Germany's leader surrounded by a sea of followers, including SA men acting as security, while at least three handheld cameras record the moment.

It is a point of conjecture whether the Third Reich could have succeeded in its goals without the malevolent genius of its Propaganda Minister, Josef Goebbels. His control of all Third Reich media and the images and words produced under his direction conjured up a form of mass hypnosis that held a nation in sway and turned millions into either direct or complicit agents of humankind's greatest self-inflicted crime.

The Camera's Role in Documenting the New Order

The camera was seen as having 'the decisive role in forging a new German collective visual memory'. A German Labour Front text summed up the import of the new age of photography in the Third Reich (author's emphasis in bold):

Amateur photography is the patrimony of the whole people and it should perform a useful task the nature of which is more manifest in the Germany of today than it has even been before. The education of the people includes photography and should provide each and every citizen with the technical knowledge to enable them to persevere responsibly in this domain and to control their own cameras. But they should not stop there. The skill required for handling a camera is not enough to create a true photographer but it does set up all the conditions necessary for his creation so that amateur photography may aspire to be one of the major factors in the history of civilization. **Furthermore, it makes possible to leave to one's children and grandchildren a collection of images whose influence is far greater than that of any number of speeches.**

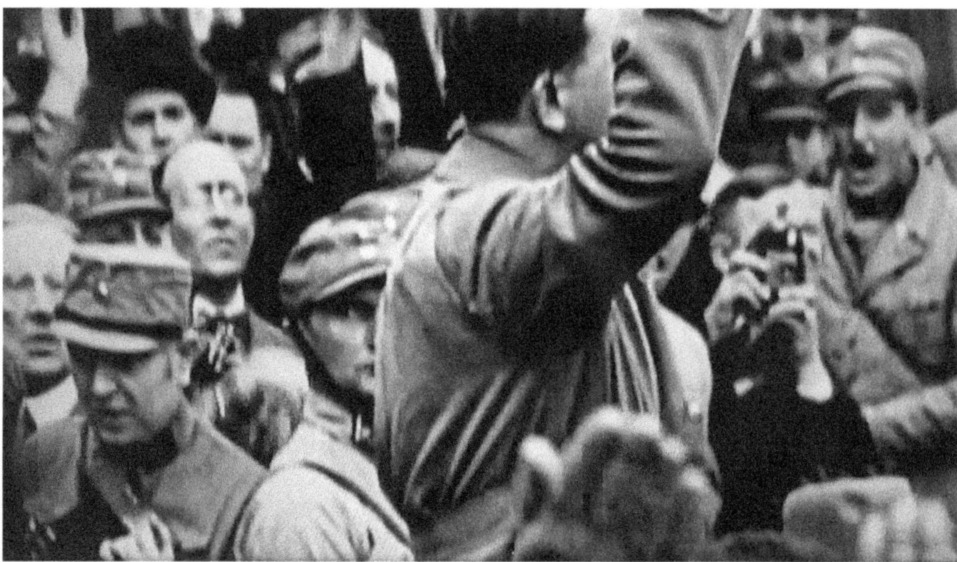

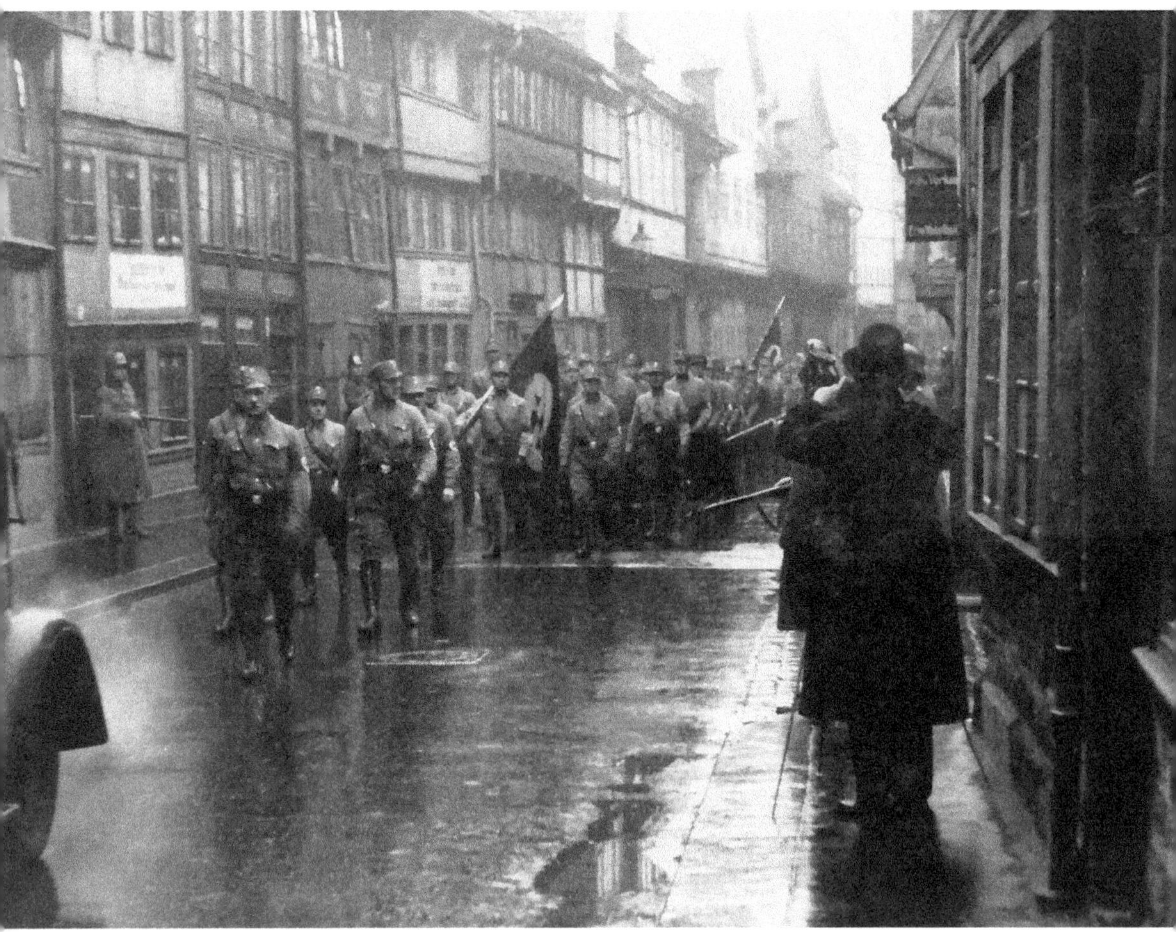

July 1925 Munich Street Demonstration
Marching along rain-wet streets, SA Brownshirts parade through their headquarters city.
Flanking them on the sidewalks, rifles are held ready by the Weimar Republic's military, who
stand aside as the demonstrators pass. An intrepid cameraman (right in hat) snaps his photo as
he himself is caught by another unseen photographer positioned behind him. The Nazi party had
previously been banned by the Weimar Government due to its inflammatory activities, but the
prohibition had been lifted in January 1925.

Specialised Photographic Units – Imagery 'Sells' an Ideology

Propaganda of all types was an integral part of any dictatorship and nowhere else was it more employed, developed and exercised than by Nazi Germany, the State calling on a wealth of designers, artists and photographers to saturate the populace with 'approved' visual media both for Home Front consumption and for the international community.

Under the leadership of Josef Goebbels, Reichsminister of Propaganda as well as controller of the Third Reich film industry, no effort was spared to sear Nazi ideology into the minds of every civilian, and that included documenting the exploits of the various military branches. Joining the effort was General Wilhelm Keitel, Chief of the Supreme Command of the Wehrmacht, when he and Goebbels

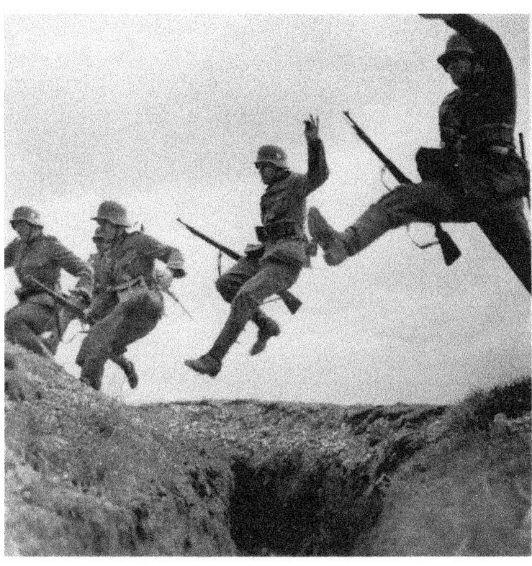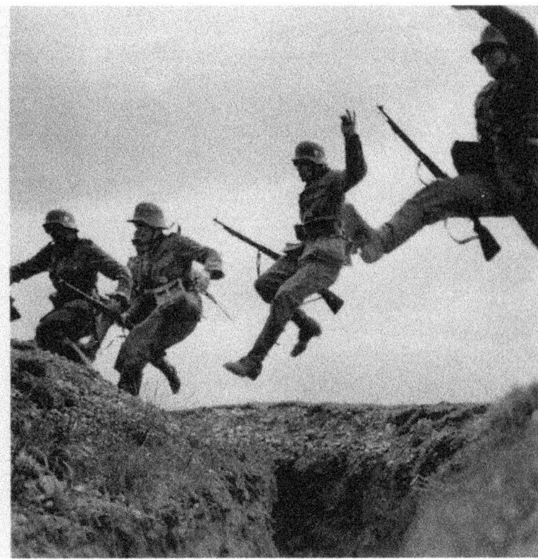

3D Soldiers
The Propaganda Ministry saw to the production and distribution of untold thousands of photos, including several series of stereoscopic images.

co-signed an overall wartime armed forces propaganda campaign in 1938 under the aegis of the *Propagandakompanien der Wehrmacht,* aka PK. As part of the overall strategy, a corps of *Kriegsberichter* (war correspondents, filmmakers and photographers) was established, the cameramen equipped with then state-of-the-art equipment.

Initially the PK units were contained with the Signal Corps, with some five divisions organized, but later finalised as a separate branch unto themselves as the *Hinsicht der Amtsgruppe für Wehrmachtpropaganda* (Official Group for Wehrmacht Propaganda).

A–Z Sampling of German Third Reich-Era Still cameras

A wide spectrum of camera designs was developed in Germany, some companies producing only a few cameras before fading into obscurity, others surviving both world wars and continuing in production today.

Adox

After beginning the production of cameras in the 1930s, Adox soon 'acquired' the already established Wirgin camera factory after its Jewish owner had to flee the country. As a result the Wirgin 35 mm viewfinder camera, the Adrette, began to be produced under the Adox brand name in 1938.

Agfa (*Aktien-Gesellschaft für Anilin-Fabrikation*)

Founded in 1873, by 1930 and the rise of National Socialism Agfa offered its first box camera, one that utilized 6x9 format roll film. In 1931 it created a frenzy of sorts when it began selling its Box 44 camera for only four Deutschmarks, the strategy paying off in the resulting massive sales of the camera's required 120 roll film that the company also offered. In 1937 Agfa launched its first 'modern' 35 mm format, and eventually its cameras and film were well-represented in the hands of German soldiers.

Balda

Models included the 35 folding strut Baldina, which was first produced in the mid-1930s, and the Super Baldina. The camera was also marketed under several different names and remained in production from 1935 to 1941.

Bilora

The company, based in Radevormwald in the North Rhine-Westphalia area of Germany, began making cameras in 1935 starting with a 'box' design known as 'Bilomatic' and continued in production until 1975, by then having produced over 1 million cameras. During the Nazi era, 200 of the Bilora factory town's residents were accused of anti-Nazi sentiments and were sent to the notorious Kemna concentration camp, one of the first established. In the summer of 2005, the story of the camp was documented by the Radevormwald museum exhibit, with a plaque also being commissioned.

Certo

Like the famous Zeiss opticals concern, as of 1905 the Certo company was headquartered in a suburb of Dresden. Its best known pre-Second World War camera was the 35 mm Super Dolina. During the Nazi era the owner hid the production machinery for the camera in the homes of the company's employees, apparently escaping the catastrophic fire-bombing of Dresden. Production resumed post-war, but in East Germany under Soviet control.

Contessa-Nettel Donata

Founded in 1908 in Stuttgart, the company produced the folding bed plate camera 'Donata' and several other models during 1919–26. The hyphenated name was produced by the 1926 merger of two companies, Ica with Ernemann and Goerz, to form the mega-optics company Zeiss-Ikon.

Eho-Altissa

Another Dresden-based camera maker, the brand produced successful medium format box cameras in the early 1930s. These included the unique 'Altissa' line, the 'Altiflex' Twin Lens Reflex in 1937 and then brought out its one and only 35 mm viewfinder camera series in 1939, the 'Altix.'

Ernemann

After launching its first camera, called 'Bob', in 1914 the company brought out a series of folding, roll film and plate designs, including 4x6.5, 6x9 and 8x10.5. The last model was produced in 1926, at which point Ernemann merged with Zeiss.

Eumig

Located in Austria since 1919, its movie camera production included the Eumig C1 for 9.5 mm film in 1932 and the C3/4 using 8 mm in 1937. The C4 was the first 8 mm amateur movie camera to feature electric power drive.

C. F. Foth & Co. (Foth)

Founded in 1926, the Berlin-based company produced cameras and lenses until 1943, in the midst of the war. Their best known is the Foth Derby vest pocket strut folder using 127 film. Also marketed in Third Reich ally Japan, it was touted in ads as a 'Sportscamera'.

Franka

In 1936, the company brought out its Solida 6x6 folding camera in various forms.

Goerz

Founded in 1886 by Carl Paul Goerz and based in a suburb of Berlin, it produced optical instruments as well as searchlights for the German and Austrian military.

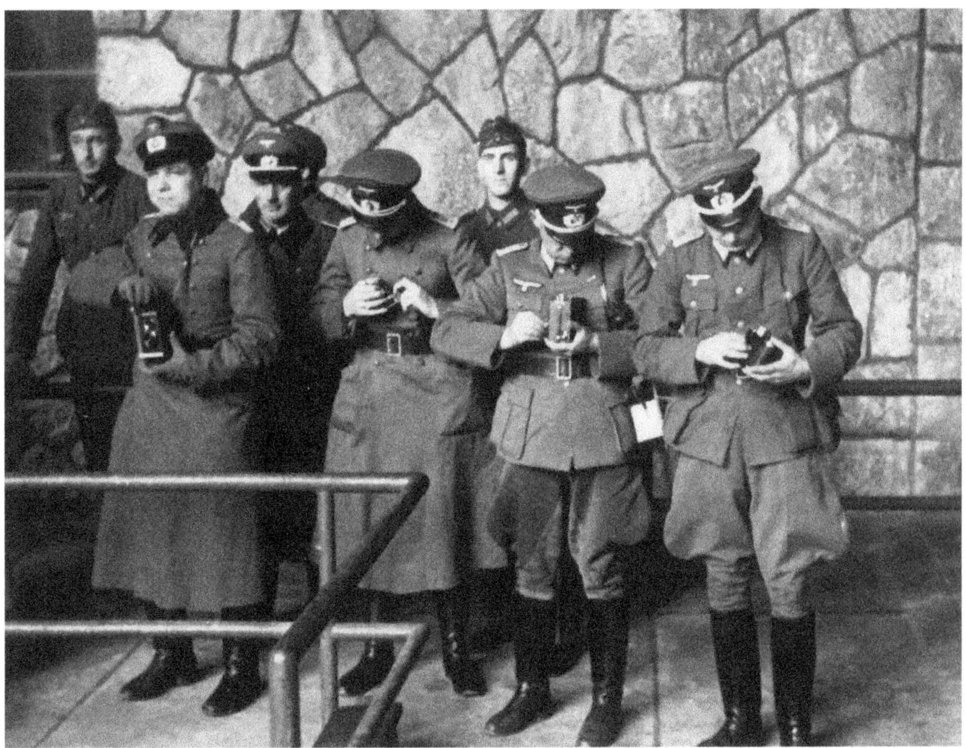

A New War Coming into Varying Focus
A group of army officers struggle with various types of cameras, likely in France. One man, second from the right, appears to be cranking his movie camera; another to the far left operates a Twin Lens Reflex while the two others work with strut 127 or 35 mm cameras.

Its most famous design was the advanced Dagor lens. Post-war restrictions brought near bankruptcy, but the company was saved by a merger with Zeiss-Ikon.

Ica
Having produced an outstanding 4.5x 6 cm miniature camera, the Ica Bebe, in 1906, Ica later became well-known for its series of folding cameras. Another of its folding bed roll film cameras, the 9x12 'Volta,' was first introduced in 1920. By 1929 by Zeiss Ikon had taken over the company, the Icarette series absorbed by Zeiss Ikon and produced until 1934.

Ihagee Kamerawerk (Exakta)
Founded in 1912, by 1925 the company was producing 1,000 roll film cameras daily and had established many 'firsts', including the first wind-on lever (1934) and the first flash socket activated by shutter (1935). It milestone camera was the Exakta A, a single lens reflex using 127 film. When launched in 1933, the skeptics scoffed at first but it became the company's breakthrough success, particularly in 1935 when it brought out the revised Kine Exakta, considered the first SLR to utilize 35 mm film.

A 'systems' design allowed for interchangeable lens, finders, plate film backs and even microscope and telescope attachments. With the war in progress, in 1940 the Dresden company's Dutch owner transferred the rights to partners and employees because of the Nazi-era anti-foreigner mindset. War's end found Ihagee production in Soviet-occupied territory.

Kodak Retina (German branch of the Kodak company)
Known originally as the Nagel company, it was bought by Eastman Kodak at the end of 1931. By 1934 the company brought about the Type 117 Nagel-Retina, which became the Kodak Retina – the first camera to use daylight-loading Kodak 35 mm cartridge film. After the summer of 1941, wartime mandates shifted its production from cameras to munitions time-fuses.

Korelle Innovator
In 1921 Franz Kochmann Fabrik of Dresden began producing high-quality professional and amateur cameras. After the owner was forced to flee the country after the Nazi takeover and anti-Jewish repression, the company was 'appropriated'. During the Dresden bombing in 1945, the factory was completely destroyed.

KWG aka KW (*Kamera Werkstatten Guthe & Thorsch*)
In 1920 the company had brought out its novel and well-received pocket-sized 'Patent Etui' model, which was produced until 1938. Another innovative design was the Pilot, the first Twin Lens Reflex using 127 film. One of its owners, Guthe, fled to Switzerland in 1937 to escape anti-Jewish repression. His partner Thorsch escaped to the US in 1938 where, oddly enough, he teamed up with an American of German ancestry, Charles H. Nobel, who owned a large and prosperous photographic business in Detroit. Exchanging companies, Nobel moved with his family to Dresden in Germany, taking over KWG and focusing on what he saw as the future of photography – the 35 mm camera, launching his new design in 1939. That camera became known as the Praktiflex 35 mm SLR (also known post-war as the Praktica). Falling into Soviet hands at war's end, Charles Nobel and son Henry were sent to a special prison – formerly the Buchenwald concentration camp. Charles survived seven years, being released in 1952 and returning to the US, but the Soviets added fifteen years in a Siberian work camp for his son. Through the efforts of President Eisenhower, he was released in 1955. In 1990, after the fall of the USSR and reunification of Germany, John tried to reclaim his father's business and camera brand, and despite only being granted the old factory, he managed to carry on in his father's name by producing panorama cameras.

Leica
The name has become synonymous with the finest achievement in camera development, specifically its 35 mm, which was first launched in the spring of 1925. Employing over 1,000, the optical company also designed high-quality binoculars and microscopes, as well as aerial cameras and movie cameras.

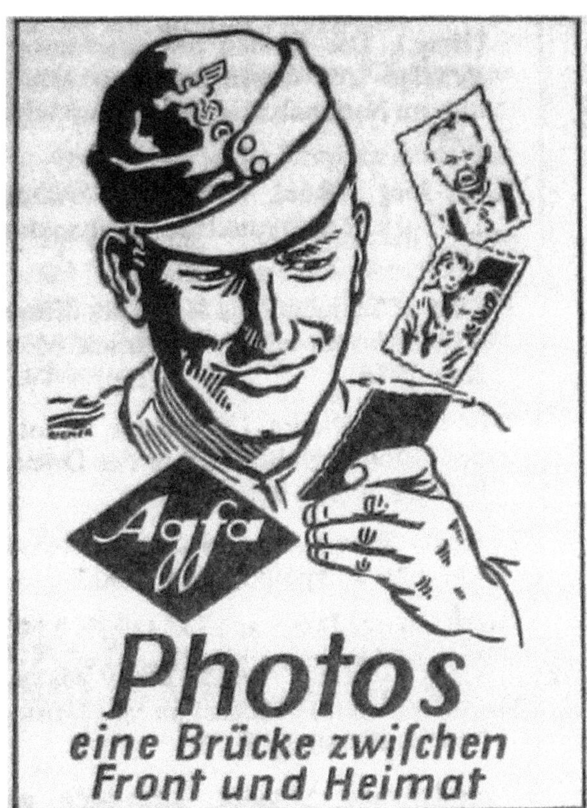

'A Bridge Between the Front and Home'
This Agfa ad appeared in German newspapers and magazines during the Nazi era, spotlighting its connection between the military and the civilians back home.

Linhof

Founded in Munich in 1887, after first making camera shutters its reputation resides with top-line rollfilm and large format film cameras. The first all-metal folding field camera, the Technika, was introduced in 1934, with camera production continuing until 1943, and then resuming post-war. After the demise of Kodak, Linhof became the oldest still-producing camera manufacturer in the world.

Mentor

In 1936 the Dresden company introduced its Mentorett Twin-Lens Reflex (75 mm) using 120 film (6x6 negatives) with its novel incorporation of a focal plane shutter. Other special features included a lever serving three purposes: film advance, shutter cocking and shutter release, all allowing for rapid firing. The company produced an estimated 55,000 cameras but few apparently survived and they are now considered rare.

Mimosa

Named after a colorful flowering tree, as of 1904 the Mimosa company was located in Dresden. During the Nazi era, Mimosa's Jewish employees and directors were forced from their jobs, its director Von Dobschinsky being sent to a concentration camp. Production was shifted to producing war-related materials, and though the facility escaped the worst of the bombing, with Red Army troops advancing the company's assets were moved westward. However, it still came under Soviet control. Von Dobschinsky was restored as custodian of the now East German state-owned company. Taken over by Zeiss Ikon in 1950 under the brand name Mimosa, it began production again by making compact 35 mm cameras.

Minox

Perhaps the most famous of subminiatures, the Minox – the so-called 'spy camera' – was first commercially produced in Riga, Latvia, in 1938. Self-taught inventor Walter Zapp came up with the design, which relied on German lenses and stainless casing material from England. He envisioned a camera for the everyman, but it turned into a premium for the wealthier customer. In June 1940, after 6,000 of the original Minoxes (aka Minox Rigas) were made, further production was disrupted by the arrival of Soviet forces, who were then displaced by the arrival of German troops in September 1941. The cameras continued to be sold under occupation and purportedly Goring gifted several to his cohorts. In spring 1944 the Red Army returned, driving out the Germans and once again taking over production of Minox.

Nagel

Stuttgart-based, the company founded by Dr August Nagel became well-known for its rigid small-format (3x4 cm) Nagel-Pupille. Nagel became a co-founder of Zeiss-Ikon, and in 1931 the company joined Kodak as its German branch, the brandnamed Kodak then becoming its offered range of cameras.

Plaubel

While the company was founded in 1902, camera production actually began in 1910, eventually resulting in the introduction of the famous series of medium and large-format Makina press cameras as well as some smaller folding strut cameras. Production resumed post-war.

Richter

The Tharandt-based company took on a name change in 1932 to Kamera-Werk C. Richter Tharandt after its founding in 1900. For 1933, the birth year of Nazi Germany, it produced the 6x6 format Reflecta Twin Lens Reflex.

Rollei

In 1921 Rollei came out with its first camera, a stereo design with Carl Zeiss lenses, followed by the milestone Rolleiflex in 1929. The latter literally rocketed to success, with some 20,000 being built the following year. The economy version, the Rolleicord, was introduced in 1933, and in 1937 the Rolleiflex Automat won top honors at the Paris World Fair. The history of photography and the Braunschweig-based company go hand in hand, especially when focused on the Twin Lens Reflex, the Rolleiflex eventually becoming almost mandatory for newspapers worldwide. Braunschweig became a garrison city for the 31st Infantry division, which took part in the invasions of Poland and Russia. As a result thousands of eastern European slave laborers were brought to work in the city. The war years saw no new camera developments, the factory being bomb damaged during 1944.

Voigtländer

Another longstanding top of the line brand, and also based in Braunschweig during wartime, the original optical company can trace its beginnings to 1756 Vienna, thus owning rights as the oldest name in cameras. Achievements include many of the first advanced lenses, and the first all-metal daguerreotype camera in 1841, followed soon after by the introduction of plate format exposures. Introduced in 1929, its Bessa 6x9 camera was its first entry into the mass market, and ten years later, at the beginning of the war, its first 35 mm, the Vito, was introduced.

Welta

Having initially brought out its Superfetka Twin Lens Reflex in 1932, in the following year and during the rise of the Nazi State the company brought out its Welta Solida, a medium-format fold camera with coupled rangefinder, the dual format design being able to use both the 6x9 and 6x4.5 cm film format. The 'modern' Welti 35 mm film format folding viewfinder model appeared in 1935.

Wirgin

Brothers Heinrich, Max and Josef founded the Wiesbaden company in 1920 and by 1932 brought out their compact and very popular viewfinder Type 27 film camera, the Gewiritte. By 1935, and keeping up with the times, it was marketing its Edinex 35 mm viewfinder cameras, which were also badged as the Adrette, made by Adox. Prompted by anti-Jewish edicts, Heinrich and Josep escaped Germany, joining their brother Max who had previously made his way to the US. Post-war Heinrich (now Henry) returned to successfully reclaim his company, which was now in US occupied territory – later also acquiring the aforementioned Franka camera company.

Emil Wunsche

The Dresden concern founded in 1887 first sold various cameras by other makers, then in 1884–85 purchased several of those companies and marketed them under the Wunsche name along with a host of photographic accessories including lenses, viewfinders, shutters, flash units, film and enlargers, as well as detective cameras. In the process, the company became the second largest photographic concern in Dresden.

Zeiss Ikon

The last in the list but certainly the most famous, Zeiss Ikon was created by the merger of Contessa-Nettel, Ernemann, Goerz and Ica in 1926, though the original company was founded by Carl Zeiss in 1846. In the process, Zeiss ordered its

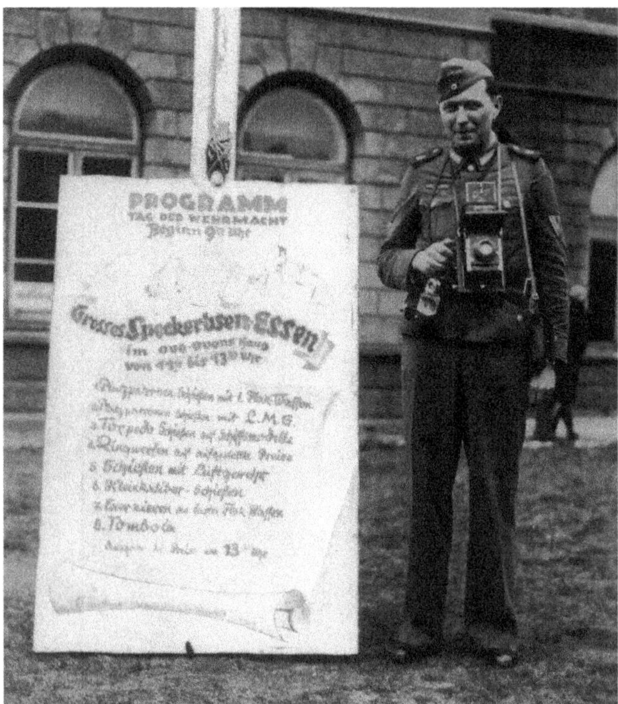

'**Day of the Wehrmacht':
Celebrations Begin at 9 o'clock**
An army corporal laden with
state-of-the-art German cameras
poses with a poster announcing
the Armed Forces Day activities,
its design contrived as a humorous
interpretation of a 'menu'
announcing a 'great bacon and
pea soup dinner' along with
eight 'dishes' or games including
'blanks shooting at anti-aircraft
targets, shooting blanks with light
machinegun [and] torpedo shoot
at [a] ship'.

acquired companies to stop making lenses, preferring to corner the market itself.
While helping to make Dresden the photo-technical capital of Germany, if not
the world, it also operated facilities in Stuttgart and Berlin. Its star list of cameras
included the Zeiss Ikon series, the Contax series, as well as the very popular Box
Tengor. Prior to the Second World War it was also the world's leading maker of 8
mm movie cameras including the Kinamo (1926–36), and the Movikon 8 (1933–39).
As of 2014 – and as testimony to the quality of its products standing the test of time
during its 175 years – the Carl Zeiss Foundation employed nearly 25,000 workers
with annual sales of over €4.5 billion.

Notes on Film Lexiconography

Eastman Kodak was a principal innovator in film development and the catalyst for
making photography available to the general public as well as commercial applications.
It began designating its film stocks with the number 100 with 101 roll film introduced
in 1895. Its 120 roll 'medium format' film appeared for use in the Kodak Brownie No.
2 in 1901 and subsequently served untold millions in the following years as the camera
proliferated worldwide. In 1912 Kodak introduced the 127 roll film, its size placing it
between 120 and 35 mm films. Kodak 127 film production lasted until 1995.

Another milestone occurred when the German Agfa company brought out its 35 mm
cartridge film for still cameras in 1936, along with color slide film.

Cine (Movie) Cameras

Various motion picture film sizes (gauges) were tried and tested for use in both still and cine (movie) cameras:

1892: 35 mm was introduced by William Dickson and Thomas Edison and became the most popular gauge for motion pictures.

1922: 9.5 mm was introduced by the French company Pathé Frères as an economical film for amateur use and was available in both silent and sound.

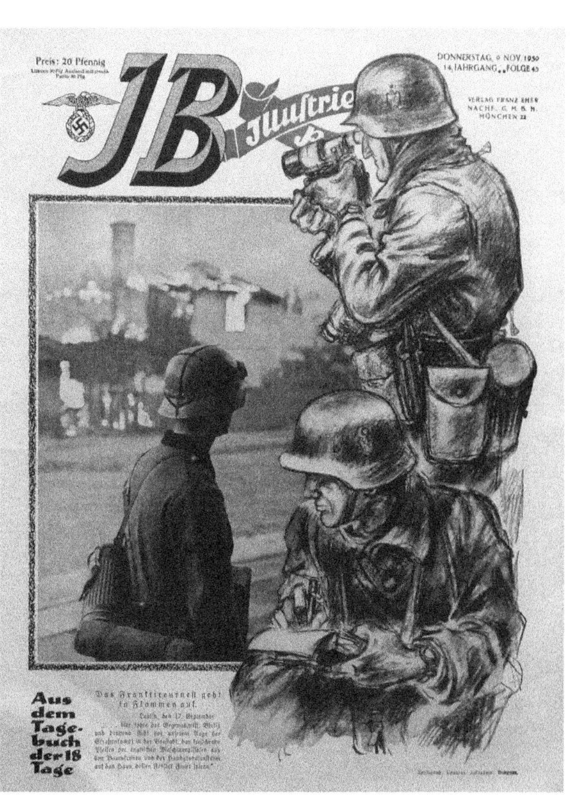

Combat Journalist Chronicles the War in Poland with Camera and Pen, November 1939
'Here the deadly counter-attack. Our eyes see the bloody and broken … our ears hear the fire of the English machine guns screeching from the treetops as hand grenades assault our refuge … the windows spitting fire.' (The cover illustration depicts a soldier filming with a compact 16 mm movie camera, the drawing credited to an artist identified only as Lazarus – an appropriate name for a war correspondent).

1923: 16 mm film was introduced by Eastman Kodak as an economical alternative for the then prevalent 35 mm film. 16 mm was extensively used during the Second World War, including for use in military training films.

1932: 8 mm, aka Standard or Regular 8 mm or Double 8 mm, available in silent and sound, was introduced by the Eastman Kodak company as an economical replacement for 16 mm film.

Milestones in the Development of the Cine or Movie Camera

1898: The first amateur cine camera is credited to a British photographer and film pioneer, Birt Acres, who designed a combination motion picture camera/projector, the Birtac Home Cinema. For film it relied on then available 35 mm film, then split into usable 17.5 mm film. He also came up with the promotional sales phrase 'home movies' to fire up amateur interest in his invention, focusing on making his camera available to the 'average man'.

1907: This year saw the founding of the Chicago, Illinois-based Bell & Howell Company, and three years later the Victor Animatograph Corporation in Davenport, Iowa, initially both involved with movie projectors. By 1917 B&H had designed a cine camera using 17.5 mm film for amateur use.

1922: 9.5 mm film emerged, as created by the French firm of Pathé Frères. Initially designed for economical commercial use in place of 16 mm film, it became popular for amateur filmmakers as well.

1923: This was the 'birthday' year for the 16 mm movie-making phenomena when the US company Eastman Kodak, previously a longtime maker of still cameras, came up with its 16 mm reversal film. Immediately popular, it motivated Kodak to begin populating the globe with film processing plants, which in turn encouraged more movie camera sales to the public. Kodak introduced the world's first 16 mm motion picture camera in July of the same year. It featured the then standard hand-cranked design, as this was prior to the development of the spring-wound clockwork design.

That credit for the next innovation, the spring-driven cine camera, goes to Bell & Howell with the advent of its Model 70A Filmo – a single lens design targeted for use in producing 'home movies'. These cameras found their way into the hands of legions of adventure/travelers, the era also seeing the popularity of steamship cruises to exotic locales around the world.

1924: The famous Swiss-made Bolex movie camera made its international debut.

1927: Bell & Howell upped the ante with its three-lens turreted Model C 16 mm movie camera – the first of its kind.

1932: While the 16 mm format reigned supreme, Eastman Kodak launched the smaller, less expensive 8 mm film along with its new spring-driven Cine-Kodak 8, which was designed specifically for that film.

1935: Bolex brought out its beautifully designed, state-of-the-art and industry-changing H16. A year later the Spanish Civil War erupted, the prelude to the Second World War. In Germany between the 1930s and 1940s, the leading cine camera makers in 16 mm and 8 mm were Agfa and Siemens, while Arriflex produced 35 mm cameras for commercial, film industry and military use.

Arriflex – State-of-the-Art in Motion Picture Camera Design

Founded in 1917 by veteran German motion picture industry cameramen partners August Arnold and Robert Richter, the so-named Arriflex company found its home in Munich in the midst of the First World War. The company would design one of most famous film camera in 1937 with the advent of the world's first reflex mirror shutter in its Arriflex 35, which functioned much like a single lens reflex camera and provided for parallax 'live' focusing. It was widely used as a 'battlefield camera' as well as for Wehrmacht training films and propaganda films. Eventually some 17,000 were built, and Arriflex is still the world's largest manufacturer and distributor of motion picture cameras.

The Role of the Big Screen in Nazi Germany

As master manipulators of imagery as a tool for social engineering, National Socialism infiltrated all forms of media, including the country's extensive and internationally acclaimed film industry. Filmmaking in Germany was considered high art and so were its motion picture cameras such as the Arriflex 35 mm, as used in the over 3,000 films made during the twelve years of the Third Reich.

Film was recognised as a teaching tool in the early 1900s by German educators, some of whom began introducing their own works to the classroom. By the 1920s an official board was established to develop guidelines resulting in the formation of the *Reichsstelle fur den Unterrichtsfilm* (RfdU) in 1934, which was tasked with the production and distribution of educational films to German schools and universities. After the rise of the Nazi state, it was renamed *Reichsanstalt fur Film und Bild in Wissenschaft und Unterricht* (RWU), or Films of the Reich Institute for Film and Picture in Science and Education. Funding for projectors and film was financed via a small charge to each student, the program being instituted in some 80,000 schools. For reasons of economy of production and the odd belief that the images without sound had more impact, the films were for the most part silent, although accompanying written materials served as a teaching aid.

While assimilated into the Nazi State apparatus, the RWU retained both a large measure of autonomy and 'open thinking' as regards to selecting its staff based on abilities rather than political affiliations. Propaganda and Film Minister Josef Goebbels sought to reign over the organization, but was initially thwarted by the steadfastness of Minister of Education Bernard Rust, who supported the RWU and who, although a fervent Nazi, had a strong personal dislike for Goebbels. However, Rust was also prone to making irrational decrees in his efforts to indoctrinate German youth in Nazi philosophy and was considered to be emotionally unstable. Rust is also credited with coming up with the idea in 1933 that people should greet each other with the Nazi 'Heil Hitler' salute. Additionally, he was instrumental in purging Jews from German schools. Rust reportedly committed suicide on the day Nazi Germany officially surrendered to the Allies.

Already established prior to the 1933 Nazi takeover, the principle German film company Universum Film Aktiengesellschaft, aka UFA, was a major force in world cinema from 1917 to 1945. However, its roots also lay in propaganda as it was founded during the First World War as a state-controlled organ for both public service and war-related films, whereby the government took control of then existing commercial film production companies.

History repeated itself when Josef Goebbels took control of UFA through both intimidation and the Nazi state purchase of 72 per cent of UFA's shares. Nationalisation as a Third Reich monopoly occurred in 1942, with all remaining private film companies absorbed by it. UFA survived the collapse of Nazi Germany and the Second World War, gaining new ground in post-war film production as well as television programming.

While many of the pre-Nazi film industry talents fled Germany as the result of racial and political persecution, many actors remained to star in a relentless outpouring of 'politically correct' Third Reich films. Some filmmakers and actors ran afoul of Nazi tyranny; others found a safe harbor as they practiced their craft – at least while the swastika held sway.

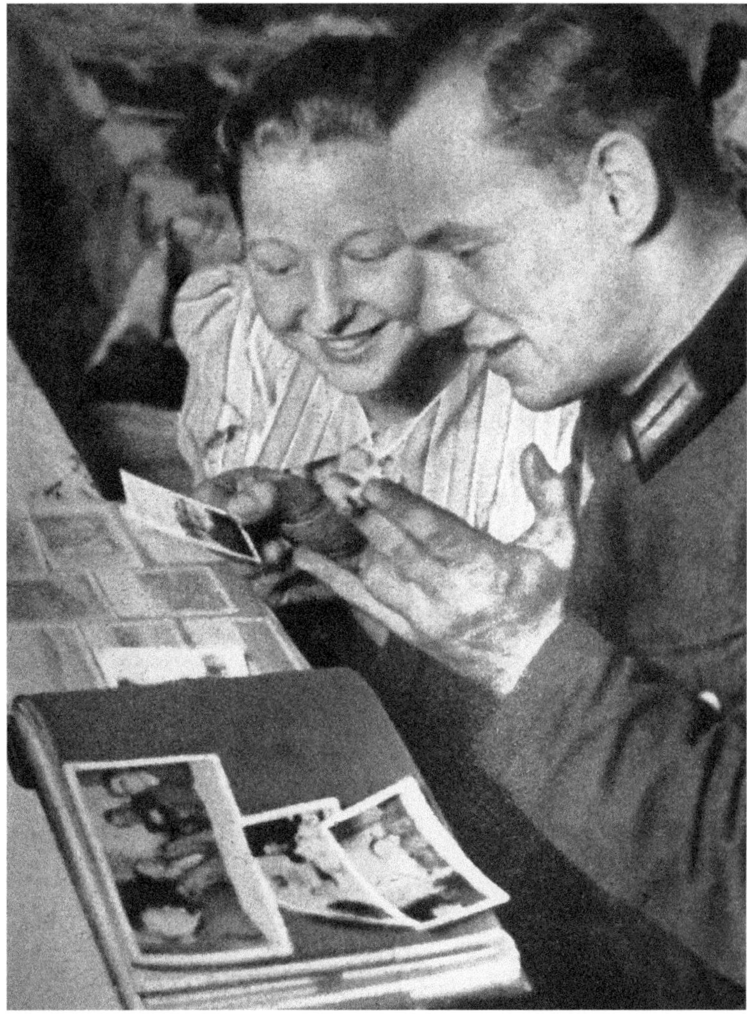

Photo of Photos
Appearing in a German newspaper, this photo finds a soldier and friend enjoying his personal photo album.

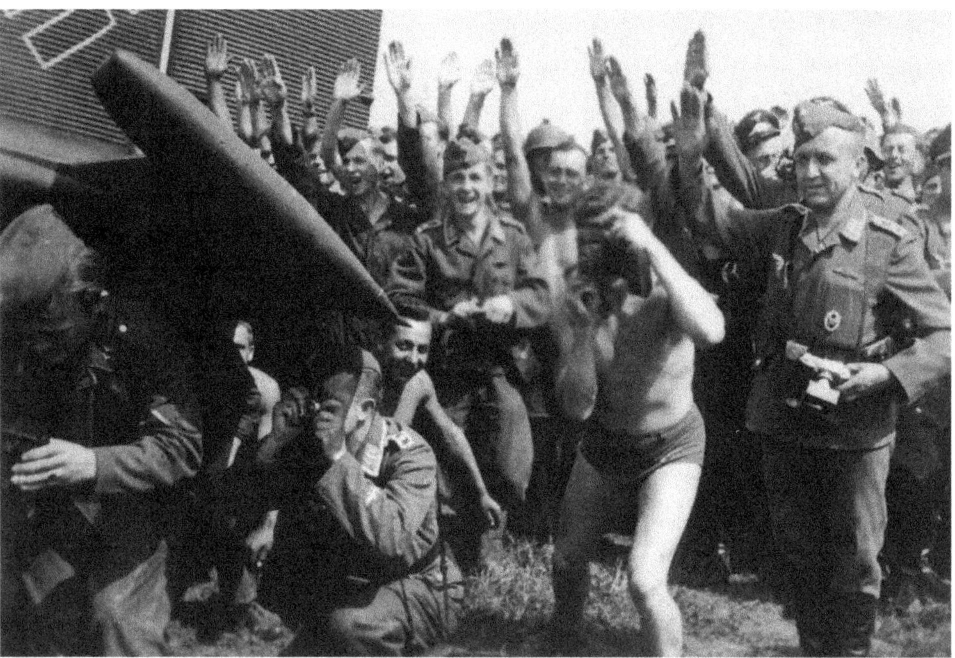

Camera Mania

At least six different cameras are detectable in this photo showing exuberant Luftwaffe personnel greeting the arrival of the Supreme Leader.

'We are simply *amazed* at the way in which the soldiers now pop up from their guns, like rabbits out of their holes, and in relays of about twenty come on to the road and snap us with their cameras. Apparently every German soldier carries a camera on him as part of his equipment.'

Englishwoman Bessy Myers in her 1942 book *Captured – My Experience as an Ambulance Driver and as a Prisoner of the Nazis.*

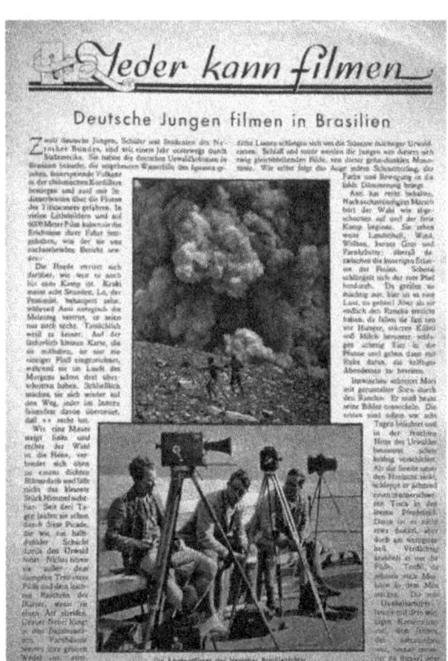

Student Project

A magazine article captioned 'Everyone Can Film' recounts a pre-war German student trip to Brazil and their photographing and filming of an active volcano. Many such photographically inclined students would go into uniform as war journalists and members of the propaganda ministry units.

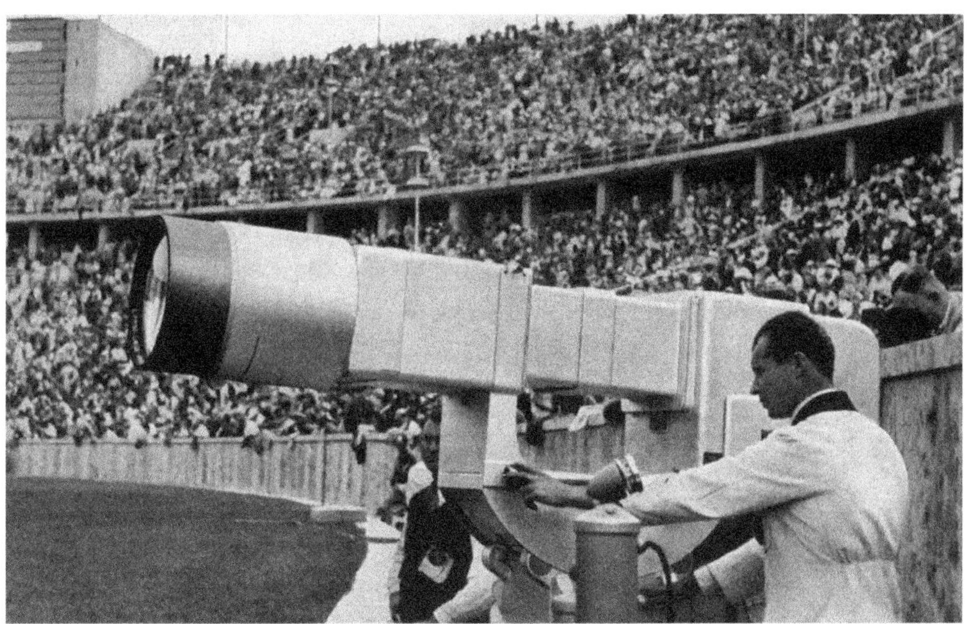

Latest in Camera Technology – Television Transmits Massive Memories
A technician operates a mammoth TV camera to film the 1936 Berlin Olympics, the first recorded televised sporting event. Broadcast in Germany via the Telefunken and Fernseh communication companies, the equipment utilized RCA and Farnsworth components, its labyrinth of wires and cables hidden out of sight beneath the Olympic stadium.

A major political and propaganda victory for the Nazi Government, the XL Olympiad was orchestrated by Propaganda Minister Josef Goebbels and immortalised by Leni Riefenstahl's notorious but award-winning 1938 documentary film *Olympiad*.

Prior to its Nazification, in 1931 Berlin was selected by the National Olympic Committee to be the host city, beating out Barcelona, Spain. More than ironically, Nazi Germany would aid the fascists under Franco in the civil war begun in July 1936, which many see as a practice run for the Nazi military plans for warfare.

Photos from the Third Reich's Big Screen

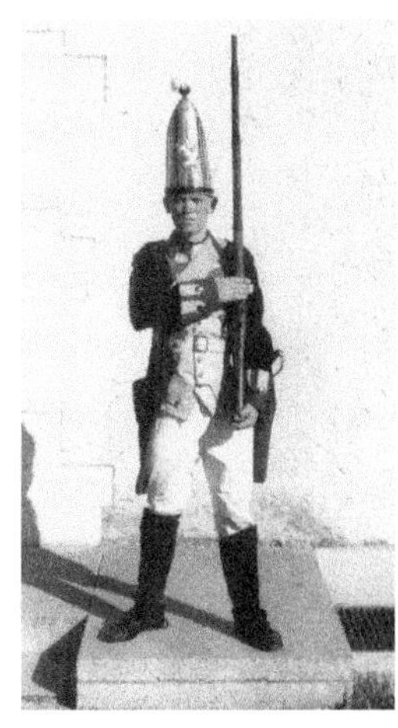

Toy Soldier
In charge of Third Reich filmmaking, Goebbels often requisitioned entire companies of soldiers as 'cannon fodder' for his many epic historical romances. The 'actor' is costumed as a 18th Prussian Grenadier, although the photo was taken in 1940, the year of Germany's invasion and occupation of France. (An historical footnote: while 30,000 German Hessian soldiers fought as mercenaries for the British against American revolutionary forces during the War of Independence, another German officer, Friedrich von Steuben, was instrumental in training George Washington's troops.)

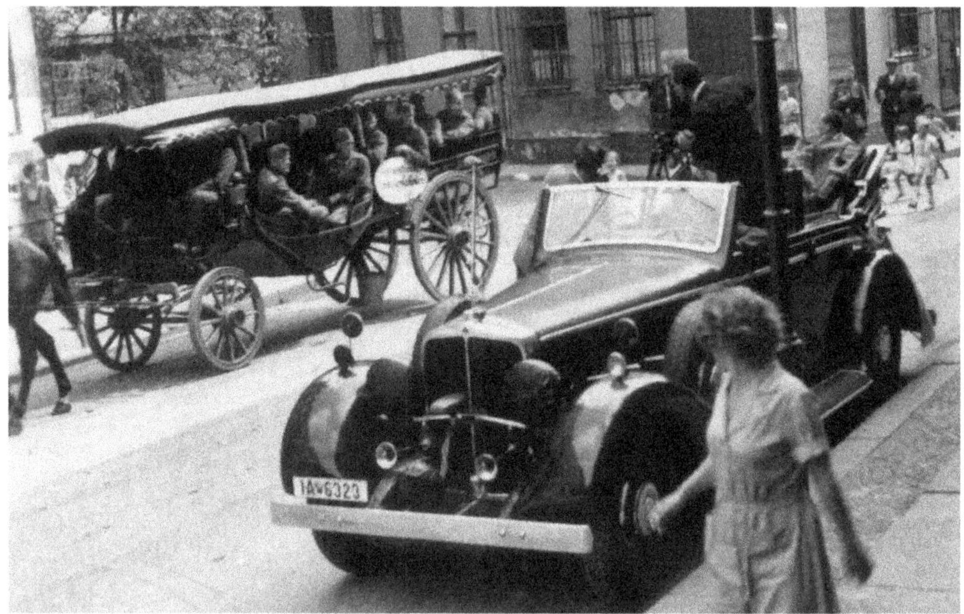

Aktion!
An open car is used as a mobile camera platform as filming takes place on a Berlin street, the subject a group of soldiers enjoying some sightseeing aboard a horse-drawn tourist carriage. The Third Reich would produce some 3,000 feature films during its twelve years, production literally lasting until the last weeks of the war in an extension of 'the show must go on'.

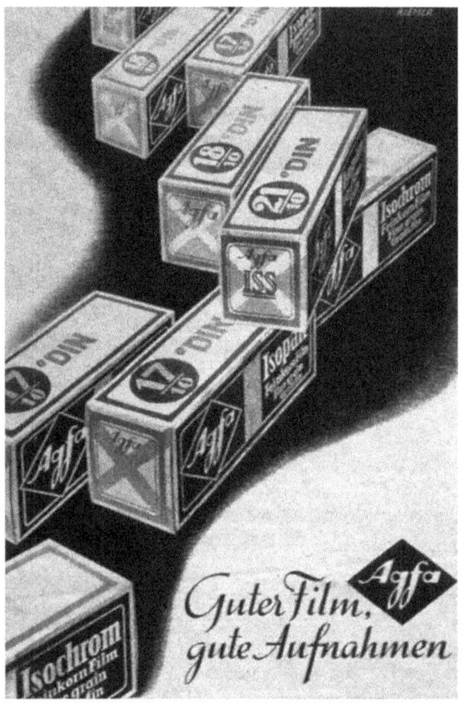

'Good Film, Good Shots' – In Living Colour
A major innovator in film development, in 1936 Agfa introduced the first colour 35 mm film in both print and transparency (slide) format for commercial and amateur use. In 1941, Agfacolor negative-positive film stock was used for the first time in a feature film, titled *Frauen sind doch Besseren Diplomaten* (Women Make the Better Diplomats). The musical, set during the German revolutions of 1848–49, involved the niece of a casino-owning uncle who goes to parliament to prevent it being closed by the government. It ranked as the most expensive production by the Third Reich film industry and was one of the most popular during the early war years.

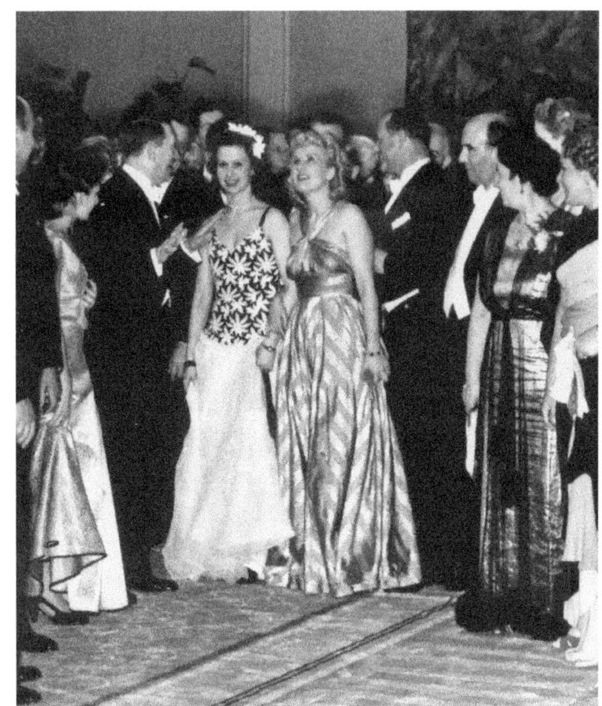

Star-Struck

During a gala reception at the Munich Museum of Art, a crowd of formally attired dignitaries seem star-struck upon the arrival of two luminously begowned young women, including blonde-haired Dorit Kreisler, a leading star of the German cinema. A closer look shows us that none other than the German Chancellor himself has fallen under their spell, his hands making some dramatic gesture. However, neither woman seems focused on the leader of the Third Reich; rather, one has noticed the cameraman and looks toward the lens while Dorit Kreisler examines the ceiling with a look of awe.

Super Star *v.* Hitler – Film Studio Promotional Photo

Hans Albers was in today's vernacular a 'top matinee idol' and was adored by German moviegoers from 1930 to 1945. He was the highest paid celebrity and exerted powerful influence outside of Germany as well. Although he prospered under Goebbels' film and arts umbrella, his fictional bravery turned real when he openly expressed his feelings about the Nazi Government and refused to enter films that aggrandized their image. As to the secret of his success for remaining immune to disaster when flouting the Nazi regime, it apparently had to do with 'attitude'. Albers believed that if the German people had been forced to choose between Adolf Hitler and Hans Albers, the majority would have chosen him.

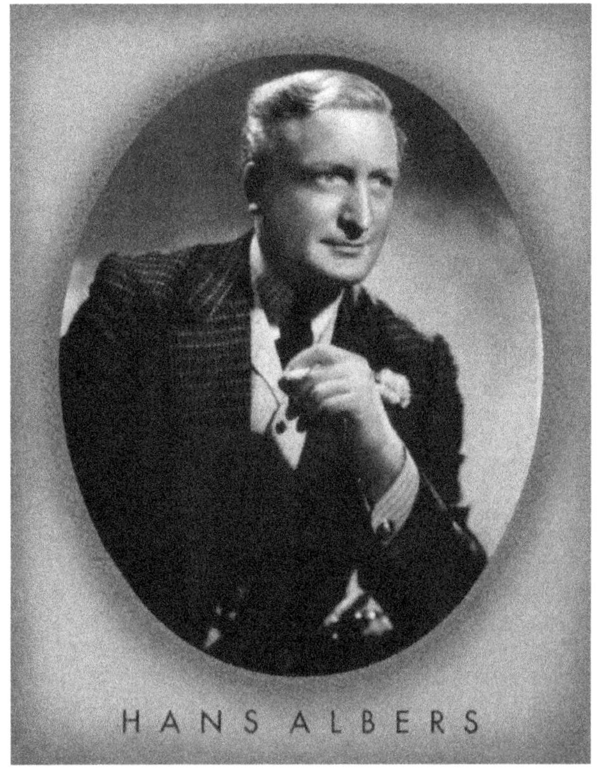

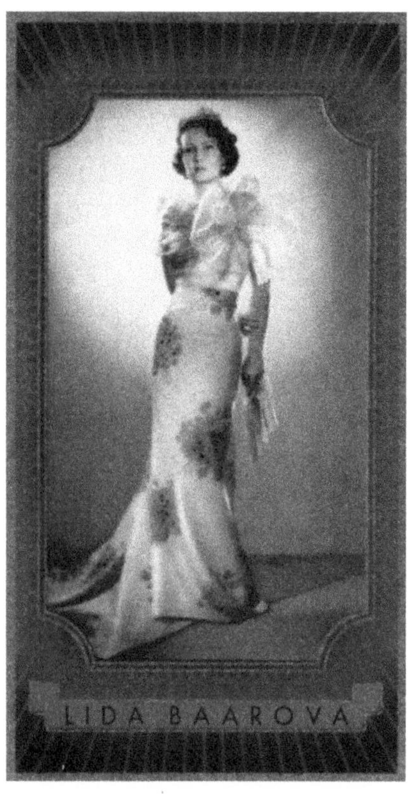

Lída Baarová – Goebbels's Near Fatal Obsession
The studio photo of actress Lída Baarová was featured on a 1937 collectible card packaged as a sales perk in packs of cigarettes. Considered one of Europe's most beautiful woman, she caught Goebbels's lecherous eye and entered into an affair with him. Reportedly he wanted to divorce his wife and resign his Reich's post and sail off to Japan with her. Hitler forbade him to leave his wife and Goebbels unsuccessfully attempted suicide in 1938. Baarová, pursued by the Gestapo, fled to Italy and worked with the famed director Federico Fellini.

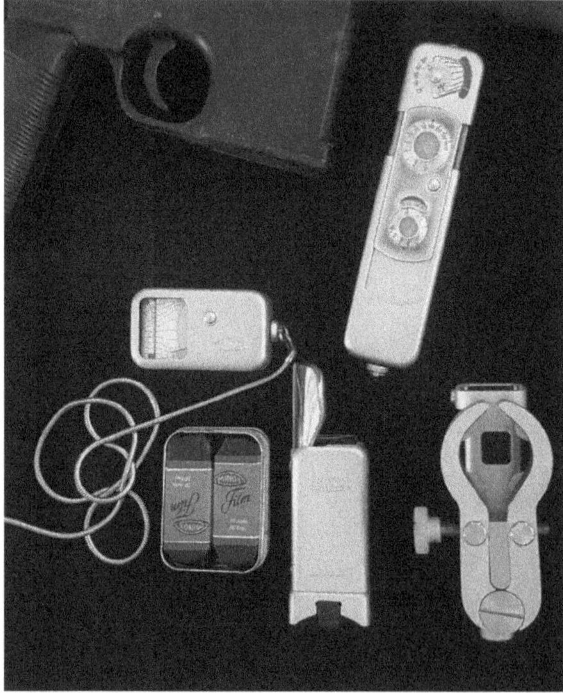

Epitome of the Spy Camera
Perhaps no other camera has acquired the status of the subminiature Minox as a tool of covert actions and espionage, especially for the clandestine recording of documents. Using ultra-small 16 mm film, it still produced ultra-sharp images, and was also very easy to conceal. The camera's 'life span' stretched back to 1932 and its evolution over the many following decades retained its original design along with upgrades including an integrated metering system. Accessories include a flash unit (center), a separate meter and an adapter for use with a binocular or monocular. Two original rolls of Minox film are seen packaged in an aluminum container. The braided chain served as an accurate measuring device when focusing on pages of documents to be photographed.

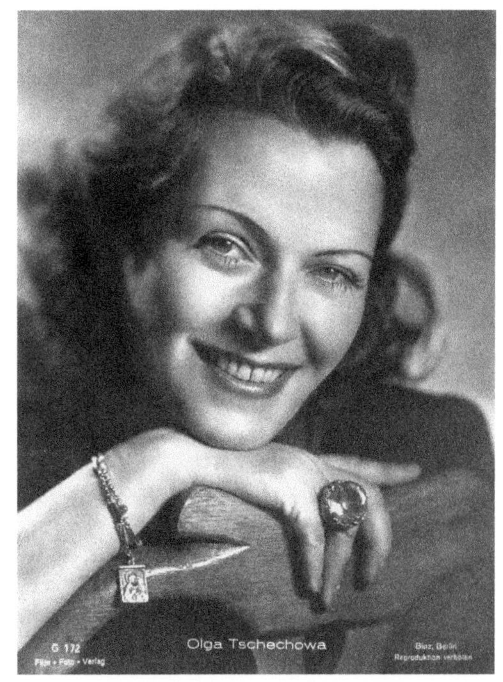

Olga Tschechowa

A Charmed Life – Silver Screen Double Agent

The official German film industry photo of Olga Tschechowa was produced under the control of Third Reich Propaganda Minister Josef Goebbels. The bracelet she has chosen to wear for the photo, taken in the Binz studio in Berlin, displays a Russian Orthodox religious icon worn as a bracelet charm, a detail that somehow slipped past Nazi censors, but not perhaps Olga's Soviet contacts in the ultra-secret counter-spy organization SMERSH ('Death to Spies'), for whom she purportedly served as a 'sleeper spy' in Nazi Germany.

Hannes Stelzer

Movie Star Mortality

Seen in costume for a film studio portrait, actor Hannes Stelzer starred as Oberleutnant Hans Wilde in the 1941 hit movie *Stukas*. Art imitated not life but death. On 27 December 1944, while flying near Komárom, Hungary, Stelzer, who had joined the Luftwaffe, was killed when his plane was shot down.

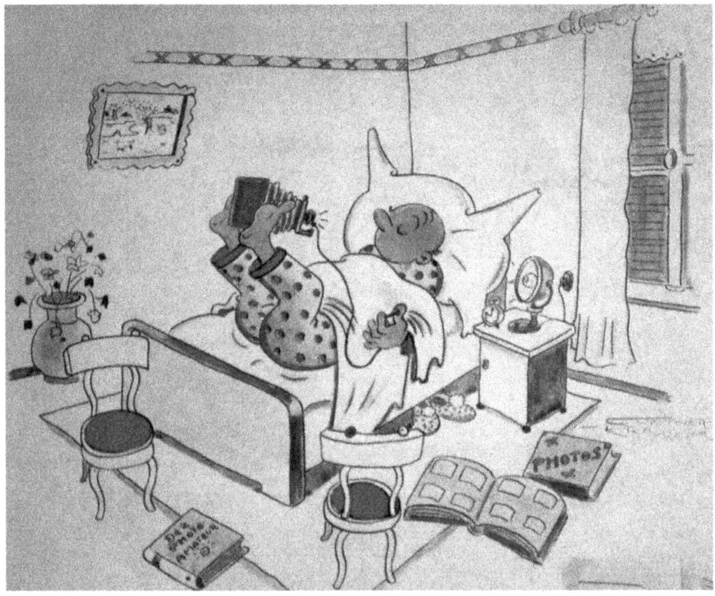

Birth of the Selfie?

The country's camera mania is lampooned in the humour section of a popular Berlin magazine published in 1940. The German fascination with photographic images extends back to the earliest appearance of cameras. As a result, individuals, both civilian and military, were often eager to have a professional capture their image, either in an outdoor setting or within a studio enhanced by a scenic backdrop. Many such studio photos were printed by both the photographer and Nazi State organizations and configured as commerical postcards during an era when literally millions of postcards were posted annually.

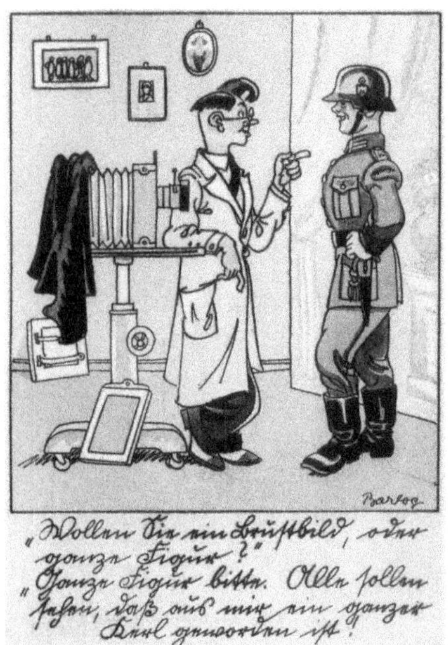

'You'd Make a Good Figure for the Camera'
This postcard with a humorous comment about a photo studio was one of several cards featuring the cartoons of the artist known as Barlog.

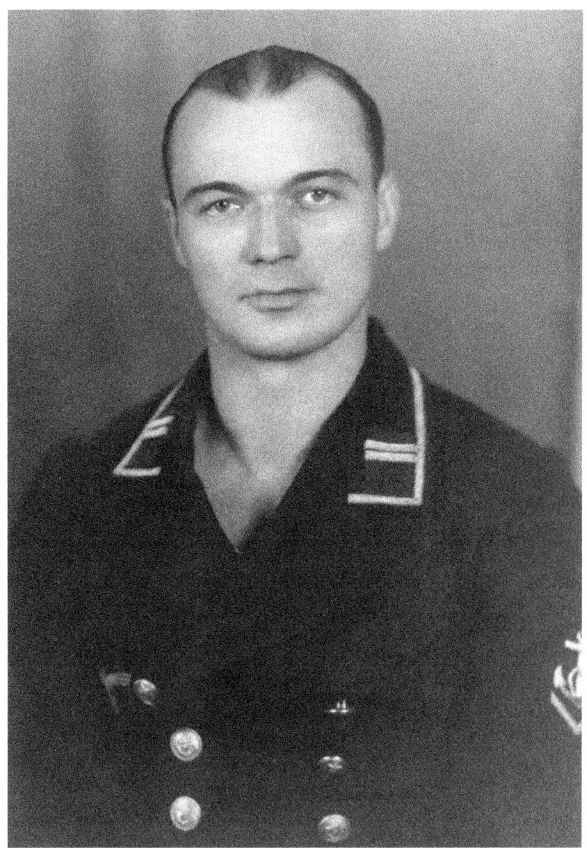

Formal Portrait – *Kriegsmariner Obermaat* (Chief Petty Officer) The studio portrait bears the embossed imprint of the photographic studio of Foto-Keil Werth, located in the Bavarian town of Selb on the Czech border.

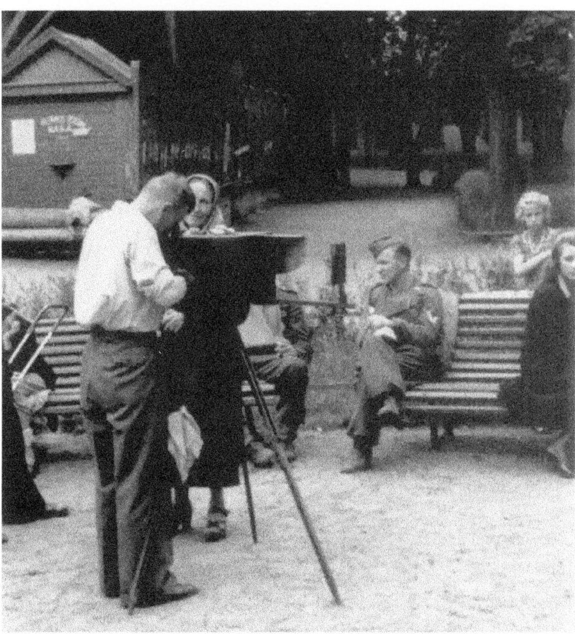

Smile for 50 Pfennigs – Instant Photo Postcards A professional photographer plies his trade in a city park, having set up his specialized photo postcard camera. A woman appears to be asking for information as the cameramen adjusts his camera, his intended clients perhaps including the corporal lounging on a bench. Sitting nearby, a young woman and girl have spotted the out of frame cameramen documenting the moment.

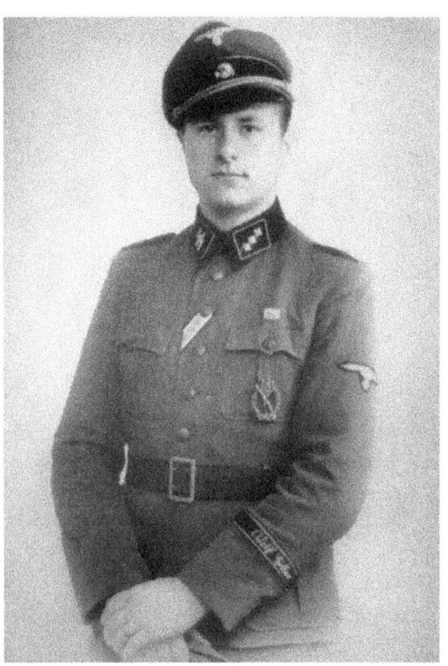

Officer of the *Leibstandarte SS* Adolf Hitler – Photo Postcard
The LSSAH *Sturmfuhrer* (Storm Leader) uniform shows an Infantry Assault Badge and Iron Cross Second Class award along with the unit's special cuff title. If the Infantry Assault badge is silver, the soldier was in foot infantry; if bronze, it denoted motorised Panzer troops. Initially Hitler's personal bodyguard, the LSSAH was reformed as a Waffen-SS detachment taking part in attack on Poland in September 1939, and by war's end had been enlarged from regiment size to a Panzer division.

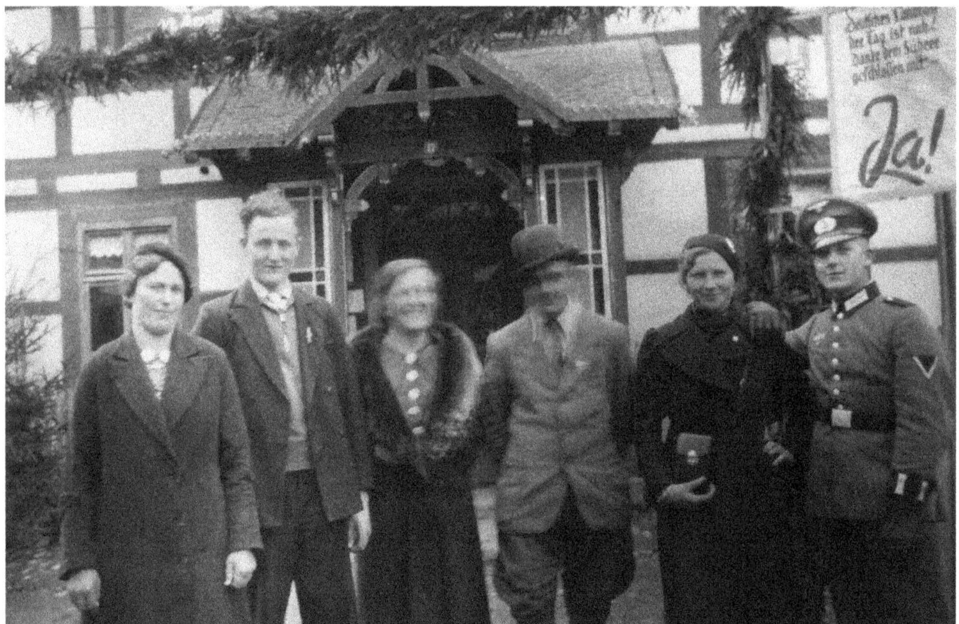

'Vote Yes ... One People, One Country, One Leader'
A family outing includes an army corporal wearing his *Waffenrock,* or formal 'stepping out' uniform with its distinctive 'piano key' cuffs, though the style was discontinued during wartime. His arm rests on the shoulder of one of the two sisters, who is carrying a camera case. The signage indicates the summer of 1934, during the political campaigning promoting granting Hitler new dictatorial powers. As the result of the voting held on 19 August, 89.93 per cent of Germany's voters said yes to Adolf Hitler's plebiscite. Within days, the campaign of terror began when many of those resisting National Socialism or deemed enemies of the State were silenced, either by imprisonment, torture or death.

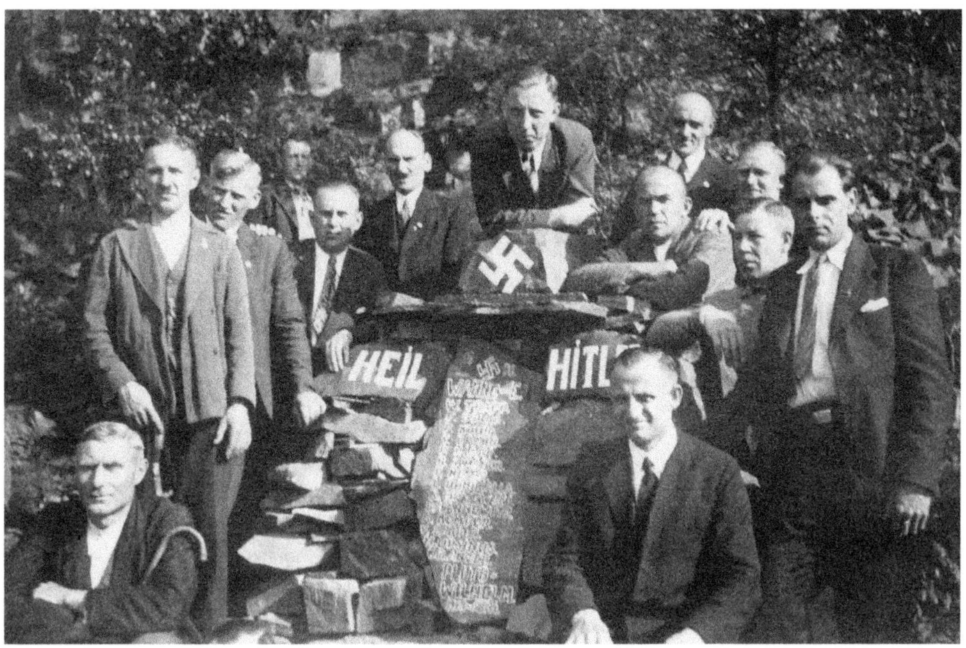

Rank and File

In a photo dated 1935, supporters of the Nazi movement, several wearing party membership pins, have erected their own personal monument and inscribed their names, including the last signatory, one Wilhelm Pluto.

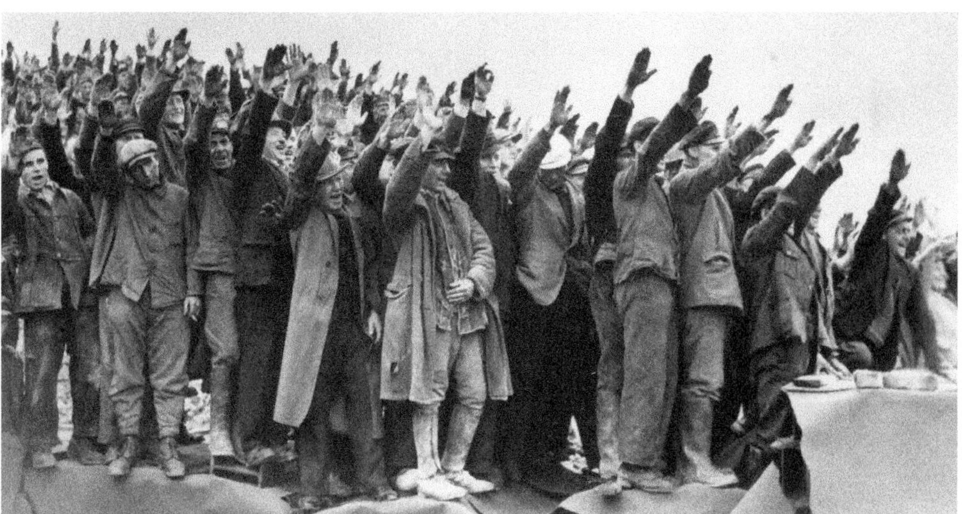

'Heil!' – Jubilation on Cue: Propaganda Ministry Photo

A crowd enthusiastically gives the Hitler salute. In a precursor to modern television show audience applause-ometers, the National Socialist Jubilation Third Stage (*NS-Jubel Dritte Stuffe*) carefully orchestrated peak-volume applause at demonstrations and party meetings. A specific decibel rating was assigned to the required level of applause by the managers of Nazi events and ceremonies. Colored lights helped heighten the effect. Even the chaos of noise was tightly regulated by the Third Reich.

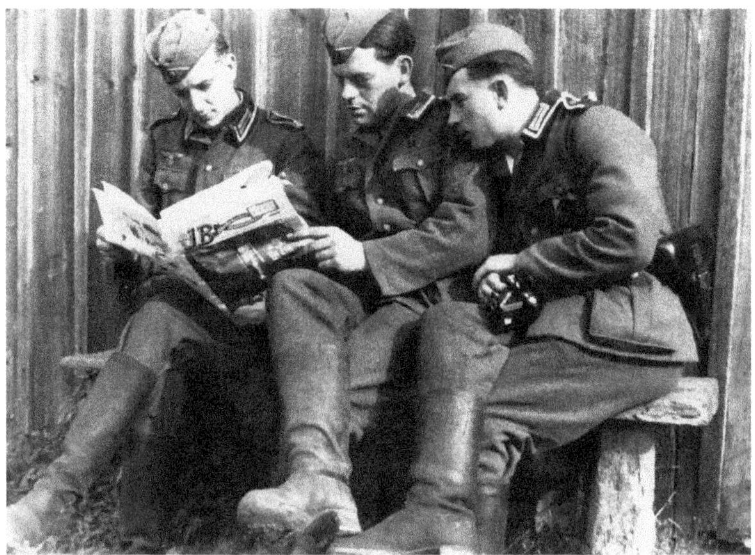

Illustrated Observer Being Observed

Three soldiers, one holding a strut-folding camera, peruse an issue of the *Illustrieter Beobachter*, a very popular large format 'photo magazine' published in Munich. Known as *IB*, it was an official Nazi Party publication with some twenty-four pages laid out in 10x24-inch format. Price per issue was a very reasonable 20 *Reichspfennigs* (12 cents US). Its contents included worldwide news with an emphasis on the course of the war, entertainment features, propaganda and cartoons, as well as the plentiful use of photographs.

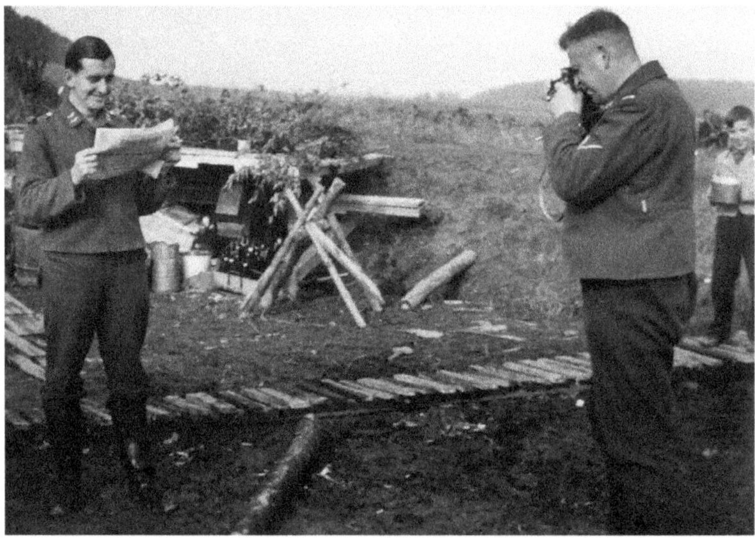

Flakmen

Using a strut-camera, a Luftwaffe corporal snaps his anti-aircraft crewmember reading a copy of the *Berlin Illustrated* newspaper. Walking into the photo, a young boy carries a hot meal along the wooden planks lining the muddy ground of the gun emplacement. Under the camouflaged workbench, a crate of beer is visible.

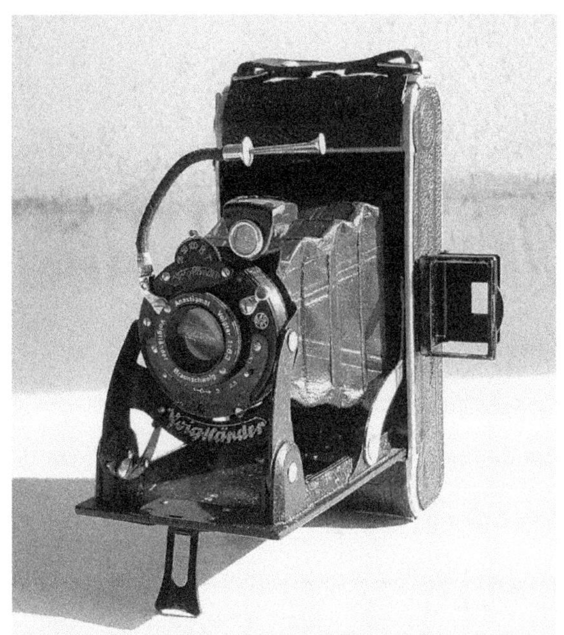

Voigtländer Bessa 6.5 x 11 cm Folding Camera for 120 Rollfilm
Bessa production began in 1931 and continued throughout the war. This example features the F/6.3 Voigtar lens with a relatively slow maximum shutter speed of 1/125th of a second.

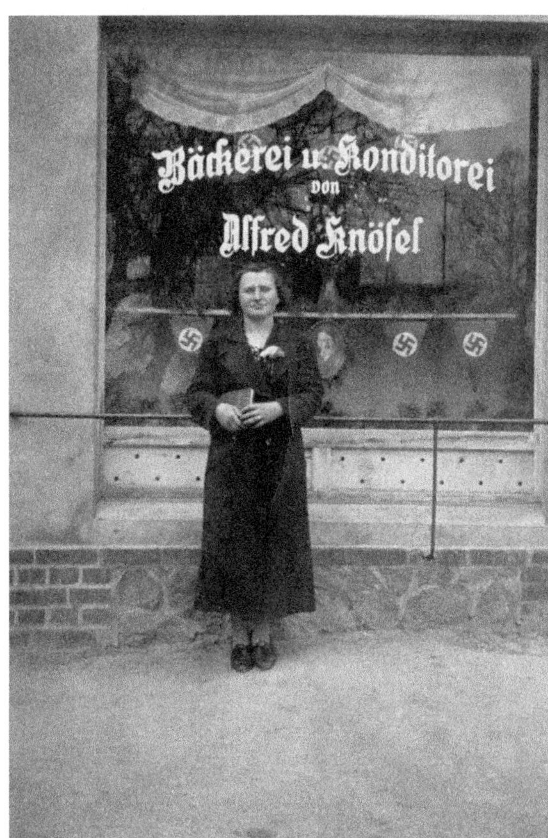

Images within Images – Sweet Swastikas
Alfred Knofel's bakery and confection shop, decorated with swastika pennants and an image of *Der Führer*, serves as a backdrop for an impromptu portrait. Everything and everything the German population saw, heard, read or even tasted bore the imprint of National Socialist political, racial and military ideology.

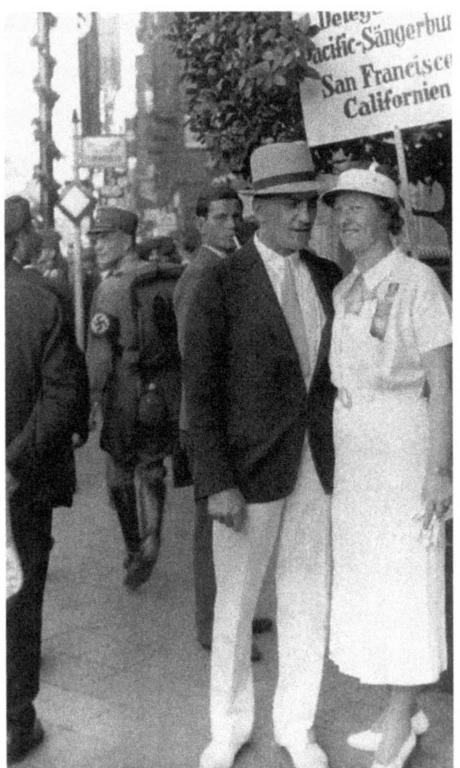

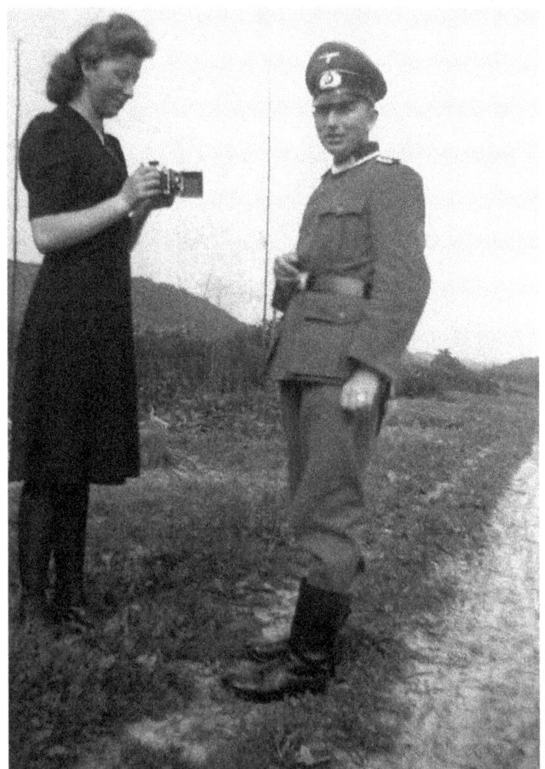

***Above left:* Rare Moment Captured – Tourists from California**
Just as an SA man in uniform casts a wary backward glance, someone photographs a sportily dressed American couple on a crowded German street. As delegates from the Pacific *Sangerbund*, an ethnic German music organization in San Francisco, they are attending a pre-war music conference in the country of their forbearers.

***Above right:* Recording the Photo Session**
An NCO checks out the off-screen photographer as his companion appears ready to take a snapshot.

***Opposite above*: Hitler Youth on the March**
A tripod-mounted camera (far right) stands ready as members of the SA and civilians return the salute given by a marching group of BdM, some of whom seem less than enthusiastic.

The Hitler Youth (*Hitler-Jugend*) program came into effect in July 1926 when all German youth groups were placed under the control of the SA and divided into geographic areas or *Obergebeite* including *Nord, Sud, West, Ost, Mitte* and *Sudost*. The female section was called the League of German Girls, or BdM (*Bund Deutscher Madchen*). By 1936 the *Hitler-Jugend* (HJ) would comprise 5.4 million members aged ten to eighteen taking part in the immersive indoctrination.

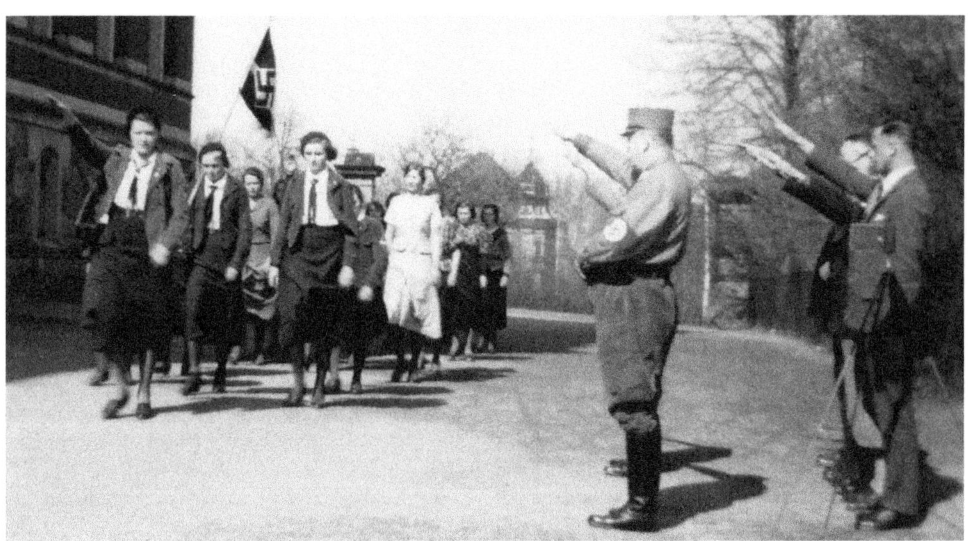

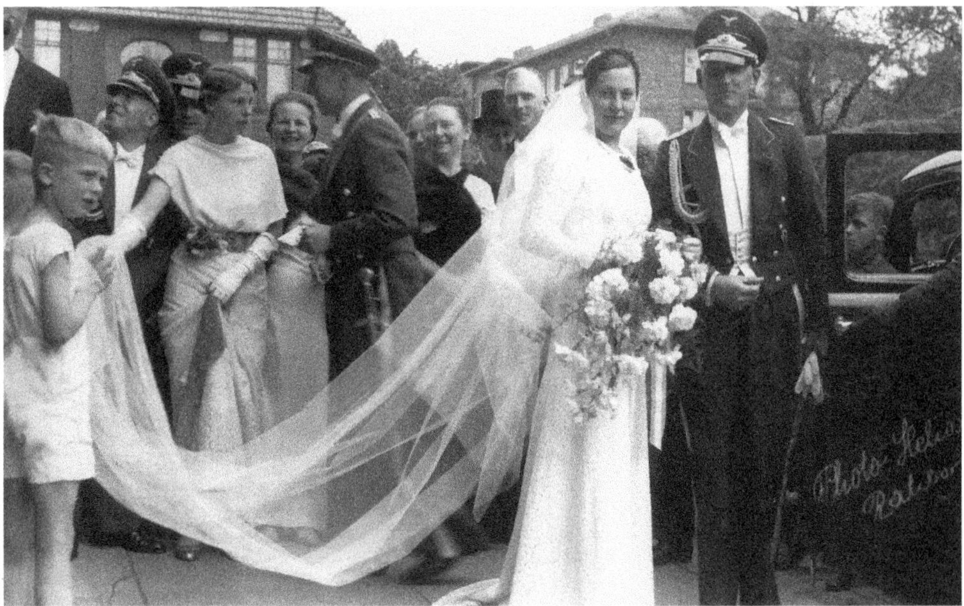

Wedding Photographer on Duty

A Luftwaffe officer wearing his formal dress uniform and his bride trailing an elegant veil appear as the picture-perfect Third Reich couple as they gaze into the camera. On his tunic he wears one medal, a DRL sports badge, along with a marksmanship lanyard, indications that the timeframe is pre-war Germany. The photo bears the stamp of the professional photographer Helios Ratibor.

While color 35 mm film had recently become available, most photos from the era were recorded in black and white. However, the spectrum of uniform colors was in fact striking. Depending on the branch of the military, the identifying color system (*Waffenfarber*) of shoulder straps alone included carmine, bright red, white, gold yellow, lemon yellow, copper brown, light green, grass green, cornflower blue, light blue, black, gray-blue, light gray and rose pink. Silver and gold threading was an additional element. Shoulder boards or epaulettes served both to indicate rank as well as branch of service.

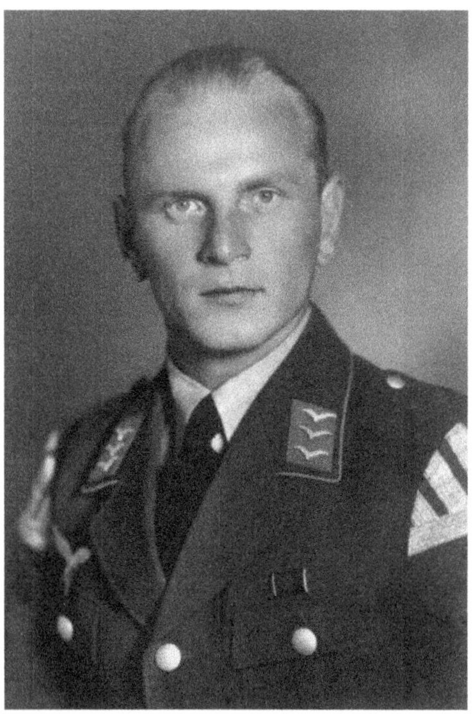

Portrait of Bandsman with 'Swallow's Nest' – Flak Unit *Obergefreiter* **(Corporal)**
All but the German Navy band musicians displayed the distinctive *Schwalbennester* (swallow's nest) shoulder insignia, including the Hitler Youth, SA and SS. Of various patterns and colors, some also included braiding and fringe that further indentified the individual; for example, drum and fife band members, trumpeters and buglers. Flak units and their ground troops came under the aegis of the Luftwaffe.

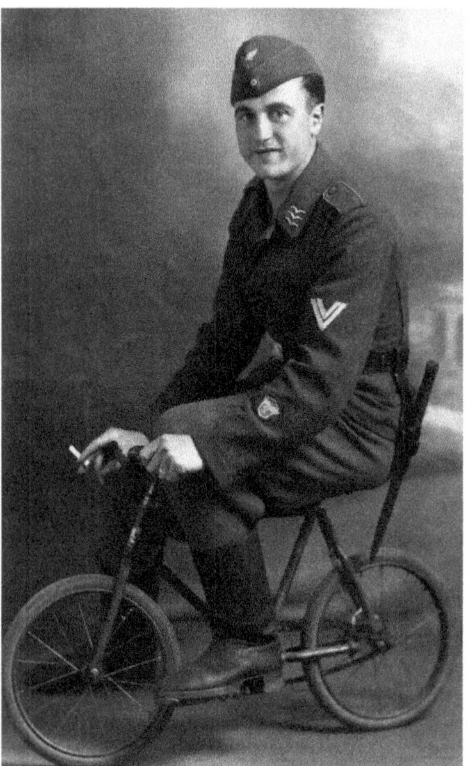

Studio Portrait on Two Wheels
A corporal in the Luftwaffe, a vehicle driver as indicated by the patch on his lower uniform sleeve, has traded his truck for a bicycle.

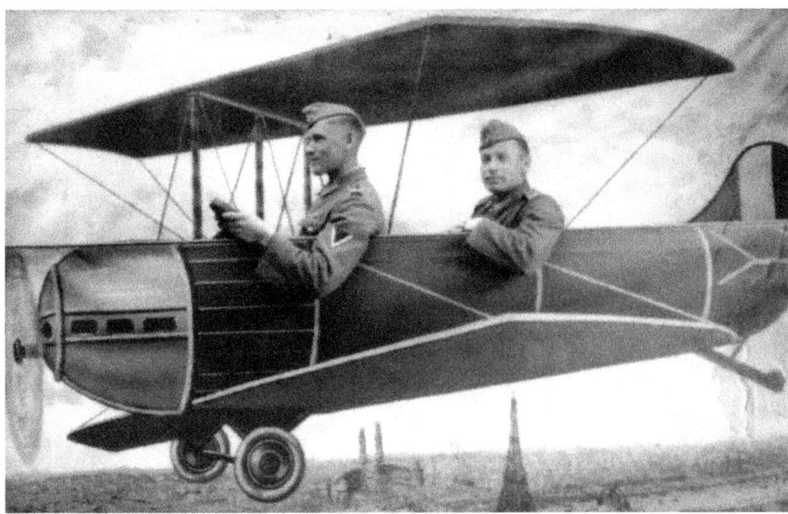

Popular Souvenir – Paris Photo Studio

An army private and corporal have taken flight over the Eiffel Tower thanks to a Parisian photo studio's special background.

The French campaign, often referred to as the 'Battle of France', perhaps because of its brevity, lasted but six weeks from 10 May 1940. The invasion also brought Belgium, Luxembourg and the Netherlands under German control. From the French beaches at Dunkirk, the Allies famously evacuated some 338,226 British, 123,069 French and 16,816 Belgian troops in Operation Dynamo. However, few remember that it was French troops who volunteered to stay behind to delay the German attack on the beaches.

In order to further humiliate the French, on 22 June 1940 Hitler forced them to sign the Armistice surrender documents in the same railway car in Compiegne in which the Germans had been forced to surrender in the First World War.

Flight of Fancy – The Past Meets the Present

Another popular studio 'trick' photo op was this one taken near Hanover, in the city of Dornitz, at Max Schutze's photography shop. Here, a rocket takes 'strong boys on a flight to their darlings'. Dornitz (aka Altengrabow) was also the location of a major military training area as well as the POW camp Stalag XI A.

Germany would lead the way in rocket design with its V-1 and V-2 'Vengeance' weapons. The first of Hitler's so-called 'Wonder Weapons' created to change the course of the war were launched a few days after the D-Day landings in June 1944, the target being London. In total nearly 10,000 of the rockets caused some 6,000 deaths and 50,000 injuries. A colonel in the SS as well as visionary scientist, Werner von Braun headed the missile projects and also developed plans for a multi-stage missile capable of reaching New York. Later, that technology would carry American astronauts to the moon.

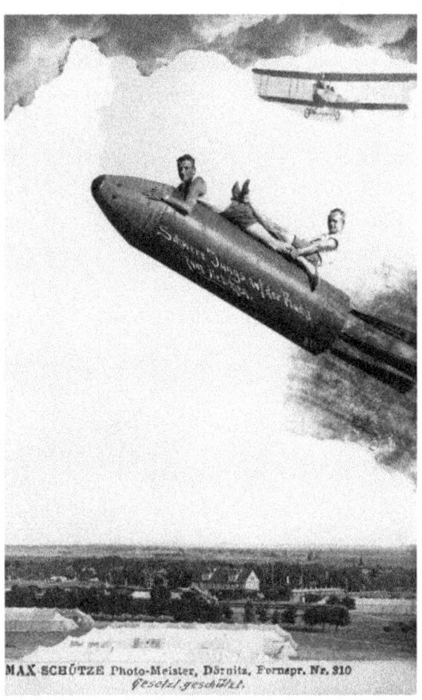

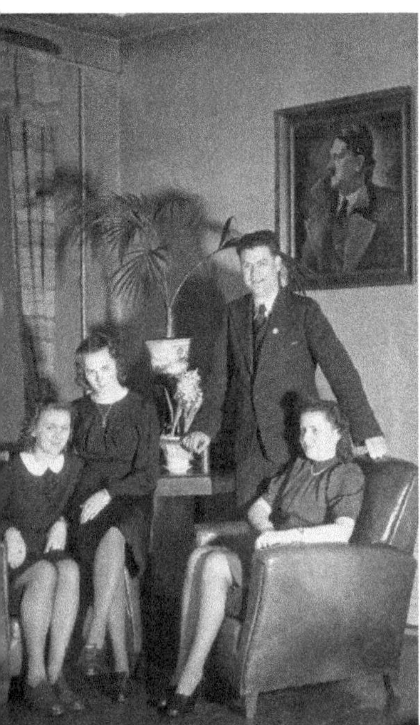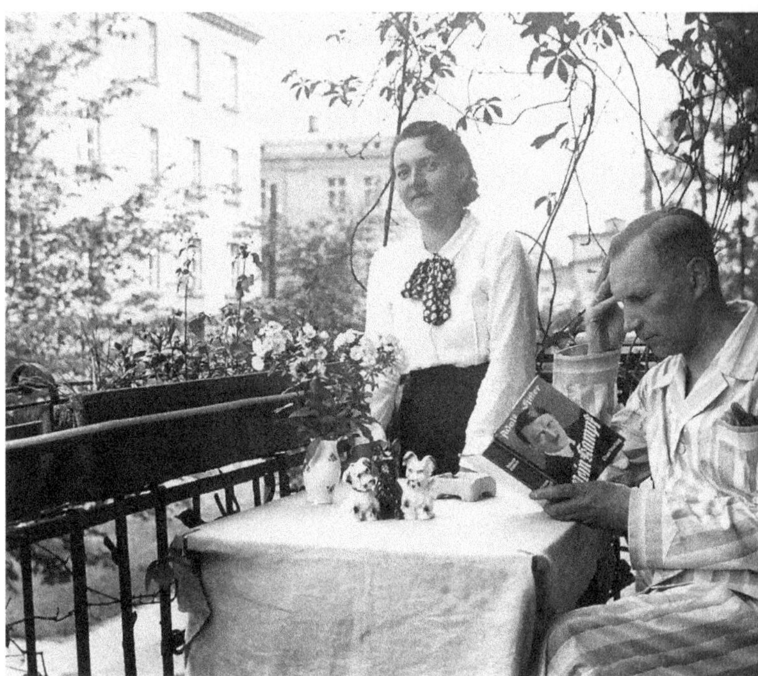

***Above left*: Studio Lighting at Home**
The glare of a photographer's lamps illuminates an upscale German family in their own home, the composition including an exotic palm tree and potted flower indicating their social status, highlighted by a large portrait of the Führer in the background. The head of the family wears a Nazi Party pin in his lapel.

***Above right*: Cover Photo**
The photo of Hitler appears on the cover of his 'best-selling' *Mein Kampf* – aka the bible and blueprint of the Nazi mindset. A copy was given as a wedding gift to every newly married couple, while millions more sold worldwide. The man in the pajamas appearing in deep contemplation was also a member of the SA (Brownshirts), who would fall out of favor with Hitler in his struggle for total power.

A fact often overlooked regarding the success of the Nazi programs, including the war effort, is the contribution of German women, with some 13 million active in the Party and many more serving as auxiliaries in all branches of the military, as nurses murdering 'unfit' children and frequently as concentration camp guards. During the takeover of Poland and areas in Russia, an estimated half million German women took part in that brutal policy of ethnic cleansing. Conditioned by Nazi doctrine, some joined their execution squad member husbands at mass shootings, often manning refreshment tables for the killers. Several even gained notoriety for killing Jews for sport or as the most sadistic of camp guards, but only a handful were brought to trial, the vast majority going unpunished.

***Opposite above*: Onsite Assignment – School Photo En Masse**
The photographer has managed to coordinate a large contingent of Hitler Youth members and their adult leaders as well as flag bearers and band members, but perhaps has not noticed some flaws.

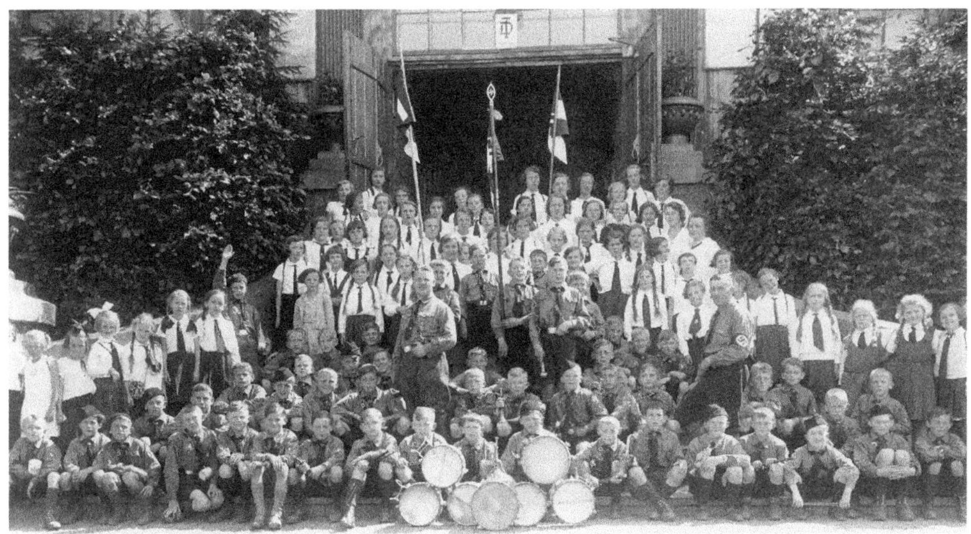

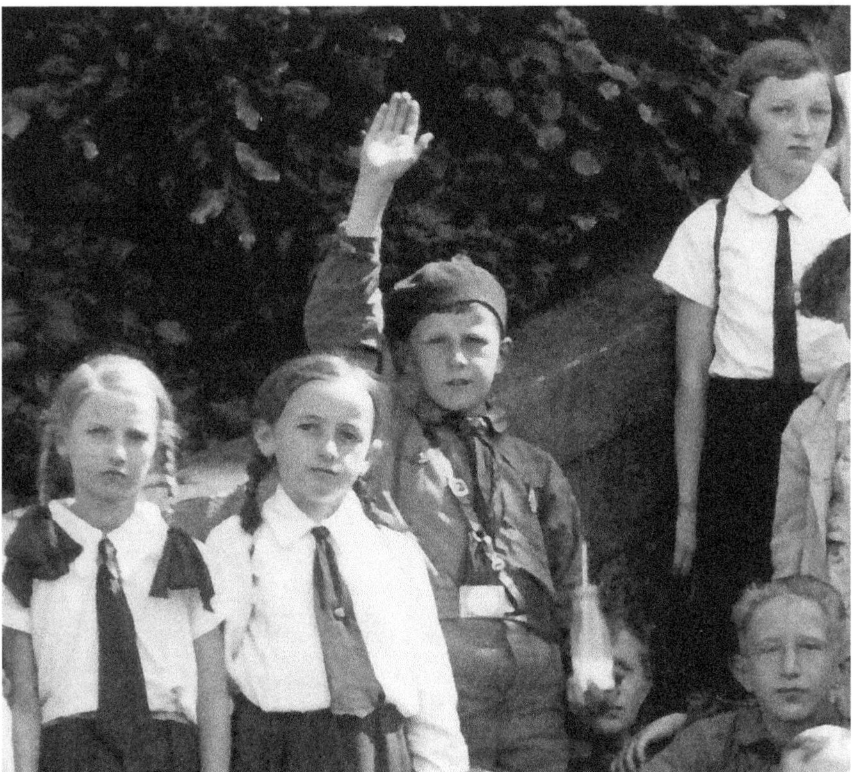

Hitler Salute with Milk
One boy, holding a bottle of milk with a straw in one hand, gives the Hitler salute with other. Another boy has crouched low as if to avoid the camera, no doubt causing concern with the photographer, not to mention the Hitler Youth leadership. It is often overlooked that tens of thousands of intensely indoctrinated Hitler Youth became part of the post-war German population.

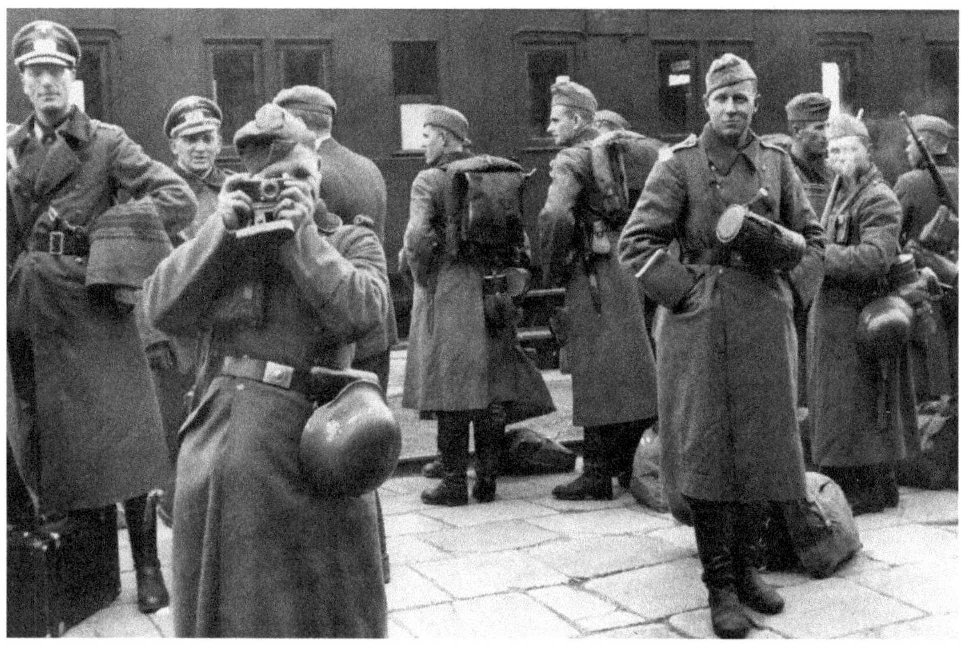

In Focus

A German soldier waiting to board a troop train snaps a photo of a fellow soldier pointing his 35 mm camera at him. A pair of officers, taking note of the photograph in progress, can be seen to his right.

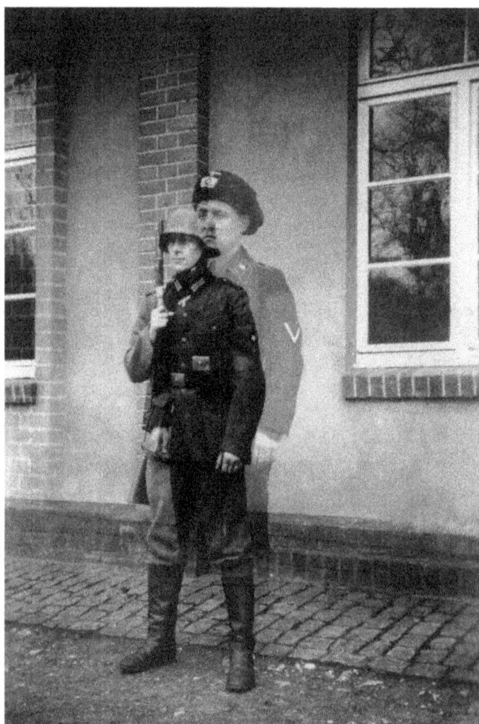

Double Exposure

A camera malfunction has seemingly captured the transformation of a field gray-uniformed *Heer* (Army) *soldat* into in a black-uniformed mechanised armour trooper, and in the process has promoted his rank from private to corporal.

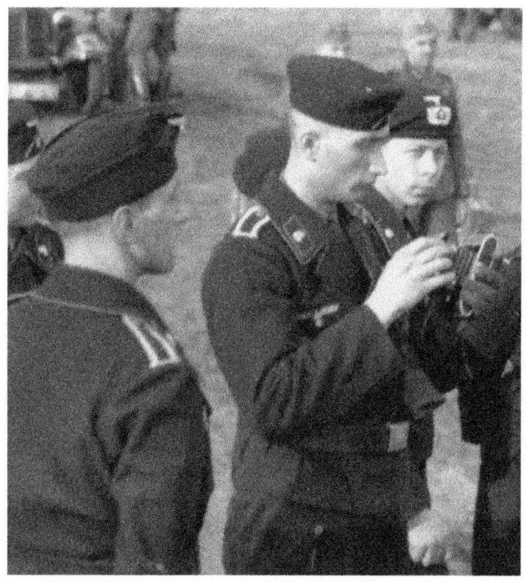

Off Came the Glove

A member of the mechanised forces, which included tanks (Panzer), armoured cars and troop transports, focuses on his camera as his colleagues look on. A variety of vehicles as well as members of the regular army appear in the background during what may be maneuvers.

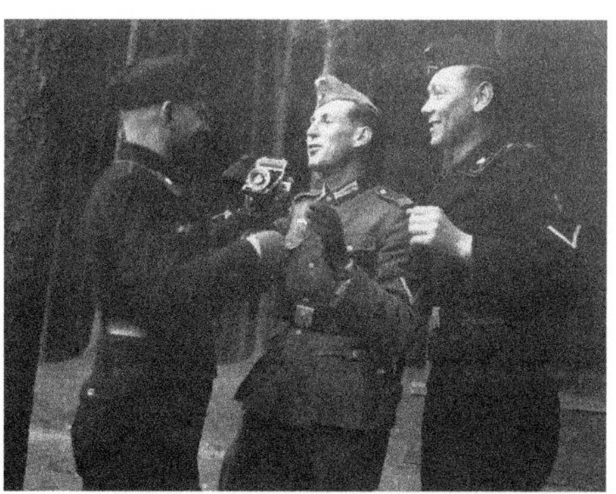

Competition for a Camera

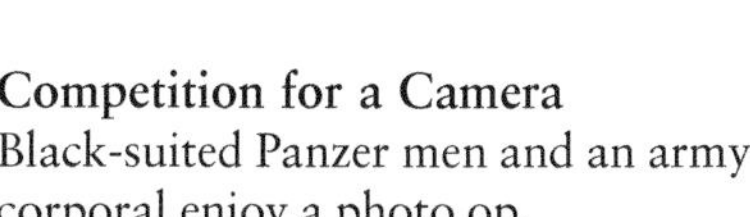

Black-suited Panzer men and an army corporal enjoy a photo op.

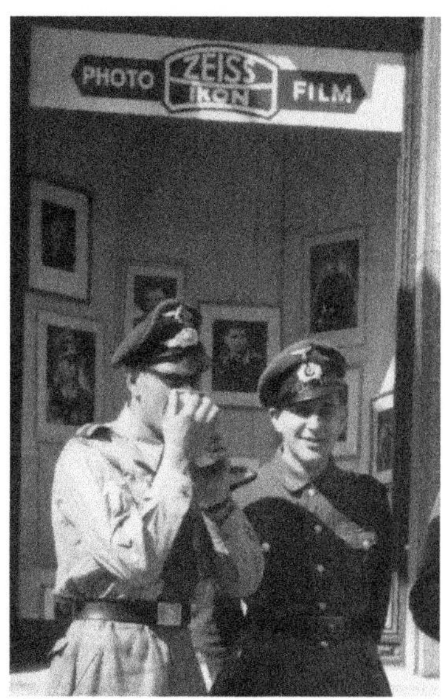

Shop of Heroes

A Luftwaffe man (left) and an army comrade are photographed in front of a photo shop advertising Zeiss products, its window showcasing a number of framed portraits of Third Reich military heroes – the German rock stars of the era, their images being marketed by the propaganda ministry. As winners of the highest Third Reich honors such as the Knight's Cross, many remained celebrities post-war, often appearing at international military conventions where they hobnobbed with their past enemies. Decades later, their autographed photos still sell briskly.

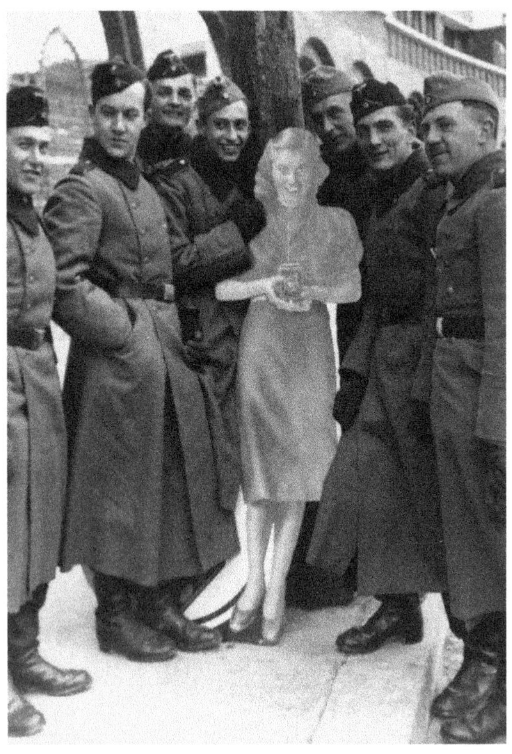

When in France
A group of soldiers clusters around a photo shop's attractive cut-out, making for a souvenir photo.

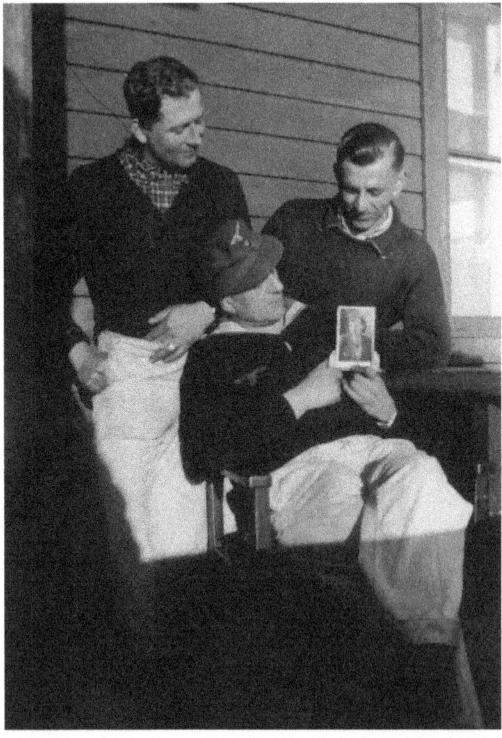

Photo from Home
Soldiers admire their comrade's photo, the young woman wearing the uniform of a Luftwaffe *Helferin* (female volunteer). Like all soldiers, Germans carried photos of their loved ones with them wherever the war sent them.

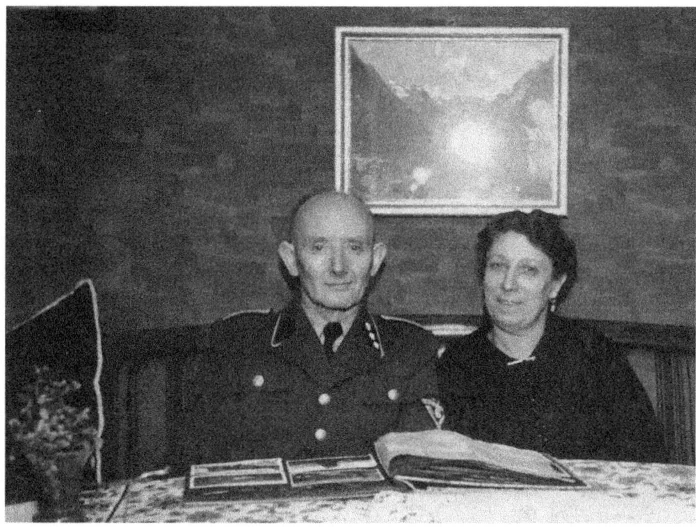

Memories

An older couple reminisces over their photo album. A First World War veteran, he now wears the insignia of a *Sturmfuhrer,* or company leader, within the NSKK (*Nationalsozialistiches Kraftfahrer Korps*), as well as the *Alte Kampfer* (old fighter) patch of honour on his sleeve, indicating him as one of the earliest supporters of the Nazi Party. The NSKK was a paramilitary organisation responsible for training automobile, truck and motorcycle operators in preparation for their military service within motorised and armored units. It origins lay within the original pre-Third Reich motoring enthusiast organisation.

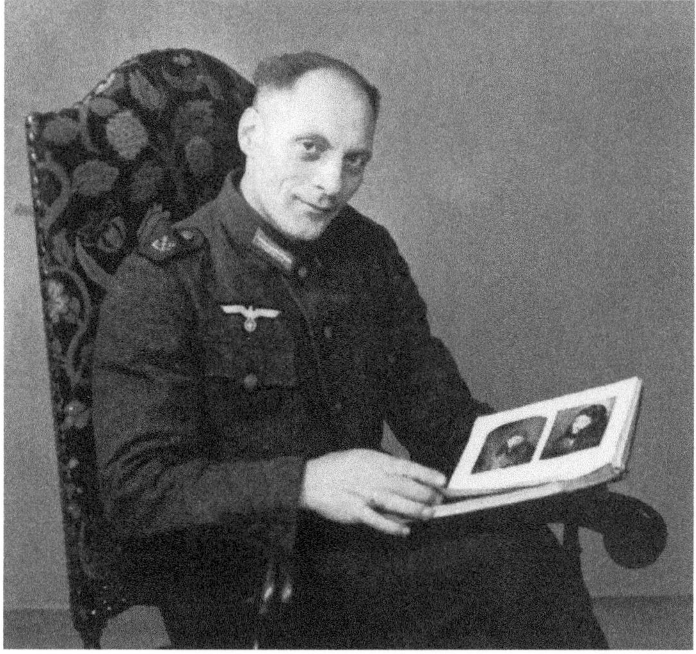

Picture Book

A member of the coastal artillery (*Kriegsmarine*) peruses an illustrated photo book.

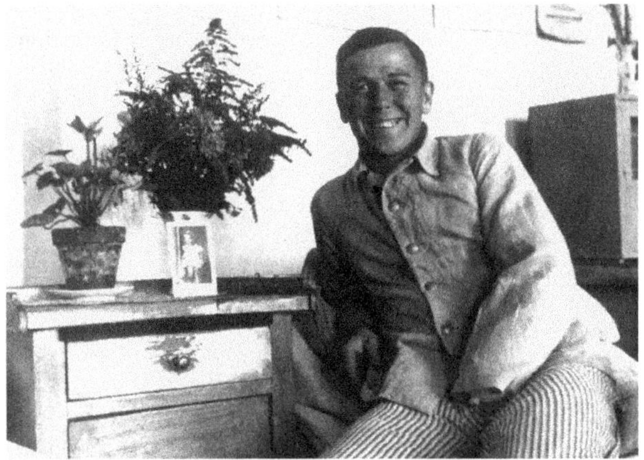

Kinderfoto in Krankenhaus
A soldier beams at the camera, the photo of a young girl propped up against a vase of flowers. He wears hospital clothing and his left hand is missing. His war is over, though the wounded were often 'reclaimed' and trained for munitions factory work, amputees being teamed up with fellow veterans.

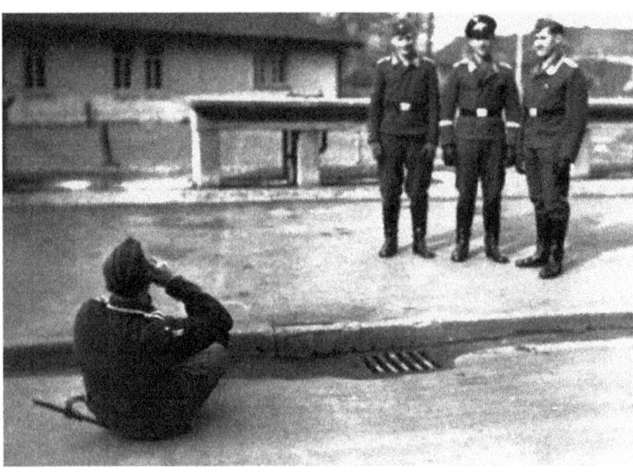

Advantage Point
A Luftwaffe NCO tries for a creative low-angle approach for the portrait of his trio of comrades, all likely flak troops.

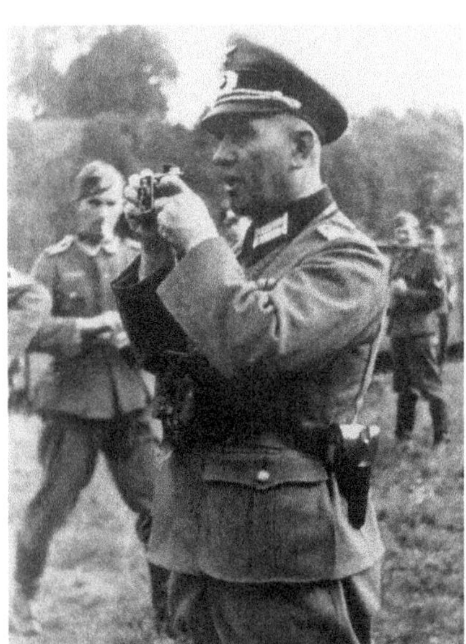

Well-Armed with Foth
Along with his Walther sidearm, a German officer aims his Foth camera in a photo dated 7 August 1941, two months after the invasion of the Soviet Union.

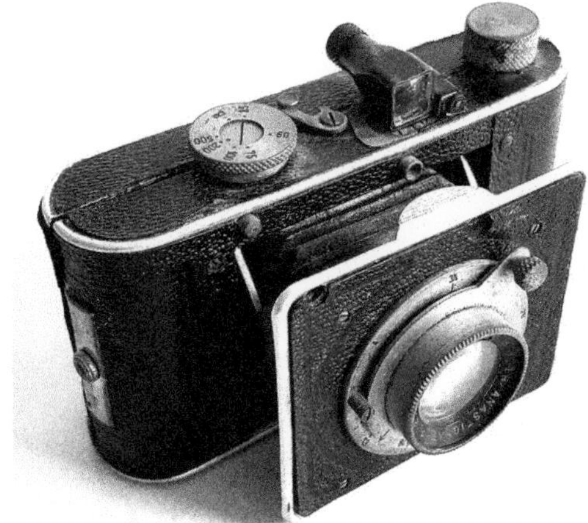

Foth Camera

The C. F. Foth optical company of Berlin produced binoculars as well as cameras from 1926 to 1940, including the 'Derby' vest-pocket strut folder using 127 film that was first produced in 1931 and continued being made until 1943.

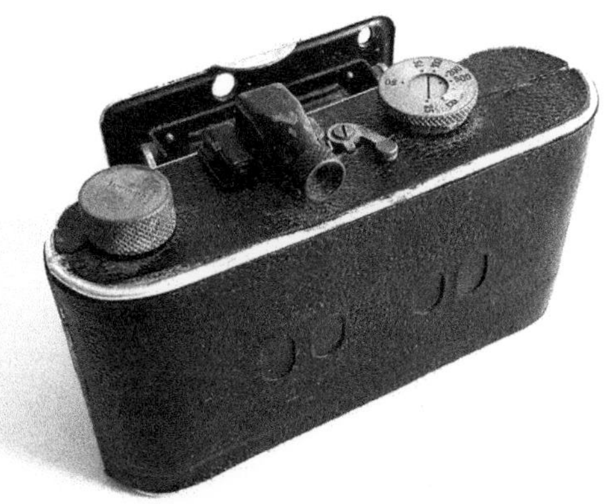

Pocketable Bargain

Featuring an advanced focal plane shutter, the Foth was offered as a low-cost alternative to the Leica and Contax cameras. It was designed as a compact, 'vest pocket' camera, and thanks to its 1/500th of a second shutter speed, was touted as being well-suited to capture fast sports action shots. The four 'windows' allow for viewing the number of the exposure in position.

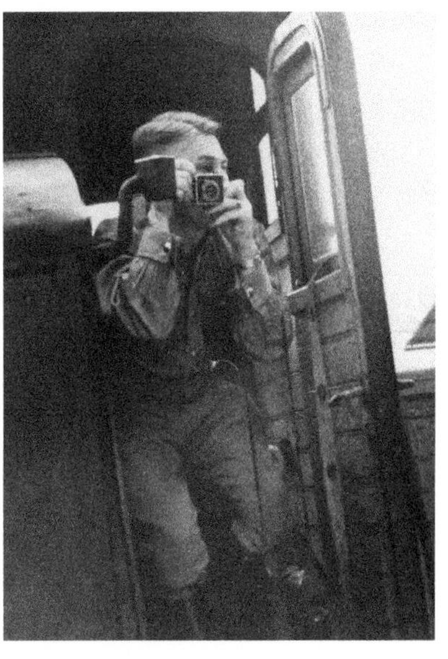

Foth Snapshot

A young soldier leans out of a doorway in order to capture something of interest. The camera appears to be a Foth Derby, its leather case dangling from the young soldier's arm.

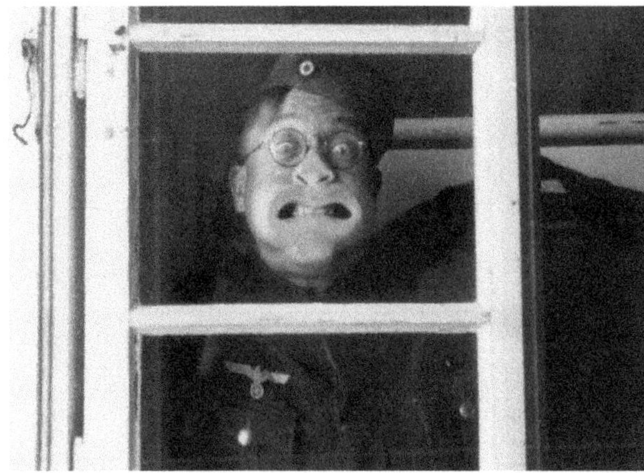

The Face in the Window
The recording of oddities was a popular subject for German servicemen, capturing humorous images in uniform or as an adjunct of gallows humour.

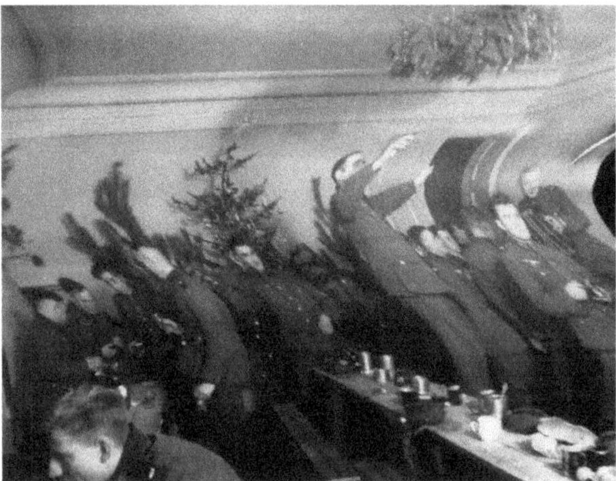

Christmas Party in Flux
The scene captured here could be the result of much beer and wine consumed while celebrating the holiday. Visible in the right corner is an accordionist adding music to the festivities. Perhaps a result of the camera motion blurring, a Christmas tree seems to have been sent flying across the ceiling by the soldier standing on the table bench.

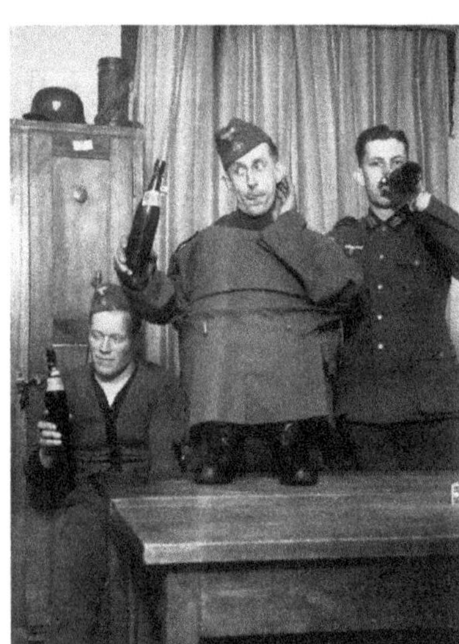

Uncommon Denominator
Beer helps compose a humorous barracks hall photo. The tenets of the Third Reich military stipulated that no privilege would be given to social rank or education, with all soldiers being seen as equal and rewards based on performance. The SS, however, had its own rigid standards of racial purity and physical prowess – standards that were downgraded as the war ground on and casualties mounted.

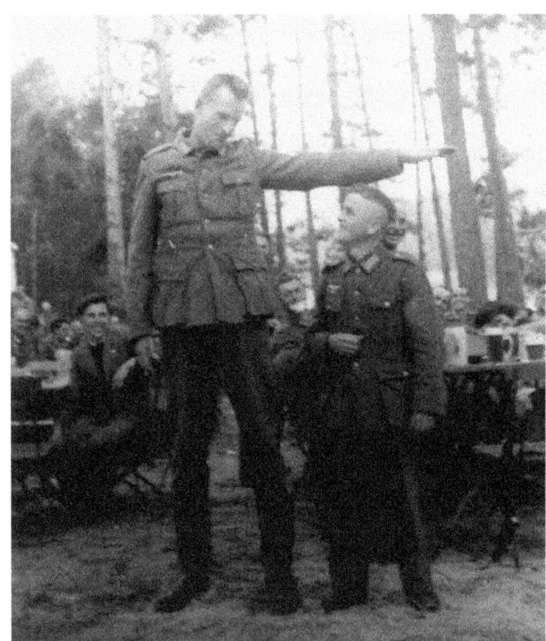

For Comparison's Sake
While their beer-drinking comrades enjoy the show, two soldiers share the ups and downs of being stand-outs in a culture of supposed homogenous Supermen.

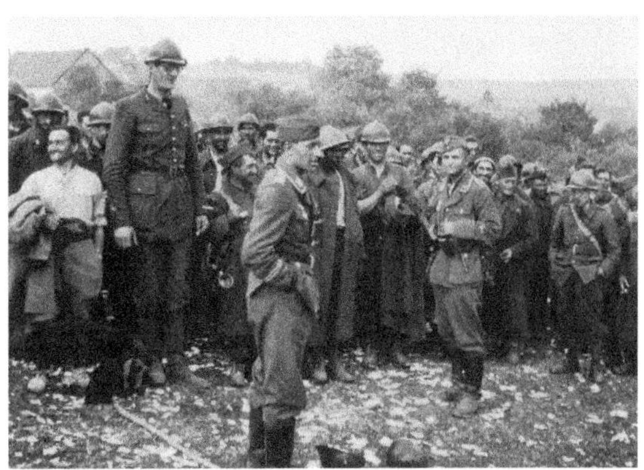

Large Target in France – May 1940
A French soldier towers above both his amused comrades and their German captors, a pair of casual-appearing Luftwaffe NCOs.

Bested by The Tallest Man in the World
In a photo dated 1942, Luftwaffe soldiers who have found themselves posted to Finland surround Väinö Myllyrinne, who stood at 8 feet 3 inches (251.4 cm). As the tallest man in the world holding the title from 1940 to 1957, he was also the tallest soldier ever to serve in the Finnish Defense Forces.

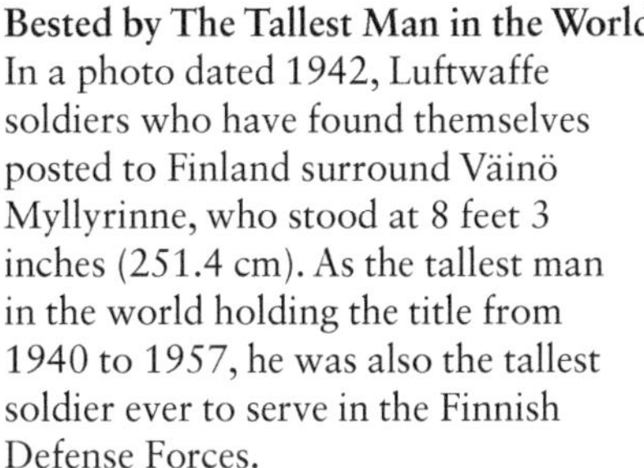

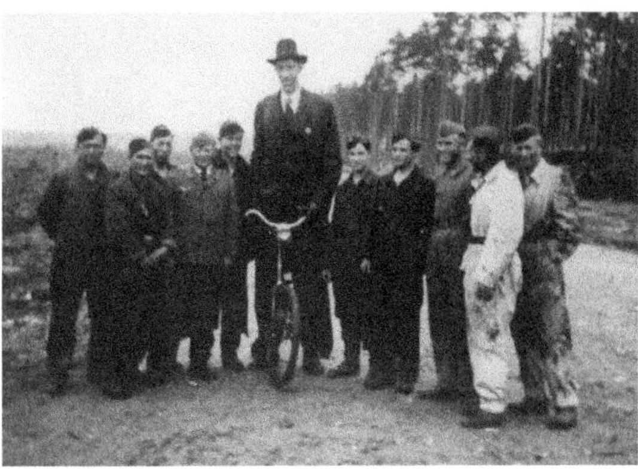

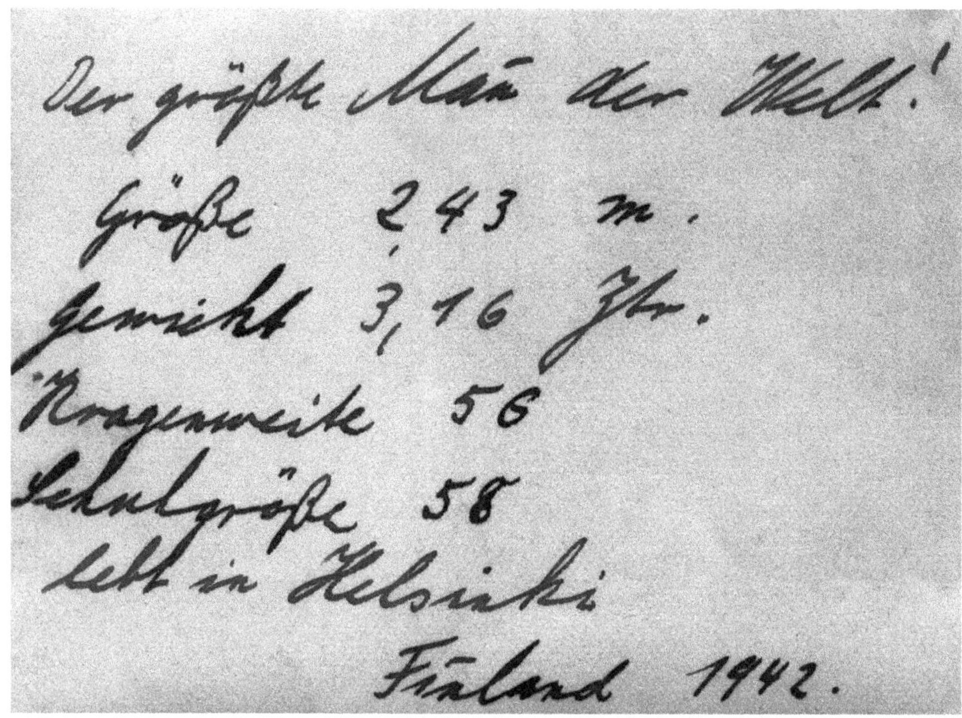

Statistics Recorded
The notations give Väinö's dimensions and that he lived in Helsinki. Väinö was also voted the twelfth 'Greatest Finn' in the TV show *Suuret Suomalaiset* (a copy of the BBC show *Great Britons*).

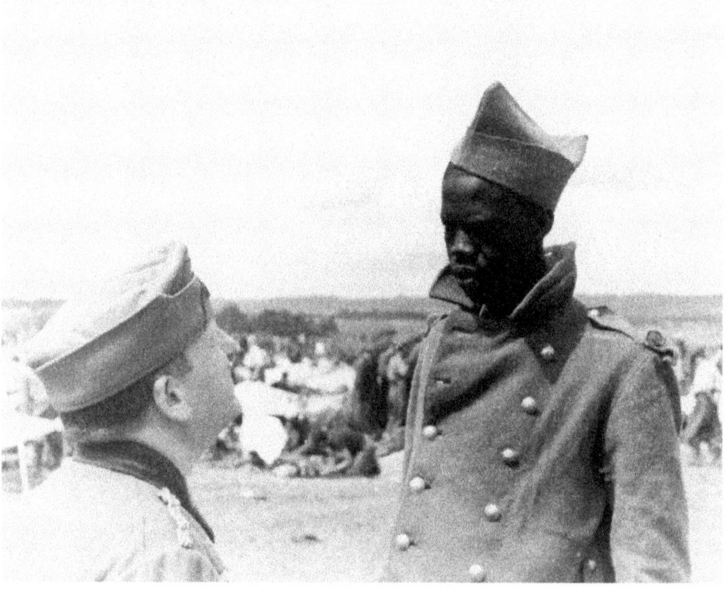

Stare-Down
A tall French Colonial African POW has been singled out for a souvenir photo. German battlefield treatment often reflected the Nazi racist edicts, resulting in summary execution.

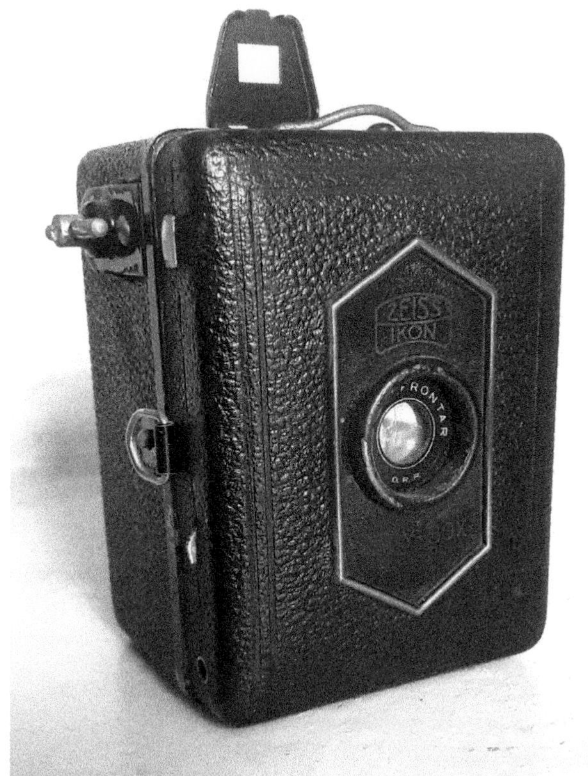

All Shapes and Sizes – Zeiss 'Baby' Box Tengor Camera with Goerz Frontar Lens
Zeiss Ikon was formed in 1926 by amalgamating four major German camera makers. The marketing plan designed to attract both beginners as well as advanced amateurs and professionals. This meant having a low-cost, simple box camera. But, being Zeiss Ikon, they had to have superior quality so modified an existing small camera produced by the well-respected Goerz company (1924–26) and came up with a series of classics, the Zeiss Ikon Baby Box Tengor, produced from 1930 to 1939.

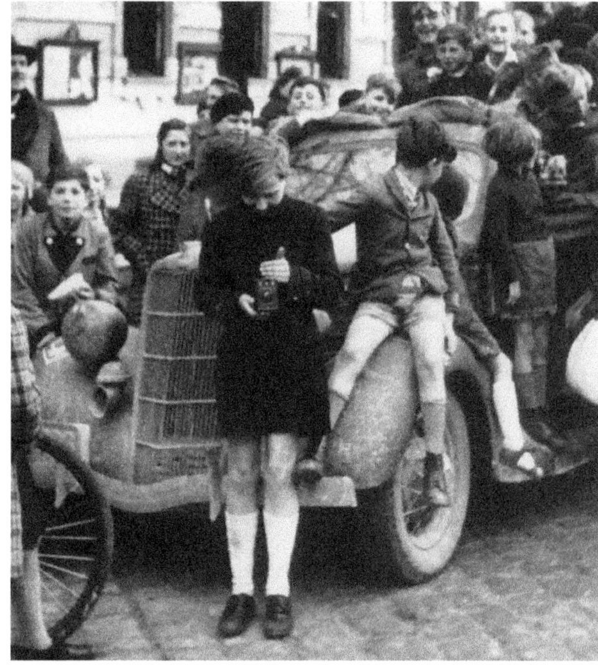

Box Camera in Action
Children in Vienna have flocked around a Wehrmacht truck during the annual Day of the Armed Forces celebration. The box camera could be one of dozens of different brands offered to the public.

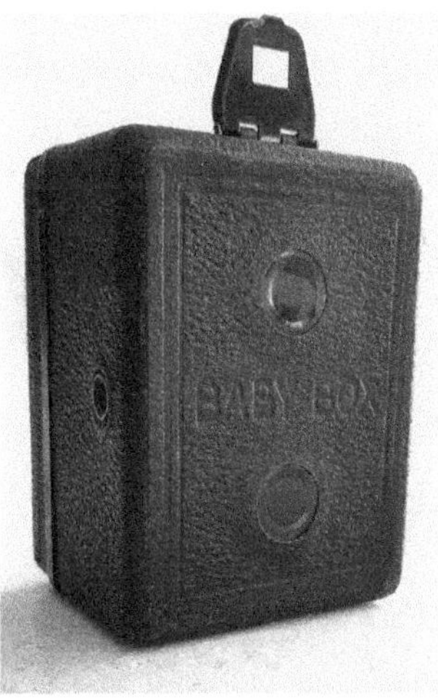 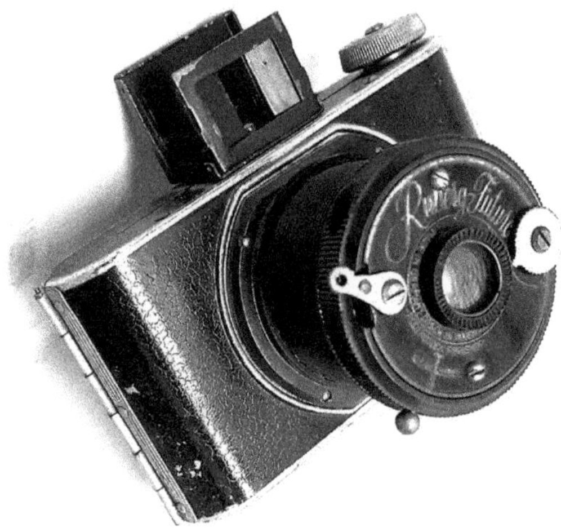

***Above left*: Palm-Sized but Potent**

Only 2 ½ inches wide, 3 inches tall and just over 2 inches front to back, the smallest was the Baby Box Tengor, the pocket camera taking sixteen pictures on 127 film with its F/11 lens and single-speed 1/25 second shutter. Designed for simplicity of use for young photographers with its one shutter speed and fixed aperture, it was suitable only for outdoor daylight snapshots. A major marketing success, thousands were in use during the Third Reich.

***Above right*: Ruberg Futurio, 1920s**

The Ruberg & Renner Company was founded in the final year of the First World War in Hagen, Germany, by Felix Ruberg, one of the industrialists who became a supporter of the NSDAP. Prior to 1930, the company designed and produced bicycle parts and chain-drive mechanisms, then ventured into simple, inexpensive cameras.

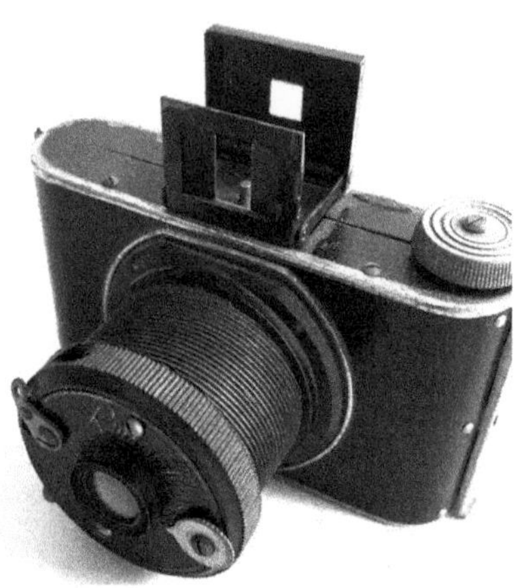 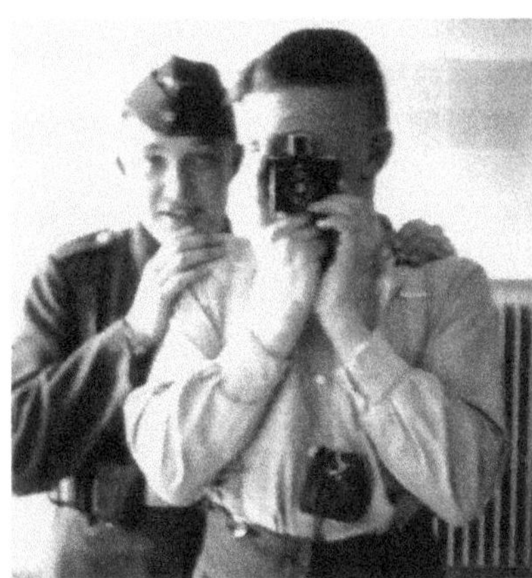

***Above left*: Helical Focusing was Manually Operated**

By 1942 camera production fell by the wayside as the company shifted to military products, including small canisters for machine-gun bullets, which were about the size and shape of the metal cameras previously manufactured. Post-war the company resumed production of earlier industrial products but not cameras; thus, the Ruberg cameras that survived are relatively rare.

***Above right*: Mirror Effect**

Two young soldiers may be facing a mirror or a fellow cameraman with one of the smaller, less expensive German cameras available in the 1930s and 1940s.

French Smiles for the German Camera

Recently captured French soldiers can't refrain from smiling for the camera. During the six-week war, the French suffered 90,000 killed, 200,000 wounded, and 1.8 million captured. German losses during the campaign included 27,074 killed. Total French losses during the war included 217,600 military deaths. In reality, more French civilians were killed as the result of Allied bombing than by the Germans.

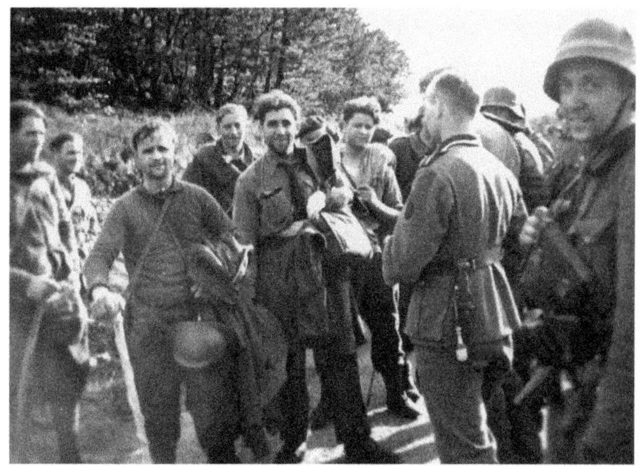

Fun with the Allies on the Run – Post-Dunkirk France

After the successful summer invasion of France in 1940, German soldiers mock their vanquished enemies by wearing British 'pie tin' (left) and French 'Adrian' (right) helmets. The French helmets bore crests and arm-of-service badges, the shiny insignia providing a good target for German snipers.

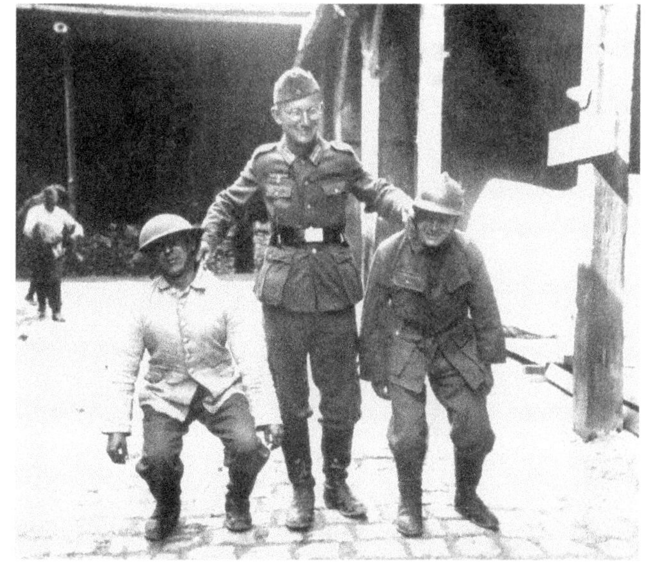

Ersatz French POWs

A group of young recruits, heads shaven for their graduation initiation, present themselves as mock POWs guarded by a German soldier who has donned a French helmet for the photo.

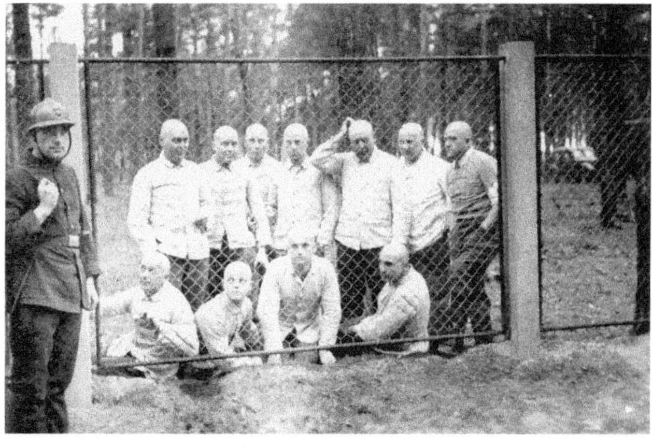

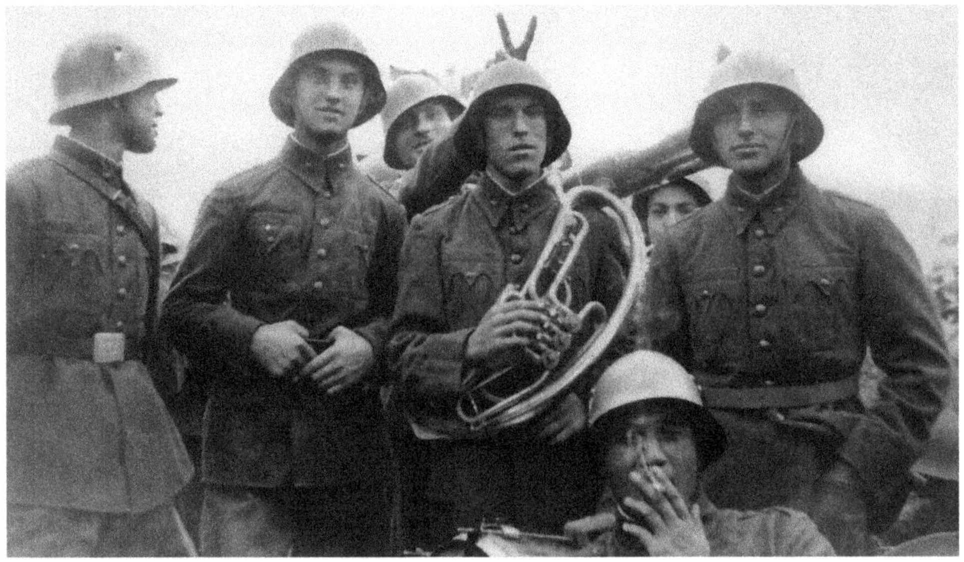

Erstwhile Axis Ally
Bulgarian soldiers clown for a German's camera sometime in early 1942. Germany secured –
either by ready agreement or forced coercion – military alliances with Italy, Romania, Hungary,
Slovakia, Latvia and Lithuania, as well as incorporating large numbers of Ukrainian volunteers
and smaller numbers of Waffen-SS volunteers from France, Holland, Belgium and Norway,
among other occupied countries. In 1944 the Bulgarians would change sides and declare war on
Germany. However, between 1941 and 1944, some 9,000 Bulgarian partisans and over 20,000
members of the underground resistance were killed by the Germans and their fascist partners.

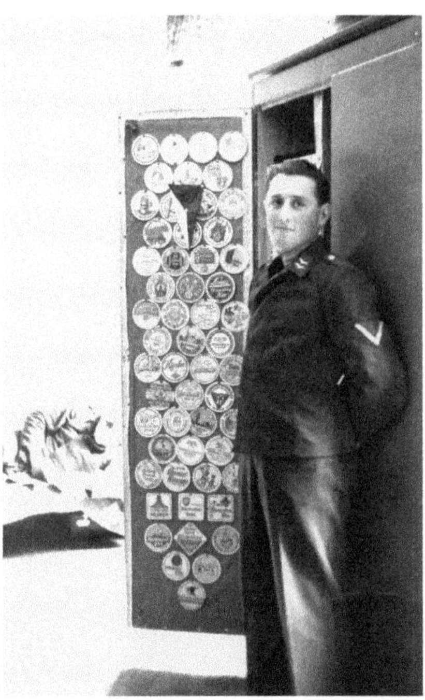

Locker Art
A Luftwaffe corporal has decorated his locker
door with fifty-six different beer coasters, which
he proudly displays for the photographer. During
the pre-war Nazi era years, German civilian
consumption of beer, already one of the highest in
Europe, rose by 25 per cent. Beer was also a staple
beverage of the German armed forces through
the war years. Hitler abstained from alcohol and
was known to drink distilled water. Himmler also
frowned on drinking and made it a punishable
offense within the ranks of the SS if taken to excess.

Celebration

Dressed in their *Waffenrock* or 'walking out' dress uniforms, a group of soldiers celebrate some occasion with extraordinarily large bottles of champagne. A clue to their location is found on the wall behind them, the signage reading 'The Two Moors is situated directly on the Rhine and the railway station,' and very likely refers to a popular restaurant. An indication of the improved standard of living under the Third Reich, at least in Germany, was indicated during the pre-war years when wine consumption almost doubled and champagne sales increased by a factor of five.

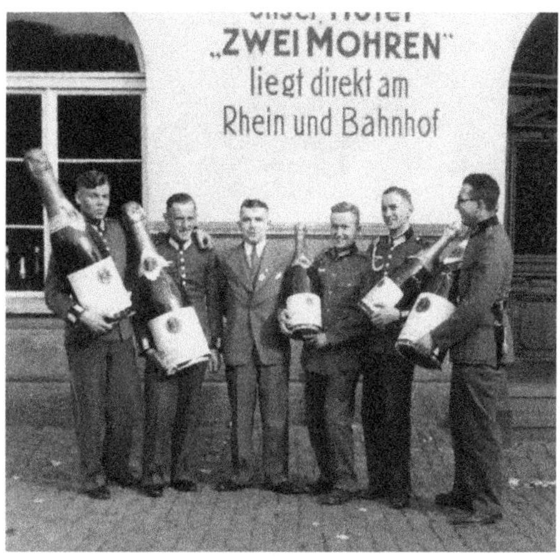

Zeiss-Ikon Ikonta 521/16

First introduced in 1935, the folding camera used 120 type film (twelve 6x6 cm negatives). This model, one of several in the Ikonta line, features a 75 mm Tessar lens matched to a Compur-Rapid shutter. Zeiss-Ikon established a well-earned and lasting reputation for high-quality optics.

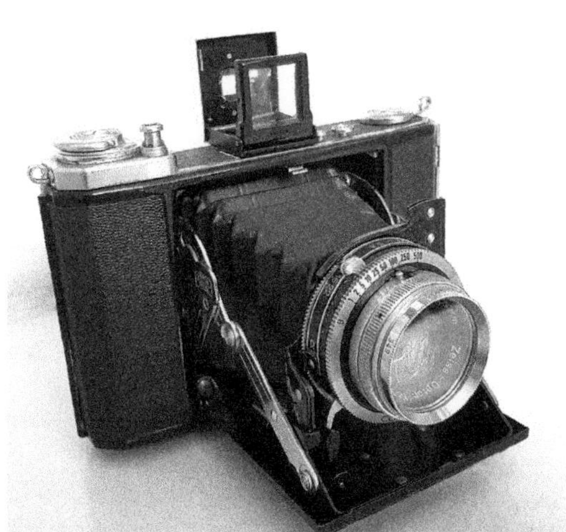

Point and Shoot

A German soldier aims what appears to be a Zeiss-Ikon Nettar 515 'pocket' strut-folding camera that could capture sixteen images on a roll of 120 size film. First introduced in 1937, it features high-end Zeiss optics and shutter speeds up to 1/125th of a second. It is similar in compactness to the modern point and shoot cameras, and in addition takes more than double the size of negatives, allowing for enhanced clarity of image. The soldier's cap shows the overseas roundel insignia, in this case indicating a location somewhere in France.

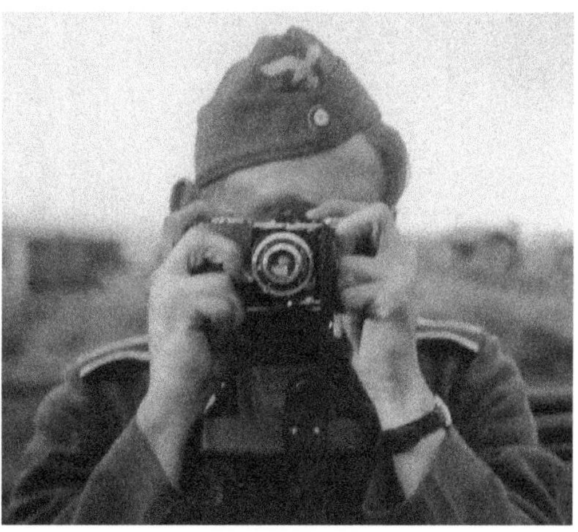

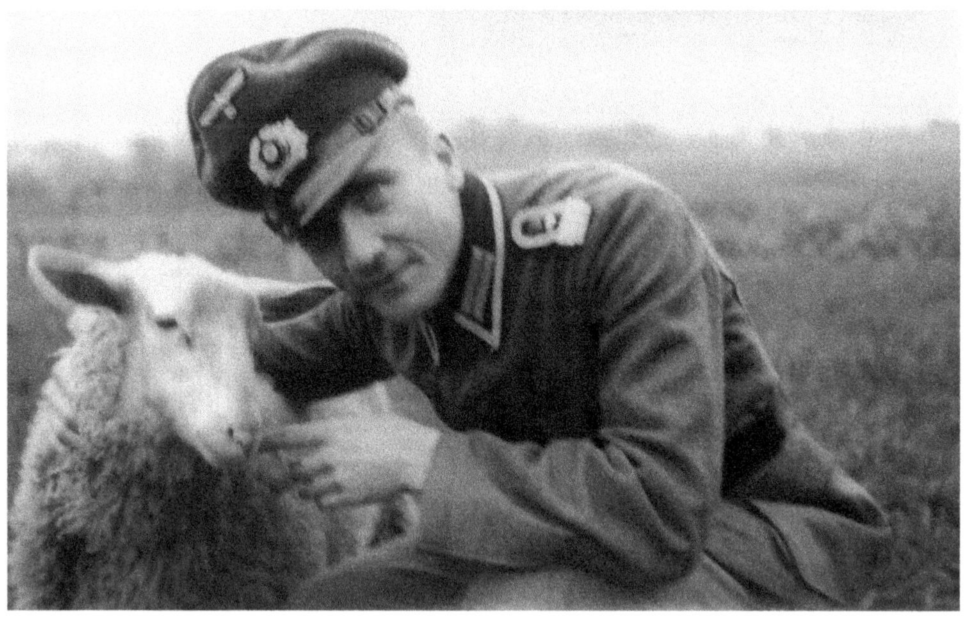

Pastoral Pastime – NCO Poses with a Farmyard Friend
Germans prided themselves as lovers of animals and during the Third Reich measures were established for their protection and welfare. Post-war West German leader Conrad Adenauer would later describe his fellow countrymen during the Nazi era as 'a nation of carnivorous sheep'.

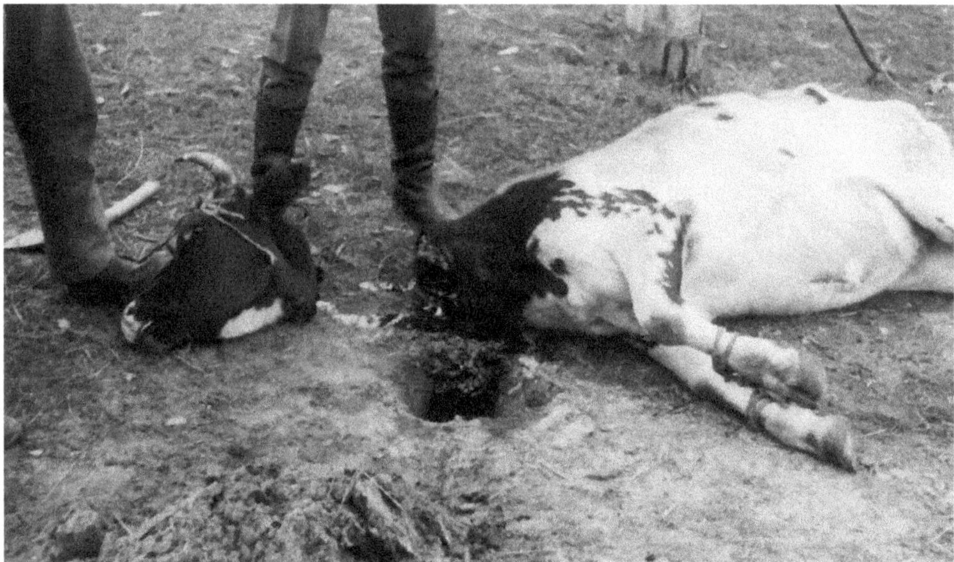

Collateral Casualty
Two soldiers stand over the decapitated body of a cow in a French farmer's field. The gaping hole could indicate a shell impact but the animal's fettered hooves may indicate it was destined for dinner, the hole dug to drain away its blood.

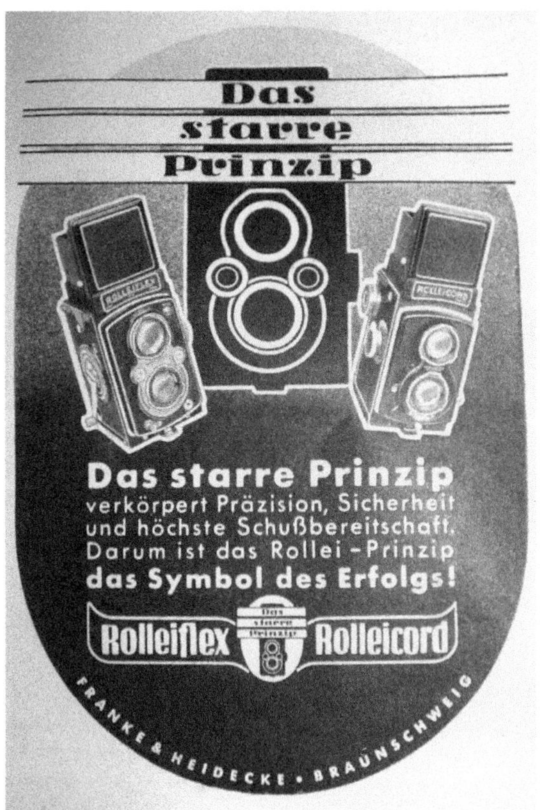

'The Prinzip Principle ... Embodies Precision, Safety and the Fastest Ready to fire! Why is the Rollei Prinzip the Symbol of Success!'
Both camera models featured Twin Lens Reflex design with the Rolleiflex targeted at professionals, the less expensive Rolleicord for amateur photographers. Both were valued for their high quality, compact size, excellent optics, user-friendly simplicity of operation and rugged dependability. The first Rolleiflex was introduced in 1929, with the improved Standard coming in 1939, just in time for Germany's invasion of Poland. The camera was also used by American photographer Frank Capra during his coverage of the Second World War. The cameras are still in production.

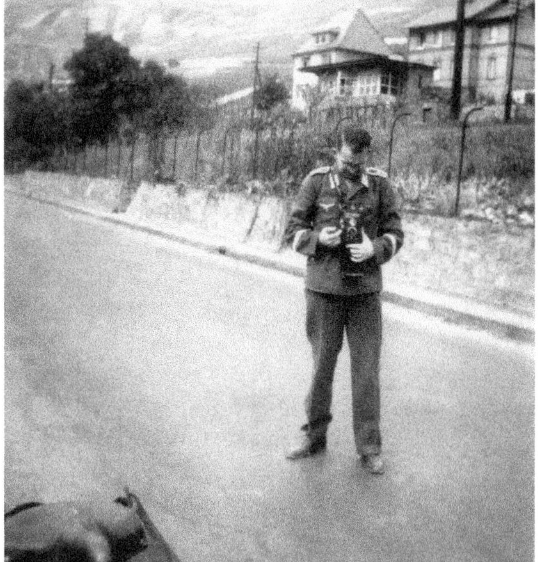

Street Scene
A Luftwaffe master sergeant adjusts his Twin Lens Reflex camera, perhaps with the motorcycle just visible in the corner of the image as part of the subject matter.

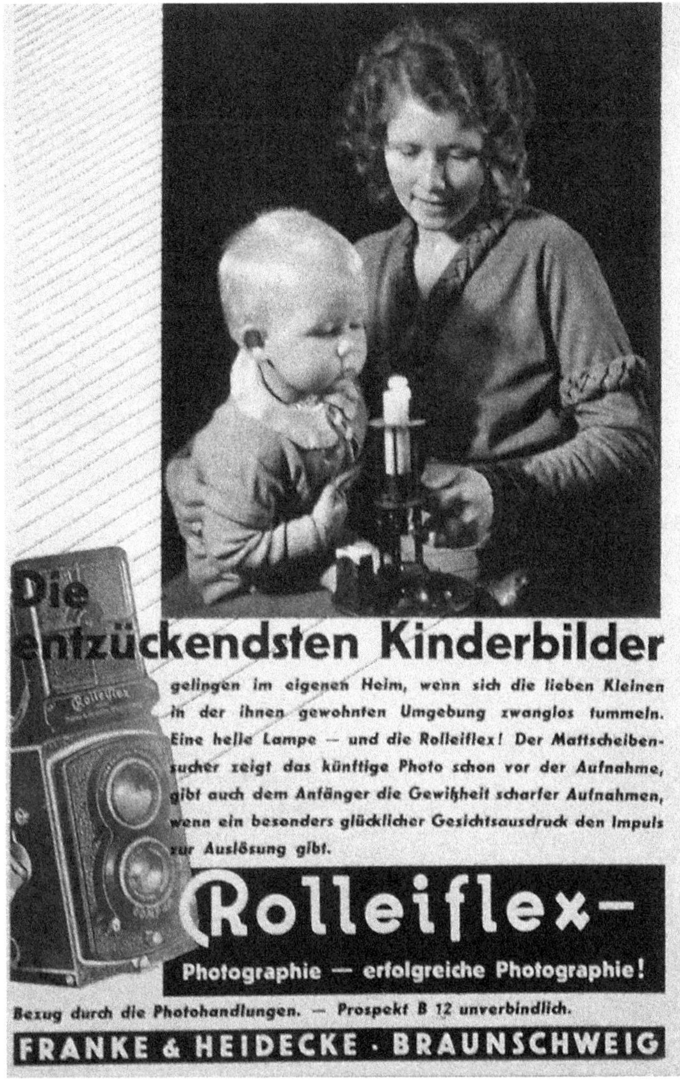

Magazine Advertisement, 1933 – *Die Entzuckendsten Kinderbilder*
The text in part reads 'The Most Delightful Children's Pictures taken in your home while the dear small ones casually play. All one needs is one bright lamp and a Rolleiflex!'

Founded in 1920 in the city of Braunschweig, the company employed 800 workers by 1930. During the night of 14–15 October 1944, 233 four-engined Lancaster bombers of the Royal Air Force dropped 200,000 incendiary bombs on the city as part of Operation Hurricane, designed to demonstrate Allied air superiority. Deliberately designed to generate a firestorm, the fires burned continuously for two and a half days. Because of its large number of excellent bomb shelters and an innovative fire department, the number of deaths was limited to 2,905. Of those, 1,286 were 'foreign workers' – aka slave laborers – who died because they were not allowed to seek shelter by their German overlords.

The Rolleiflex facility, then engaged in military production, was badly damaged, but because of its reputation the Allies aided in its recovery. The company employed over 1,000 workers by 1950, the year co-founder Paul Franke died at the age of sixty-two, followed by his partner Reinhold Heidecke in 1960 at seventy-nine, both having seen their company reborn and prospering.

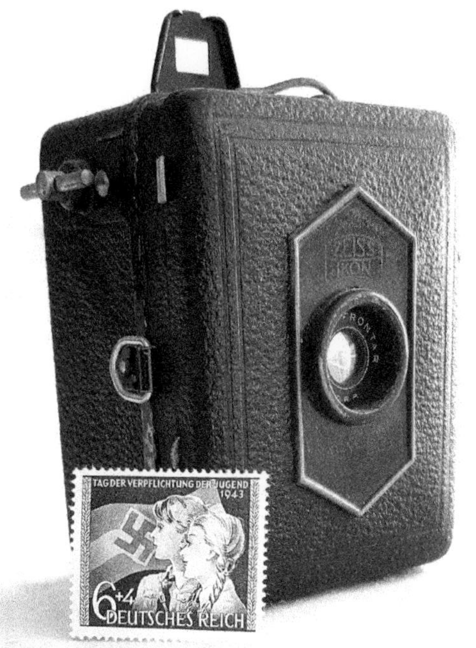

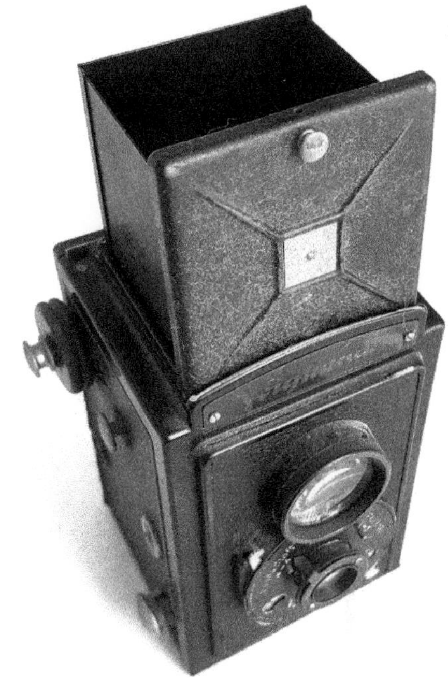

Above left: Voigtländer & Sohn, Braunschweig, Germany, *c.* 1932–37
While it has the appearance of a TLR (Twin Lens Reflex), the Brillant was in effect a basic box camera. It used 120 roll film and featured a Voigtländer Anastigmat Skopar 75 mm F/4.5 lens.

Above right: Viewfinder Open
Seen here is an early model with manual settings, including *Porträt, Gruppe* and *Landschaf*t (landscape, group and portrait).

TTL
Two army *obergefreiter* (corporals) pose with a trainload of army wagons as a backdrop. While both soldiers carry standard messenger/ courier satchels, the flowers indicate farewell gifts; they are likely off to France. The camera may be a Rolleicord or one of several other TL cameras available at the time.

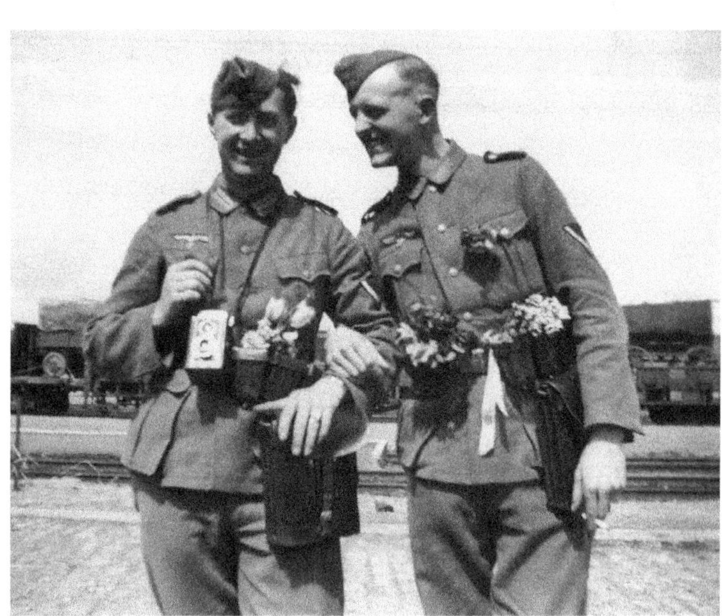

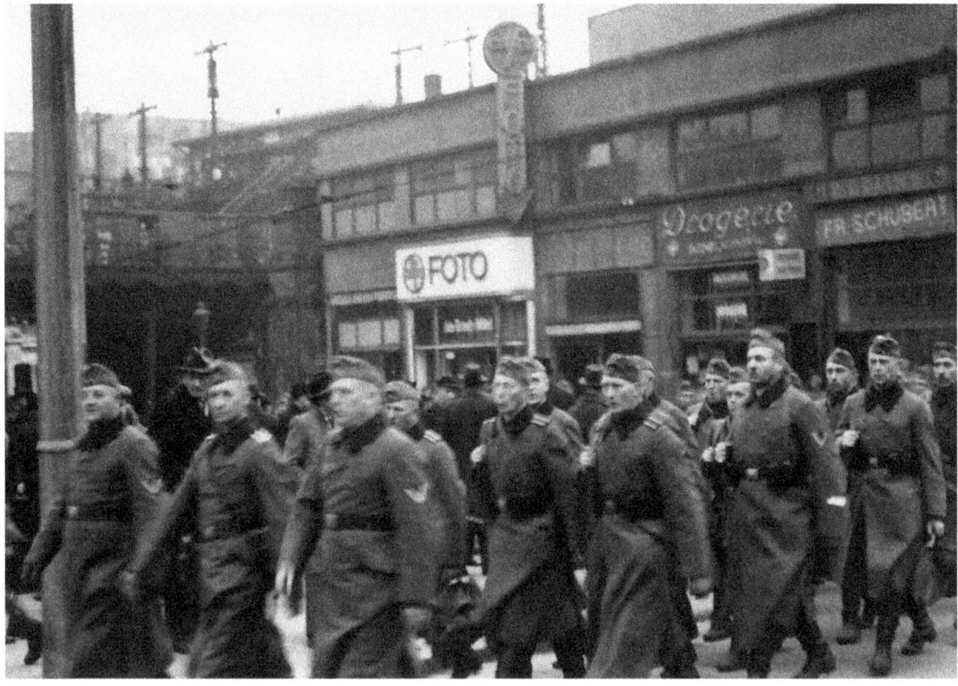

Foto Finish

Army troops, some singing, march past several shops including a photography studio advertising Agfa products in what appears to be the city of Leipzig. Founded in 1867 in the city of Rummelsburg (a suburb of Berlin), *Actien Gesellschaft für Anilin Fabrikation*, or Agfa, initially manufactured dyes and stains, the 'Agfa'-branded cameras first appearing in 1873.

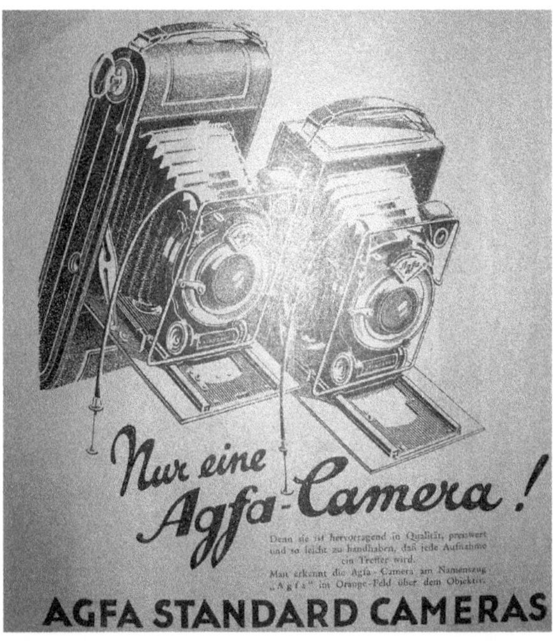

Ad Appearing in *Berlin Illustrated Times*, 1929

By the 1920s Agfa offered roll film, plate and filmpack models with Agfa cameras appearing in a folding camera/collapsible bellows design that would soon seem antiquated with the advent of compact 35 mm cameras. In 1928 Agfa USA joined with Ansco and eventually became GAF. Agfa AG, the German Agfa, merged with Gevaert of Belgium in 1964.

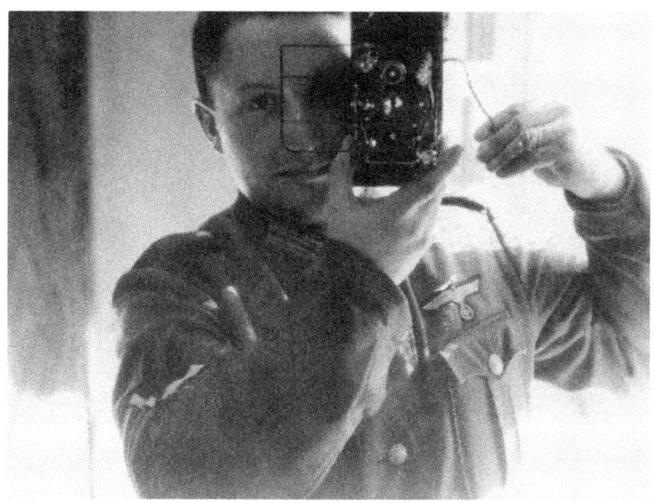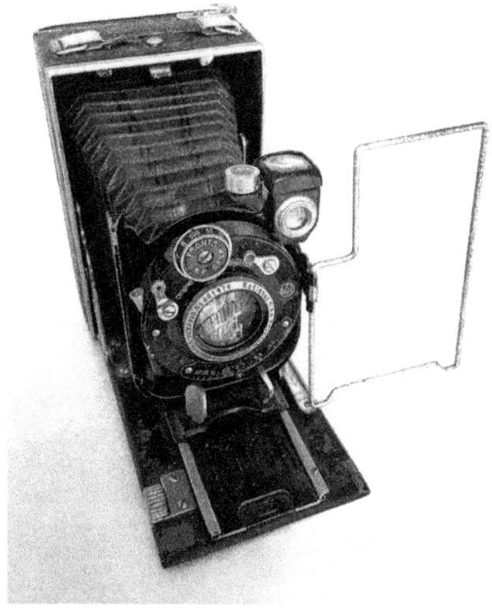

Above left: Cable Release
An army corporal snaps a self-portrait, the wire frame viewfinder extended from his large folding strut camera, one of a wide variety of German brands available from the 1920s to '40s prior to their eclipse by the smaller, lighter, more technological advanced 35 mm format.

Above right: 1930s Strut Camera – Schneider Kreuznach Radionar F4.5 Lens, Pronto Shutter and Swing-out Viewfinder
The Schneider optical company, established in 1913, produced lenses during the 1930s and 1940s for Rolleiflex and Kodak Retina. By November 1936, they had produced their millionth lens.

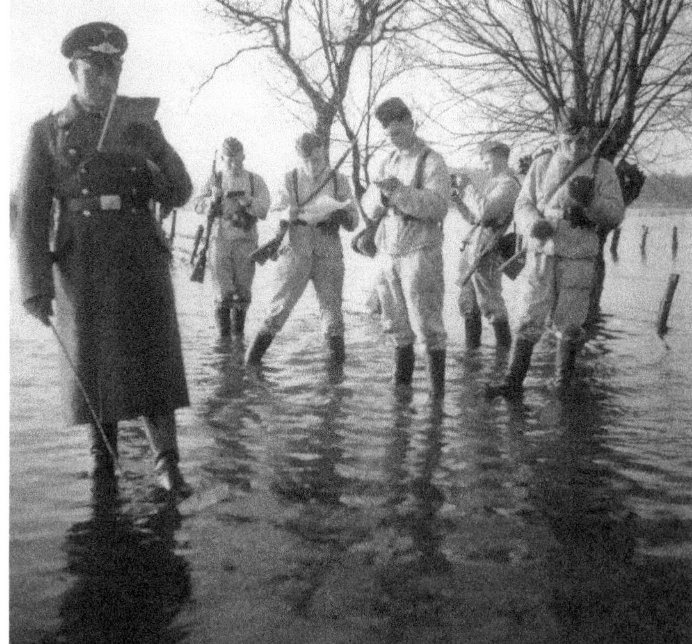

Elemental Composition in Flooded Field
No doubt standing in water himself, a soldier has brought together an exceptional composition as an officer wearing his army greatcoat consults his maps while his young recruits, wearing their protective white denim fatigues over their uniforms, check their own maps, apparently during a training session.

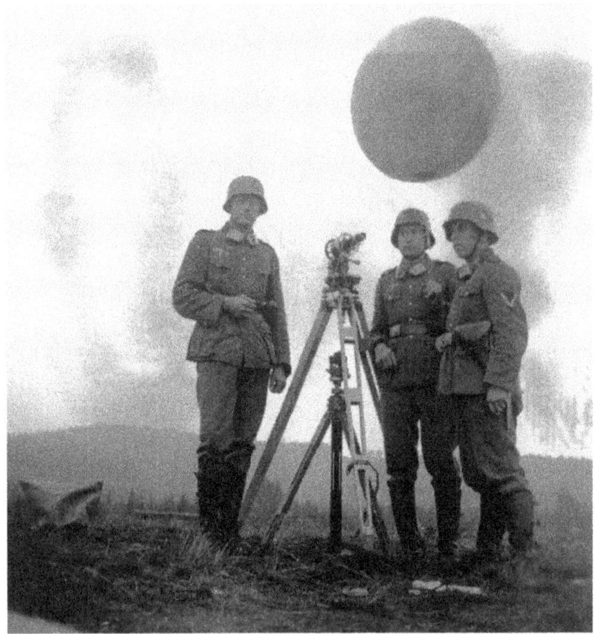

Atmospheric Composition
Another interesting combination of intent and photographing processing mishap has created an image of *Pioniers* (combat engineers) preparing a weather balloon while their tripod-mounted theodolites stand ready for measurement taking.

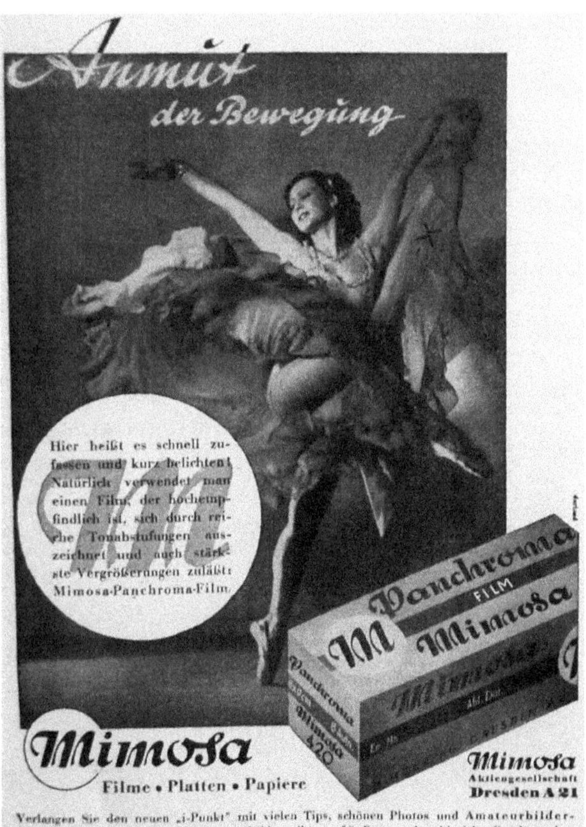

Mimosa Film, Plates and Paper – Competitor to Agfa
The ad reads in part: 'It means fast focus and short exposure. Naturally, one chooses a film that is highly sensitive, characterized by rich tonal gradations.' The company announced its new 'I-Point' film types as well as its range of prices, touting its film as just the thing for amateur film competitions.

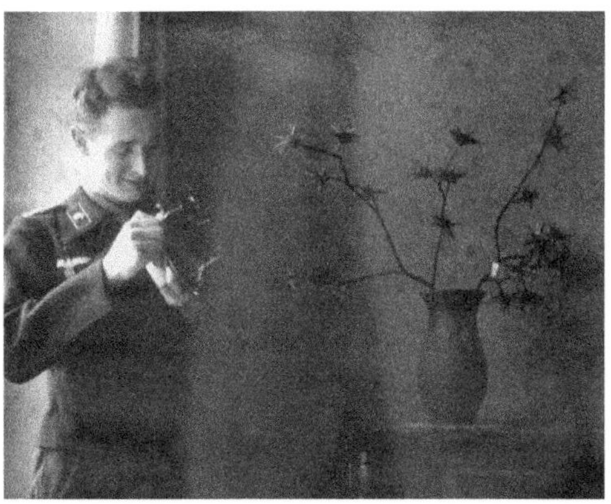

Still Life with Folding Camera
Showing the Death's Head insignia on the collar of his mechanised troop tunic, a young soldier prepares his camera. Perhaps the subject is the unusual floral arrangement.

Below left: **Top of the Line – Ica Icarette 500**
Produced by the Dresden-based company, the 120 (6x9) roll film Icarette first appeared in 1914. While it featured a position adjustable optical viewfinder, early models still carried the wire frame version. It also features the high-end 105 mm F/4.5 Carl Zeiss Jena Tessar lens fitted to some models. Shutter speeds went to 1/250th of a second. The small white plate is the distance scale and is fashioned from ivory. Beneath the leather covering is an aluminum body. The forward knobs allow for smooth rack and pinion focusing.

Below right: **Back-Up for Icarette**
The rear of the camera also featured an additional metal viewfinder that slid in and out of its sheath and which was designed for holding the camera up to the eye. For some reason it was termed the Iconometer. An additional small red window displayed the number of exposures and this was closable to prevent light seepage. Although eclipsed by the newer 35 mm cameras, the Icarettes were certainly in use through the 1930s and 1940s, and many still function perfectly today, producing very sharp images.

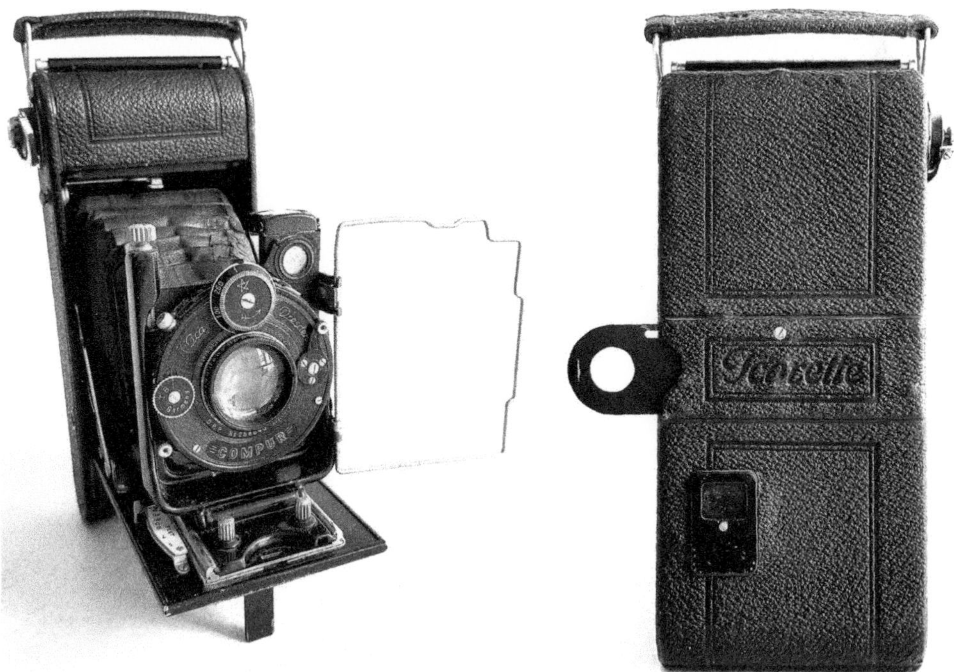

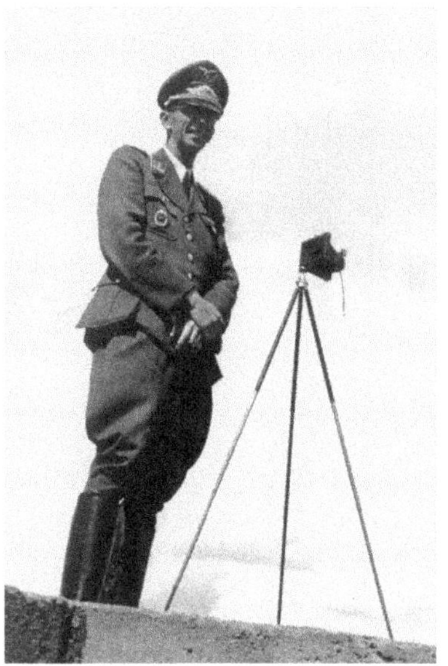

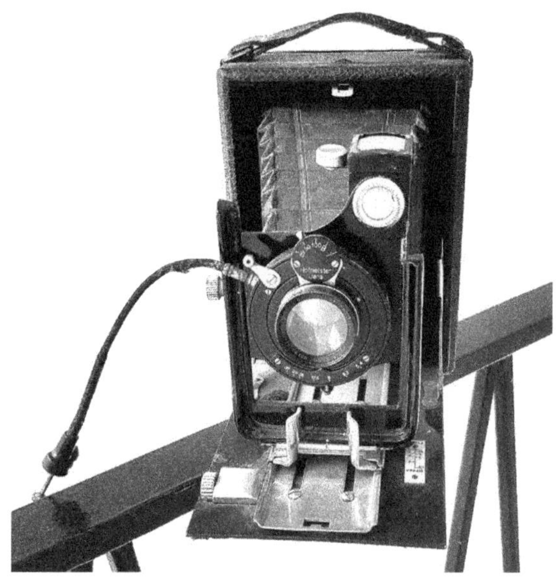

***Above left*: Top Spindly Legs**
A Luftwaffe *Stabsfeldwebel* (NCO) is photographed with his own camera mounted on a Carl Beseler foldable tripod with telescopic brass legs, the camera fitted with a remote shutter release to further minimise blurring the image. He holds the backing plate and film holder in his hands. His tunic displays the Air Crew Badge.

***Above right*: Top of the Line Hoffmeister Jena – Plate Back Folding Strut Camera with Cable Release**
Hoffmeister refers to the little-known camera maker; Jena refers to the town of that name. Jena was also the home for the famous Carl Zeiss optical company.

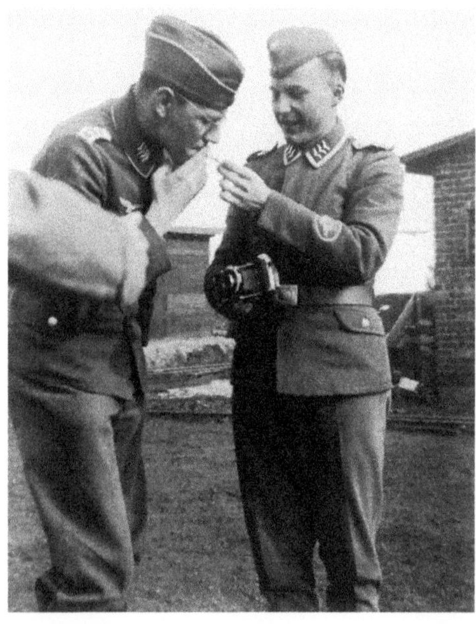

Folding Strut Camera at the Ready
Luftwaffe NCOs share a cigarette break and a photo op snapped on 14 April 1944. The sleeve insignia on the camera holder's sleeve indicates he is a member of a geographic mapping unit. At this point the 'map' of the Greater Reich is shrinking as Red Army forces devastate German armies in the East and the Allies move toward Germany after landing at Normandy, soon liberating France before entering Nazi Germany for the final conflagration.

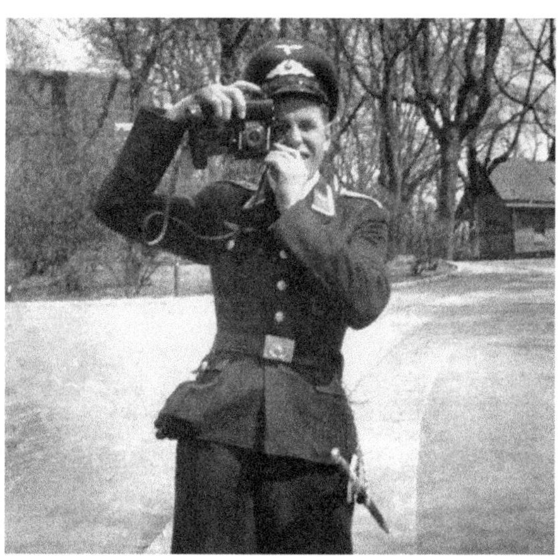 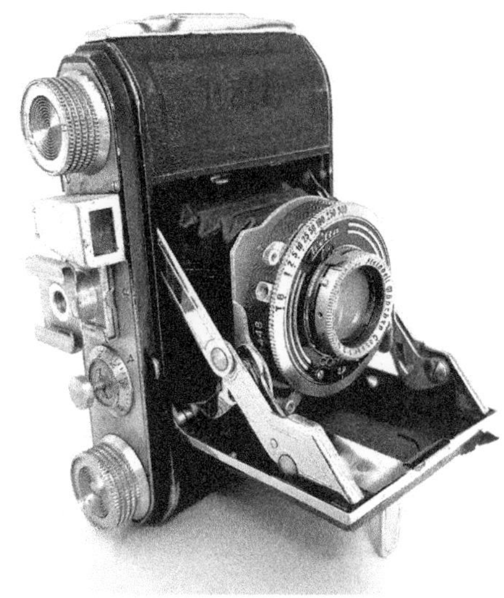

***Above left*: Shooting Vertical**
A Luftwaffe flak trooper wearing his ceremonial dagger squints into the viewfinder of his camera, still attached to its case.

***Above right*: Walta Welti Strut 35 mm Camera with Steinheil Cassa Lens**
The Welta company began making cameras in 1935. The price of its Welti model camera in New York was $19.50 as of 1938.

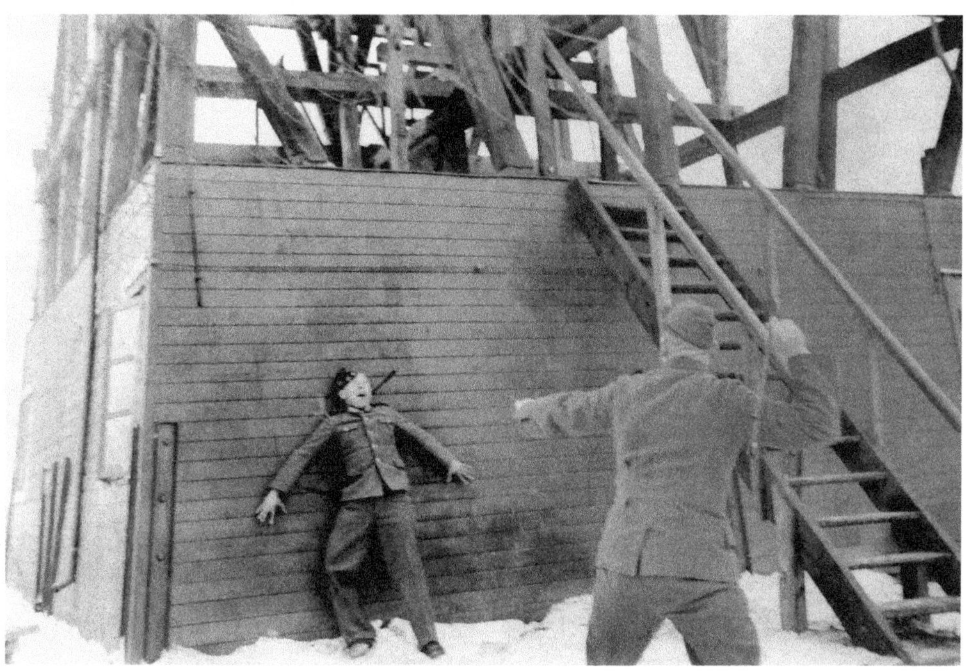

Close Call ... Even if Staged
An impromptu bayonet-throwing demonstration has caught the photographer's attention.

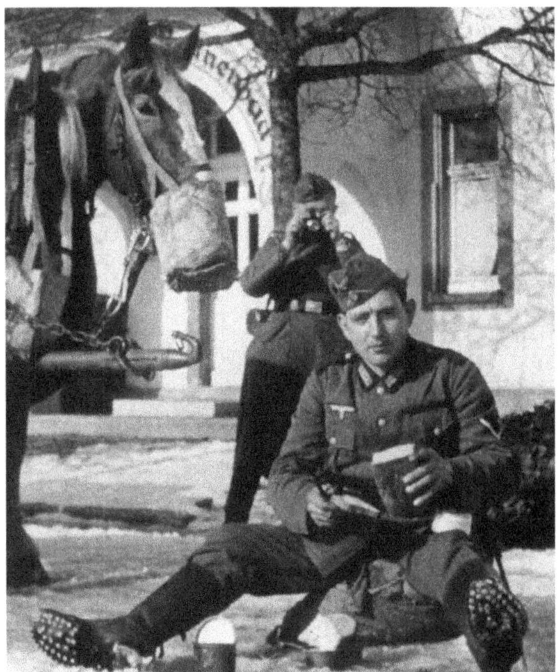

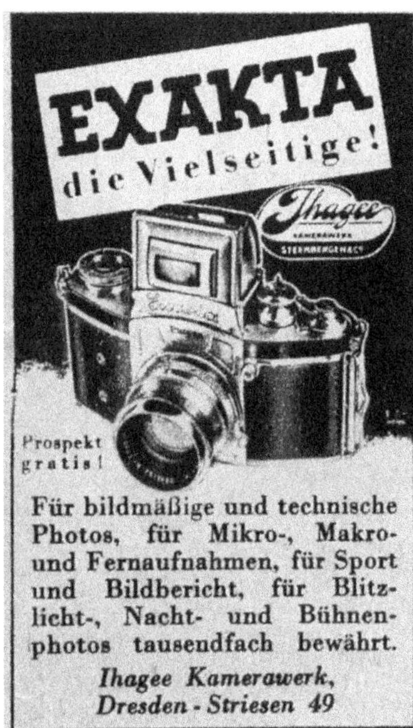

Above left: Feeding Time – Camera on Camera
Two horses enjoy a bagful of grains while a corporal, his hobnail boots showing, knife in hand, has sliced a loaf of bread. Cameramen both behind him and out of sight record the scene.

Above right: 'The Versatile One!'
The captioning for the advanced Exakta 35 mm camera reads: 'For economic and technical photos, for micro- and macro- and telephoto, for sports and journalism, for bright-, night- and scenic photos … a thousand subjects preserved.' The ad's image displays the camera's 'flip-up' waist-level viewfinder 'reflex' design. When introduced in 1935 as the Kine Exakta, it was considered the first SLR to utilize 35 mm film.

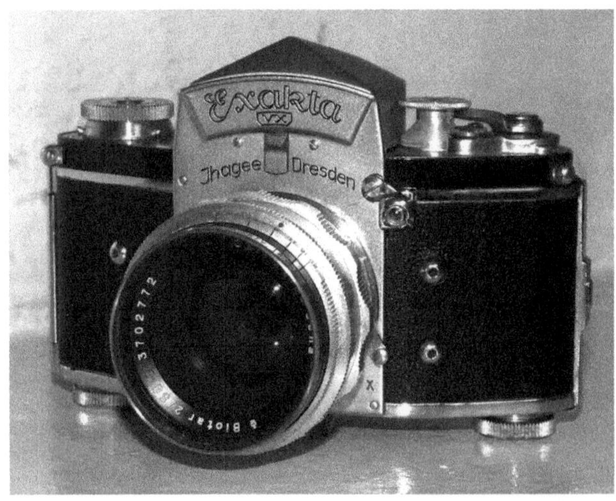

Long Lifetime
A later model produced in post-war Dresden, by then in the Soviet zone, still carries on the original body design.

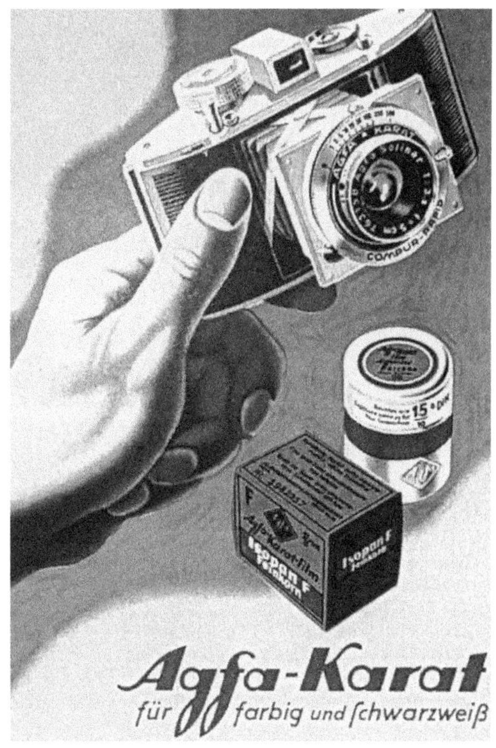

'For Color and Black and White images'
An ad appearing in a 15 July 1941 German newspaper spotlights the 35 mm Agfa-Karat and the films available for it. In 1905 Agfa had become part of the German Bayer and BASF group; twenty years later, in 1925, Agfa, Bayer, BASF, Hoechst and others merged to form the vast IG Farben conglomerate, which during the Third Reich was a prime exploiter of slave labor and also the mass producer of war materials, as well as Zyklon B gas. Production of Agfa photographic materials resumed post-war at the Bayer headquarters in Leverkusen in 1945.

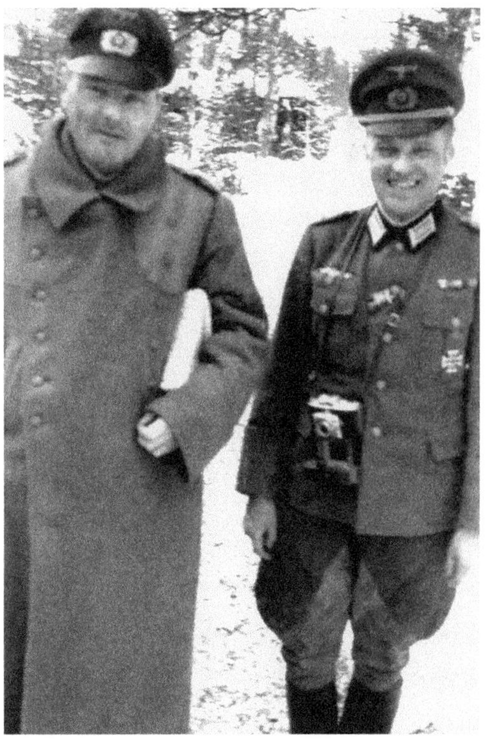

Agfa Karat and Iron Crosses in the Snow
A German army officer, showing both Iron Cross Second and First Class decorations, wears his 35 mm camera at the ready.

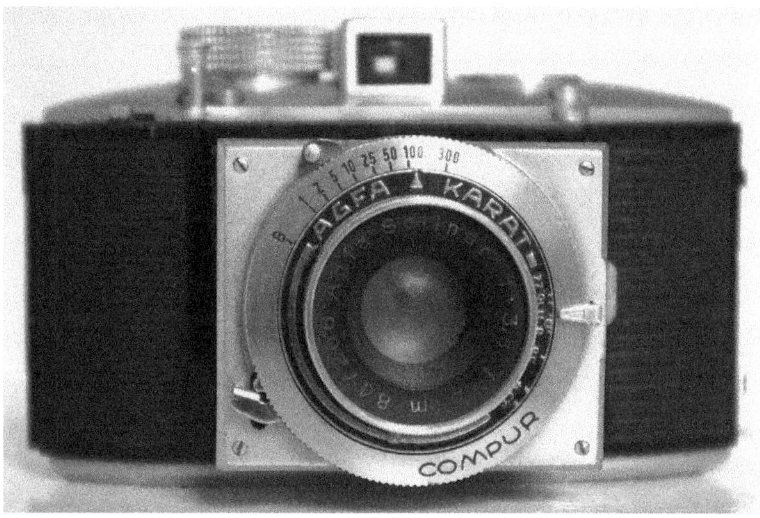

Agfa Karat 3.5 with Deckel Compur Shutter – 1938
The modern-looking German-made Agfa Karat strut-folding camera was produced by Agfa from the mid-1930s until the mid-1950s. The Karat came with the new 35 mm film cartridge developed from the Ansco Memo cassette of 1927 (Ansco and Agfa had merged in 1928). Agfa was also a major innovator in film development and in 1936 introduced the first advanced color films for commercial and civilian use in both print and slide formats.

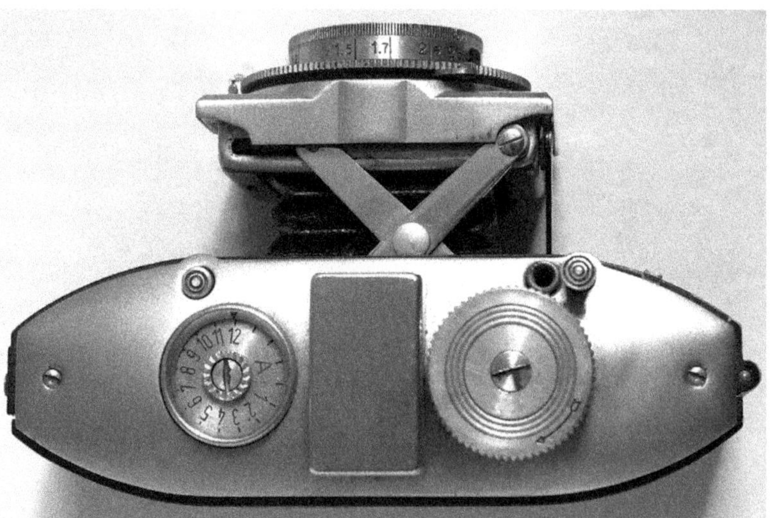

Extended Film Range
Some of the very first batches of Agfa colour slide film were utilised by amateur photographer Walter Genewelin while serving as the Nazi chief accountant and overseer of Jewish slave labour during the operation of the Lodz ghetto in Poland. His hobby, taking snapshots of the ghetto's prisoners, amounted to some 400 color slides and a rare historic documentation of the subjects' suffering. Genewelin was fastidious about his photos and complained to Agfa about some of the film stock that performed poorly. The slides were discovered more recently and provide yet more documentation of Nazi crimes.

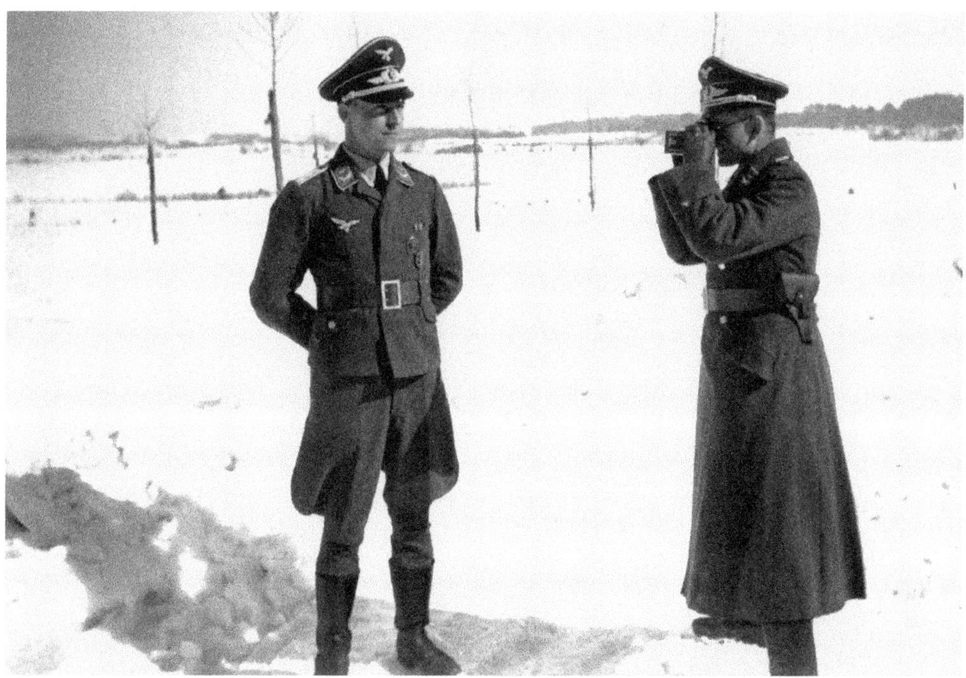

***Above*: Newly Promoted Pilot?**
One Luftwaffe *Leutnant* photographs a
fellow officer on a bright winter's day.
The subject's tunic shows two badges, the
lower of which is the Bronze Sports badge,
which came in bronze, silver and gold.
Obtaining the badge required passing
three tests – gymnastics, self-defense
and agricultural field service. Retaining
ownership further required maintaining a
'clean National Socialism record'. It was
also known as the 'SA Defense Badge',
as named by SS leader Ernst Rohm in
late 1933. The other badge is the DRL
Sports award, designed as an incentive for
physical training for eighteen to thirty-
two-year-olds, both male and female,
requiring criteria to be met over an
eight-year period; a twelve-month period
was required for those aged thirty-two to
forty.

***Right*: Top Sergeant Snowman**
Perhaps voicing his opinion about NCOs,
an army private has created the familiar
winter character but with the cuff stripes
of a master sergeant.

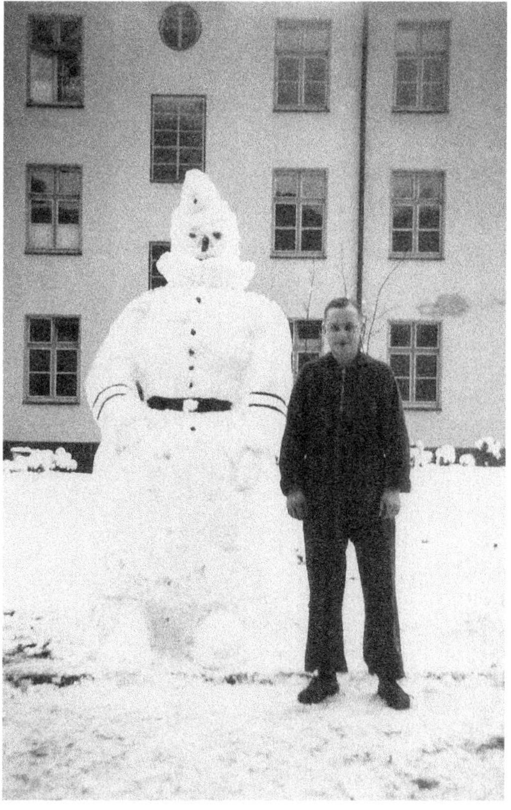

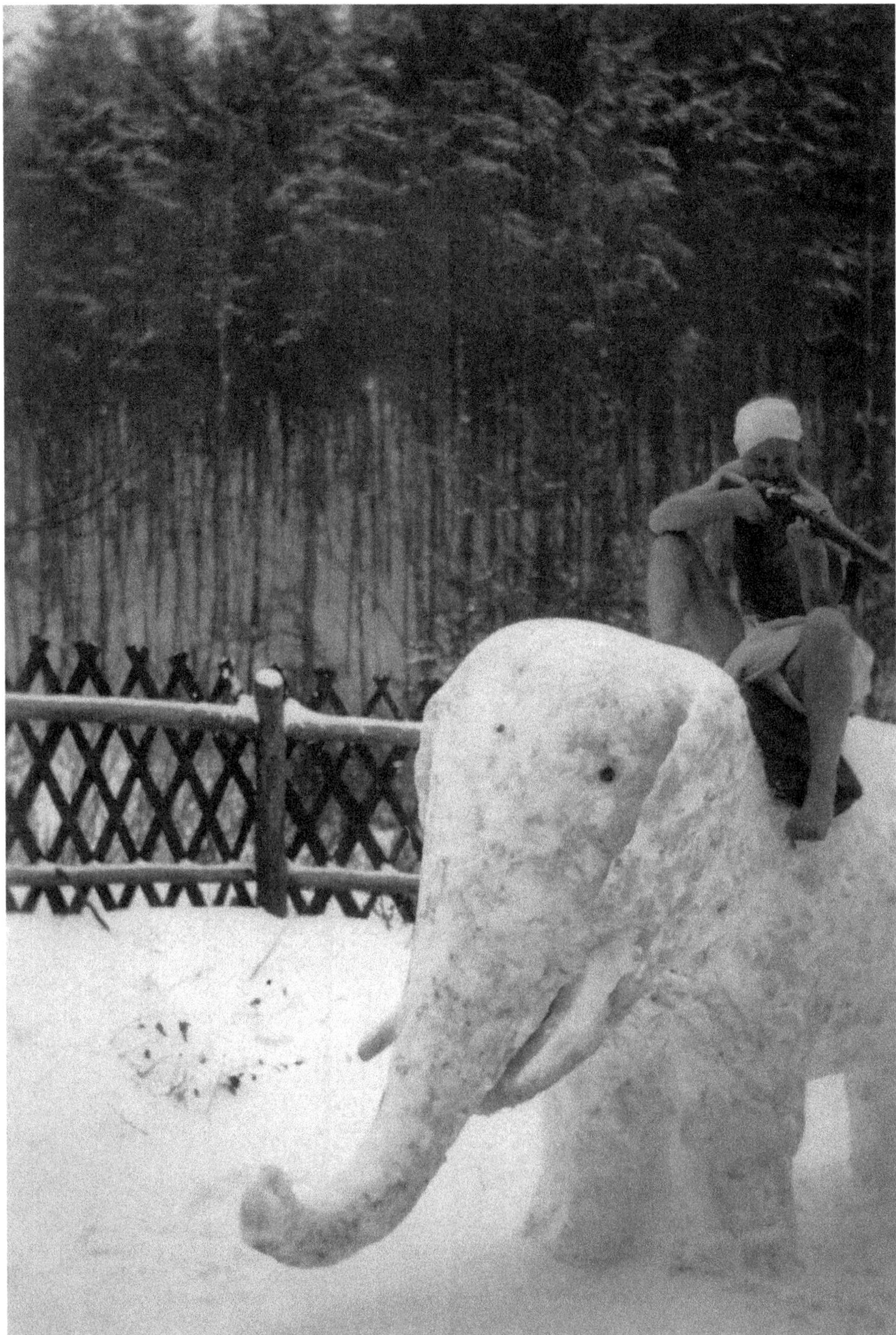

Snow Elephant
Costumed as an Indian 'mahout', a German soldier aims his rifle from the back of well-crafted pachyderm, tusks included.

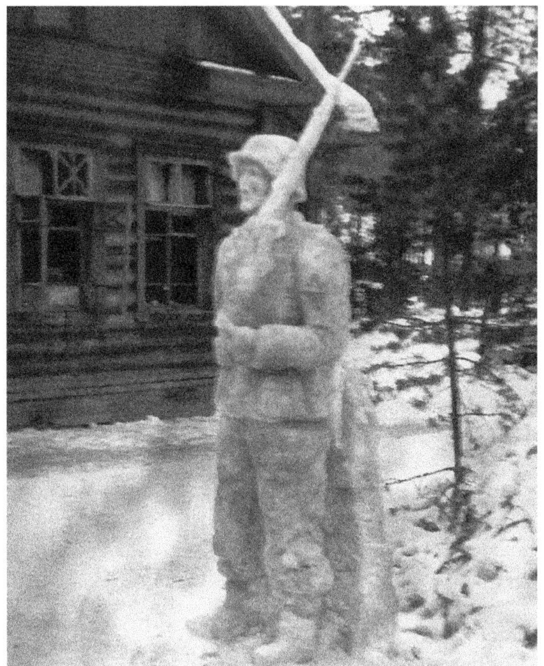

Art Imitating Death – Ice Soldier on Guard
The meticulously crafted sculpture survived until temperatures rose. Eventually the 'ice soldiers' would be of flesh and blood, succumbing to the deadly Russian winters.

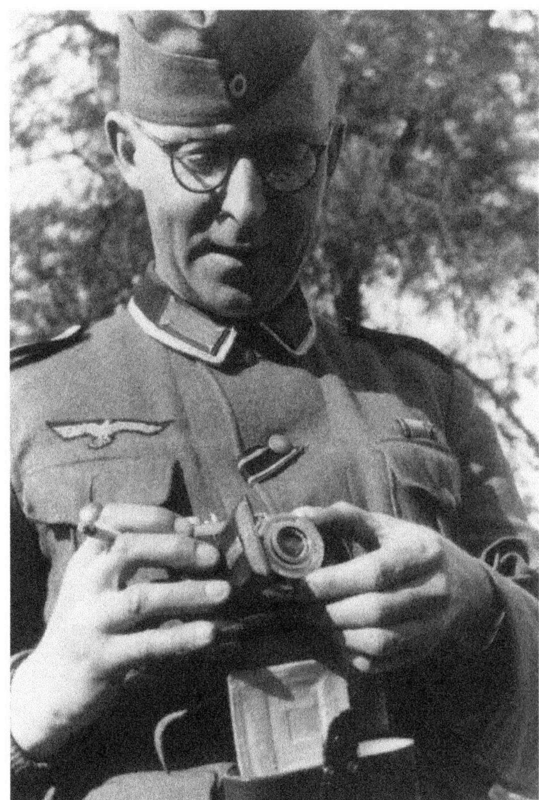

Top Kodak Moment
An army NCO displaying his Iron Cross Second Class ribbon has opened his German-made 35 mm Kodak Retina. The camera was produced in Stuttgart-Wagen by the Nagel Werk company, which the American company Kodak acquired at the end of 1931. The Retina came in both folding and non-folding types, including the Vollenda miniature folder type that, though smaller than the Leica, could use the same size large lenses.

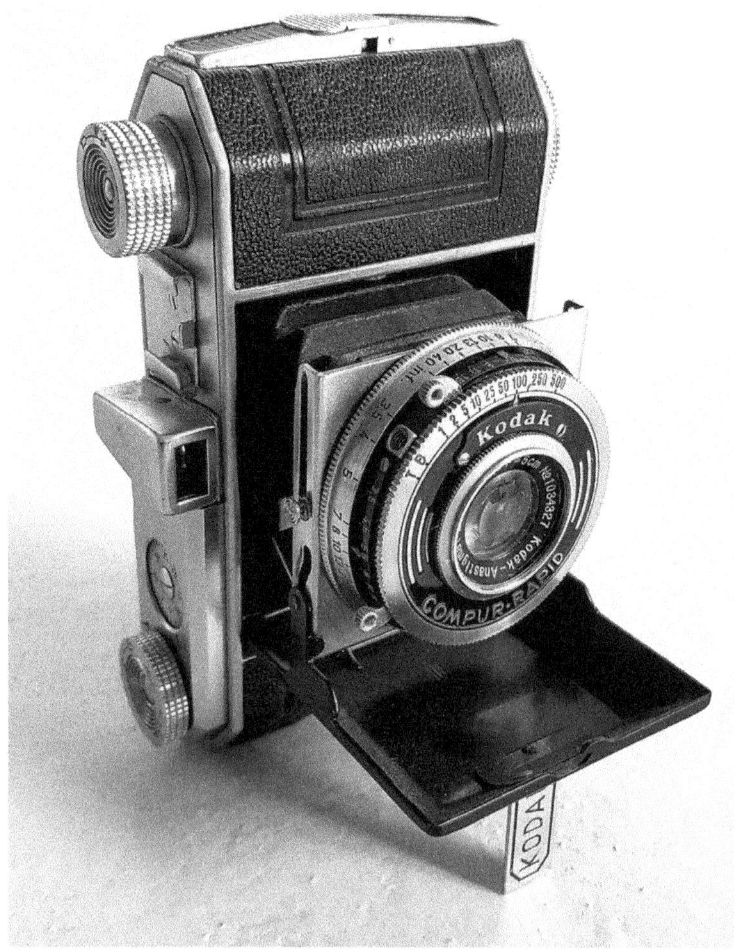

Kodak Retina I (Type 148), 1939–41
This design became Kodak's first folding 35 mm camera. A choice of either a black or chrome model was available during 1936–40 and came with a Kodak-Anastigmat Ektar 50 mm F/3.5 lens.

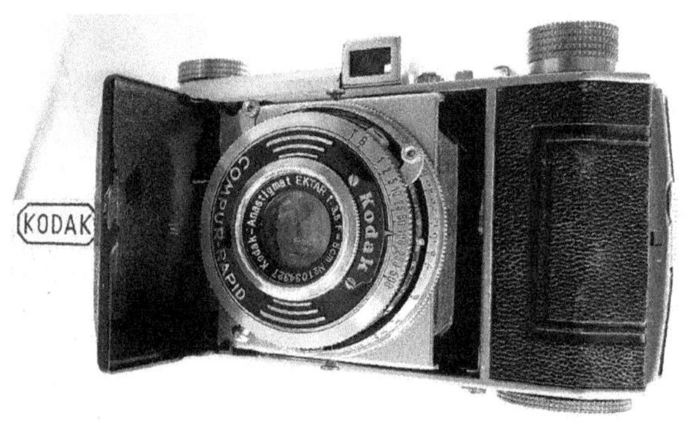

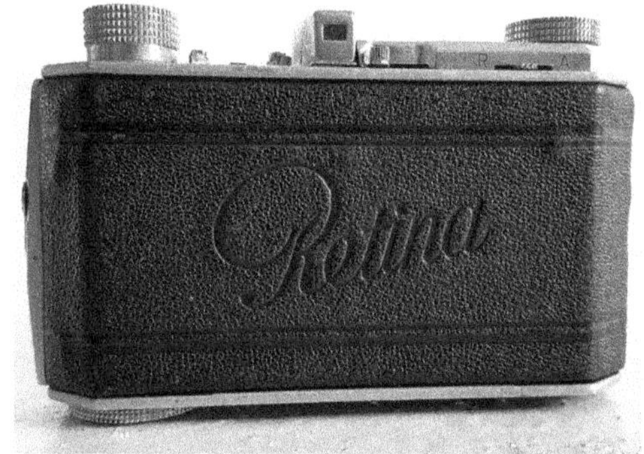

Afterimage
The Retina was produced from 1934 into 1941, at which point the German Kodak company was seized by the Nazi State. Production resumed under civilian control again post-war, before finally ending in 1950 – all the while, the cameras remained popular throughout the decades because of their high quality.

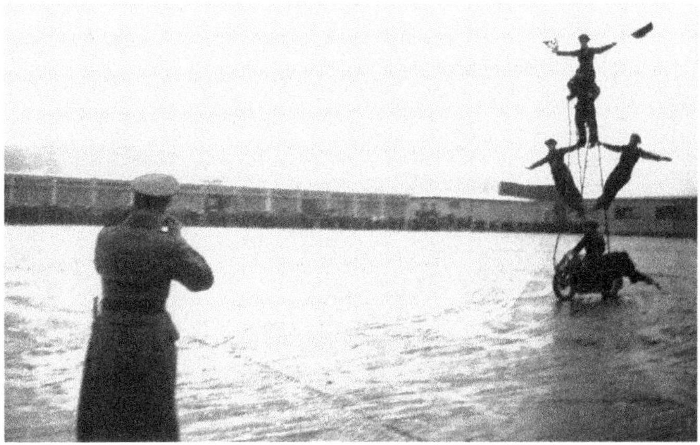

Stunt Riders
A *Heer* soldier aims his camera at five Panzer men performing a motorcycle stunt before a large audience at a military base.

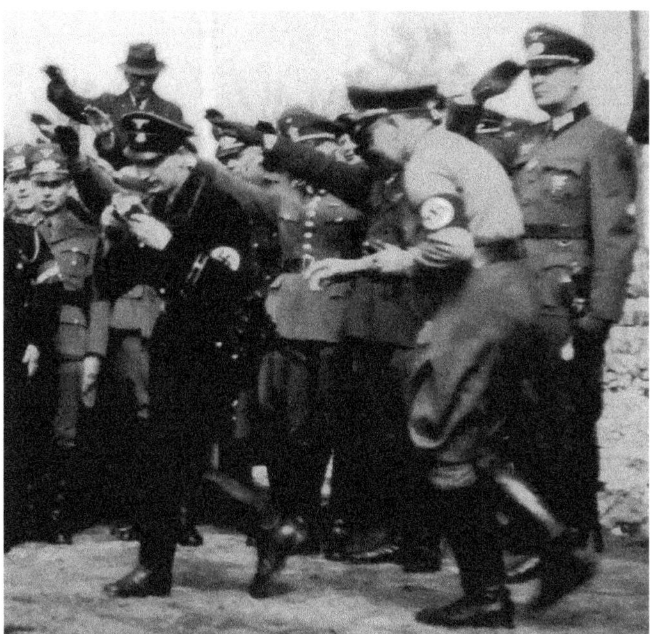

Competing Agendas/Cameras in Transition
A black-uniformed SS man uses a new 35 mm camera, while the SA Brownshirt holds an older design strut-folding rollfilm camera – a portent of the fatal clash between the two organisations ending in the Night of the Long Knives, when the SS under Hitler's orders executed a mass arrest and liquidation of SA leadership, including its leader Ernst Rohm, a longtime supporter and friend of Hitler. Rohm's radical and destabilising call for revolution was backed by several hundred thousand SA members. In order to gain legitimacy and backing from the mainstream military, Hitler acquiesced to eliminating the SA from power. It also coincided with Heinrich Himmler's aspirations for his SS 'ideological soldiers' to take over control in the formation of a Nazi State and its plans for European dominance.

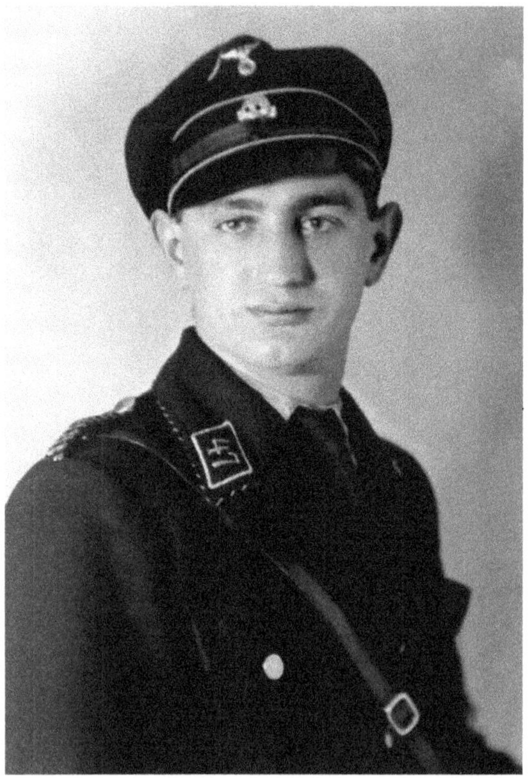

**'Death's Head' Identification Photo –
Early *Allgemeine* SS Man**
Credit for the design of the all-black
SS uniform is given to *SS-Oberführer*
Professor Karl Diebitsch and graphic
designer *SS-Sturmhauptführer* Walter
Heck. While widely seen in Nazi
propaganda newsreels as well as
post-war films, the black uniforms were
for the most part not seen in use after
the war began. In fact, the uniforms
were recycled for use by Eastern
European collaborationist police forces
and other Axis allies. SS men also had
their blood type tattooed under their
left arm, a fact that later helped identify
them in the search for war criminals.

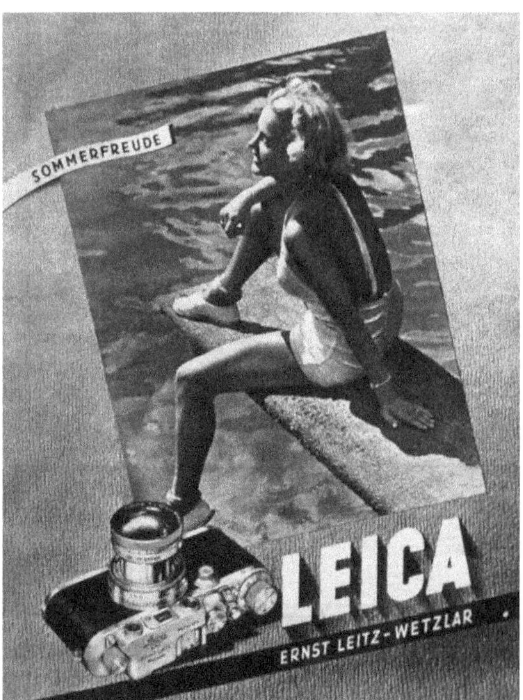

'Summer Joy'
In 1925 Ernst Leitz of Wetzlar
introduced the first Leica, thereby
leading the way in the development of
the 'miniature', aka portable, camera
in Germany. Goebbels, seeing modern
photography as a major means for
spreading Nazi propaganda, endorsed
the smaller, lightweight 35 mm camera.
In an effort to promote the use of the
'modern' 35 mm camera, Goebbels
issued a ban on photojournalists who
did not adapt to the new cameras.

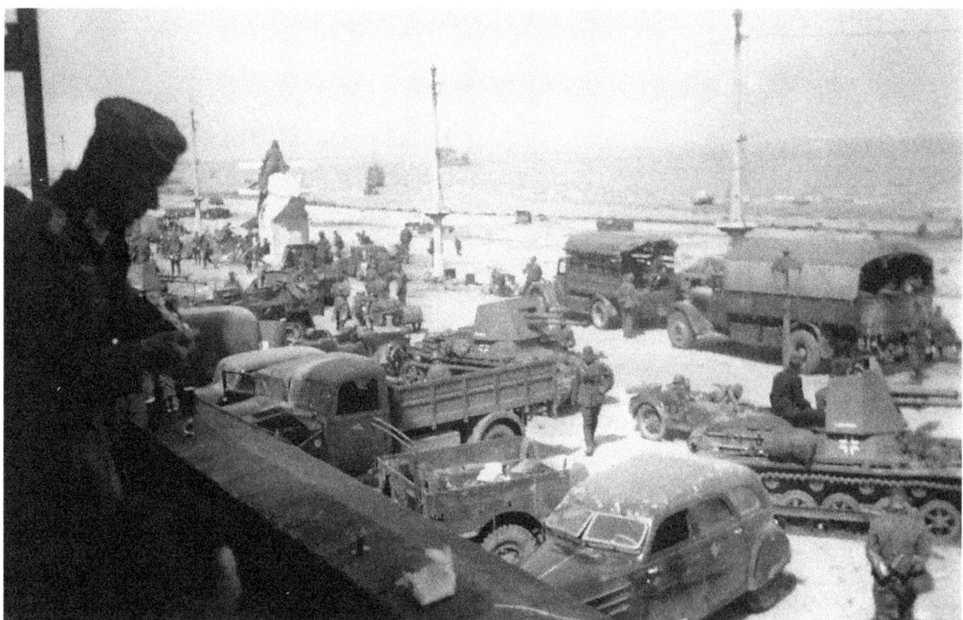

Leica at Dunkirk – Post-Evacuation

A German soldier readies his camera to record the array of German vehicles massed on the beach at Dunkirk not long after the trapped Allied troops escaped across the Channel to England via the famous 'people's' armada.' Along with the German trucks and motorcycles are a pair of *Panzerjäger*, or 'tank hunter/destroyers', each fitted with a 47 mm gun. Often recording a pivotal moment from a unique vantage point, whether in the hands of military photographic units or held by an individual soldier, cameras captured milestones in the history of Nazi Germany and the war.

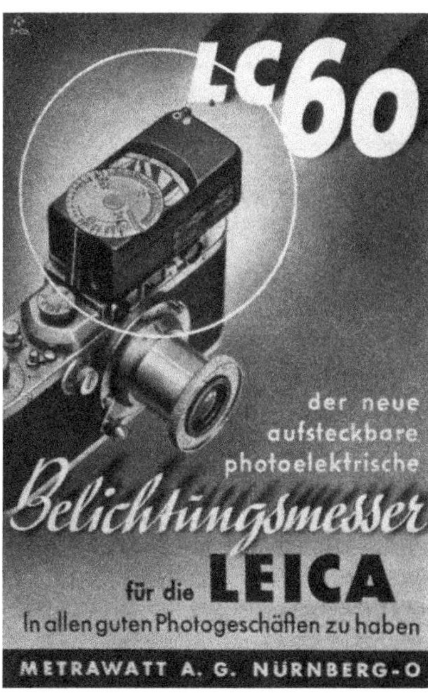

Standard of Excellence

A June 1940 magazine advertisement for the Leica 35 mm camera spotlights its new integrated electronic light meter (*Belichtungsmesser*). Leica advertising during the Third Reich promoted, among other values, the historical significance of family snapshots. Leica also helped ignite the 'camera boom' in the US, its major sales market, thanks to popular photo-laden magazines like the *Saturday Evening Post* and *Life*, especially after the introduction of color Kodak film in 1936–37.

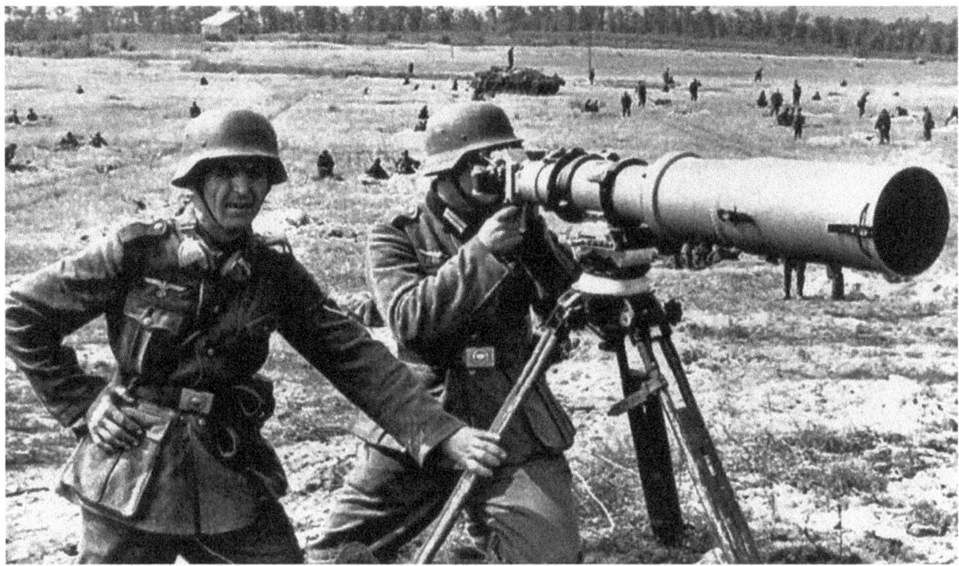

Long-Range Leica

Army troops record the action with a telephoto lens during pre-war maneuvers. The lens is very likely a product of Zeiss, the famous manufacturer of optical systems founded in 1846 by Carl Zeiss of Jena, Germany. Behind its seemingly pro-Nazi image, Leica secretly came to the aid of German Jews, not only providing humane care to its Jewish workers but also aiding many to either escape the country or find protected jobs within the organisation. Elsie Leitz, the daughter of the company's owner, was arrested and imprisoned in 1943 by the Gestapo for her activities. Surviving brutal treatment, many months were required to heal her injuries. Leica was seen in a positive light by the Allies and was therefore aided in its post-war redevelopment, regaining its international status for excellence.

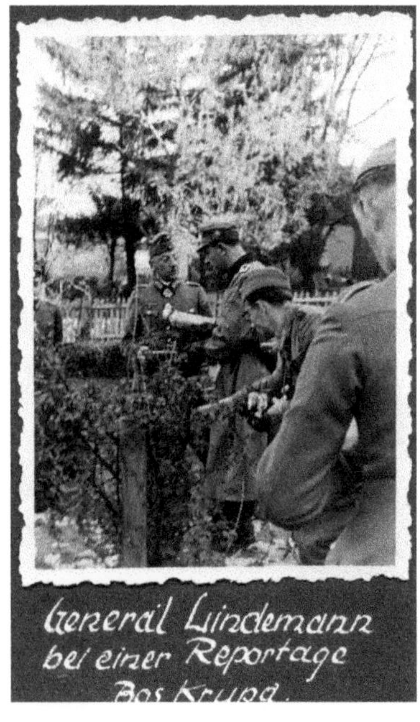

Album Page – Interviewing a General with a Leica

Members of a *Kriegsberichter* (war correspondent) unit equipped with a large recording microphone and Leica 35 mm camera gather around infantry General Gerhard Lindemann somewhere in Russia. Convicted as a war criminal, he was imprisoned by the Soviets until 1955. Released and returning home to Bremen, he lived for another forty years before dying at ninety-seven.

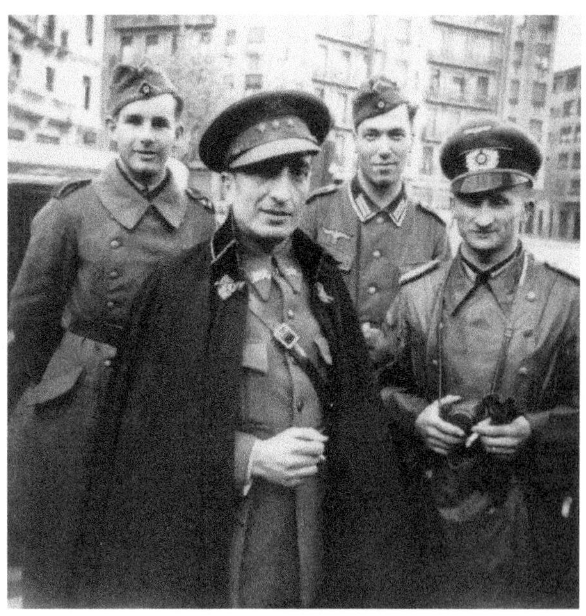

Proxy War Allies, 1936 – Camera Tourist in Madrid
A German officer has brought his camera to Spain and poses with his adjutants and one of Franco's generals. Hitler had supplied men and material in support of the fascist war that erupted in July 1936 against the Republican forces, ultimately winning victory and establishing the third fascist state in Europe along with Germany and Italy. The Spanish Civil War ended on 1 April 1939, exactly five months prior to Germany's invasion of Poland.

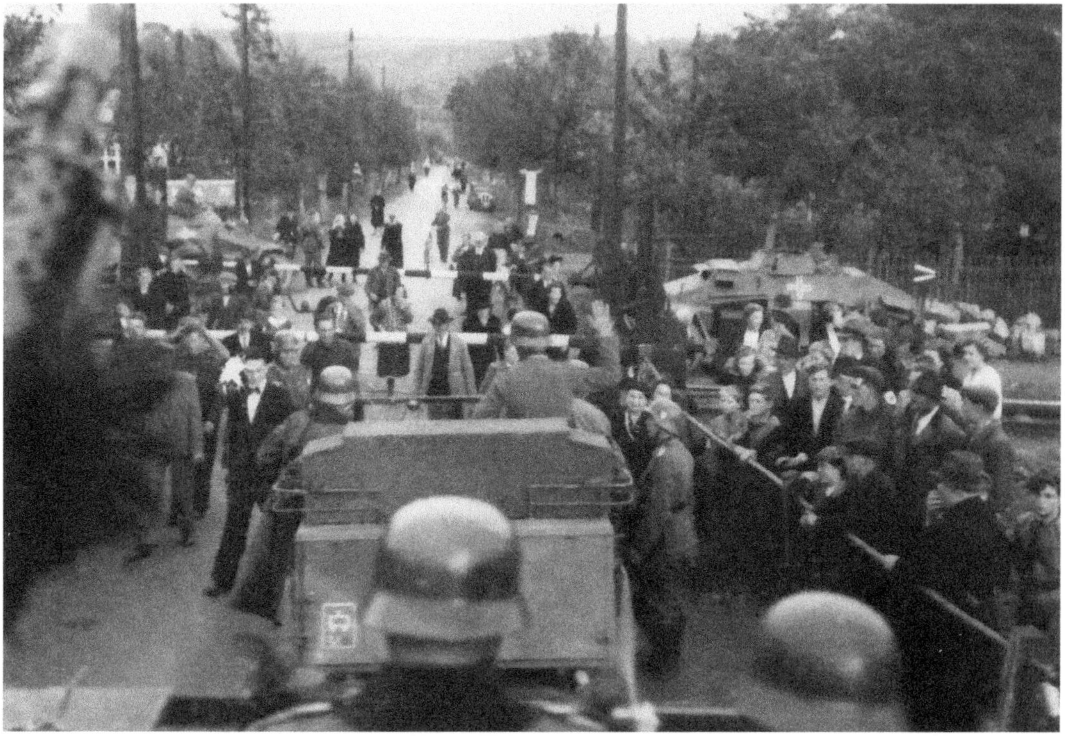

Crossing the German border into Austria, 10 March 1938
A solider aboard an armoured vehicle raises his camera to record the historic crossing that signalled the *Anschluss,* or incorporation of Austria into the German Reich. Austrian civilians have thronged the German convoy, welcoming them at the border barriers about to be raised.

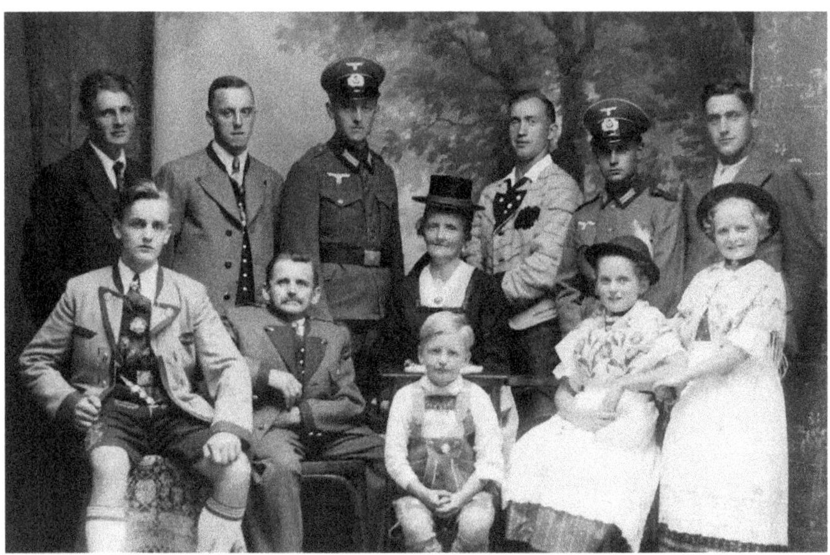

***Anschluss* in Austria, March 1938 – German by Popular Demand**
An Austrian family poses for a studio portrait, several wearing traditional Austrian attire while two of its members have donned the uniform of Nazi Germany. After the country's 84,000 square kilometers was annexed into the Greater Reich, Austria was renamed Ostmark to mark the occasion. History often forgets that Hitler was Austrian by birth and that 40 per cent of Death Camp personnel were Austrians.

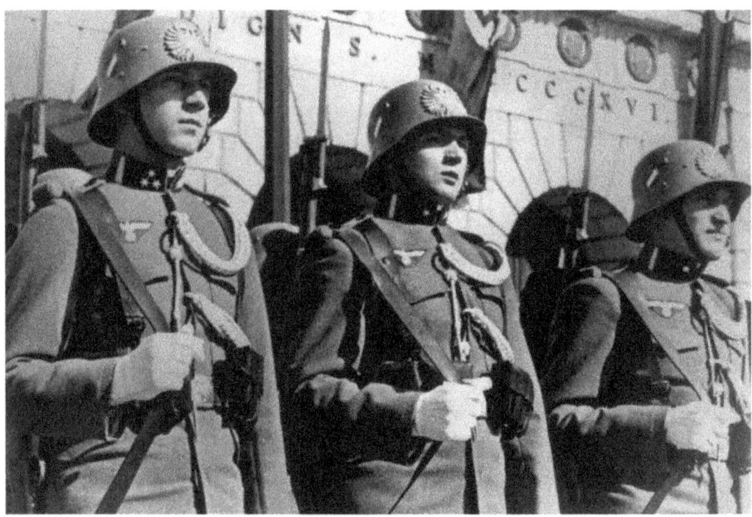

Transition by International News Photo, 14 April 1938
The photo caption reads: 'Vienna, German-Austria … Here are soldiers of the former Austrian Army, wearing the newly adapted uniform of the Nazified German-Austrian Army. The German-style steel helmet has been decorated with the brass double-eagle emblem of the former Austrian monarchy, leaving out the crown of the Hapsburgs. On the right side of the helmet, the colors of the Republic of Austria have been painted red, white and black. On the right side of the chest, the National Socialist emblem has been put on the tunic.'

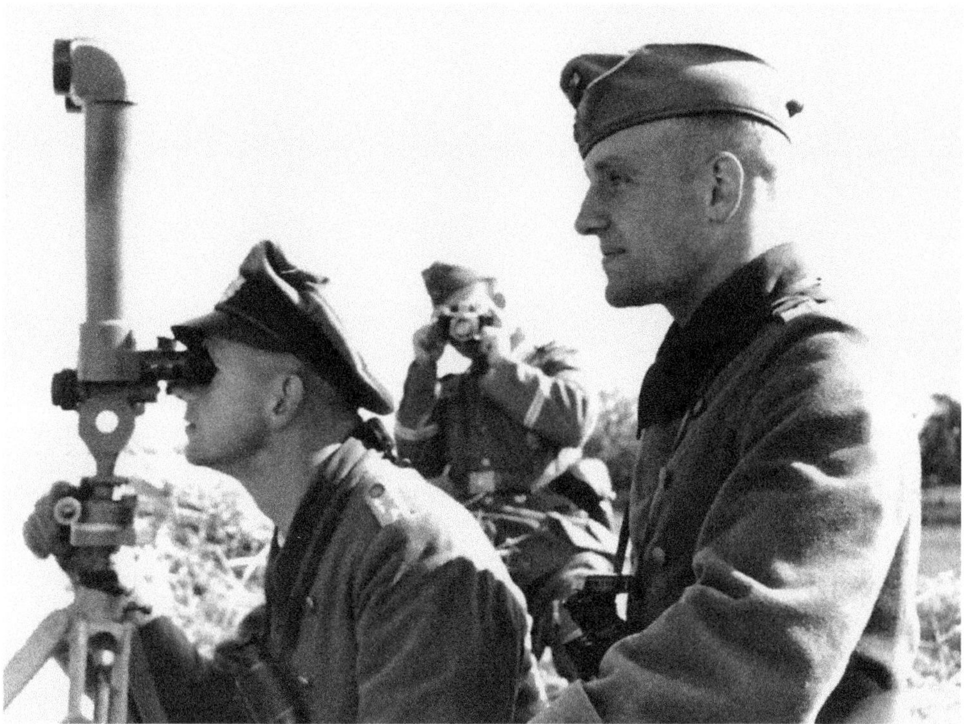

War Just Coming into Focus, 1939
An NCO cameraman serving in a field correspondent unit captures an officer peering into enemy positions with a *Scherenfernrohr S.F.14Z.Gi* 'scissors telescope' made by Carl Zeiss. The periscope design allows for safe viewing from within the cover of trenches, the observers normally being out of sight with only the top portion of the optics protruding in view. The photo is inscribed on the reverse with the date 1 September 1939 – the day of the German invasion of Poland, which ignited the Second World War in Europe.

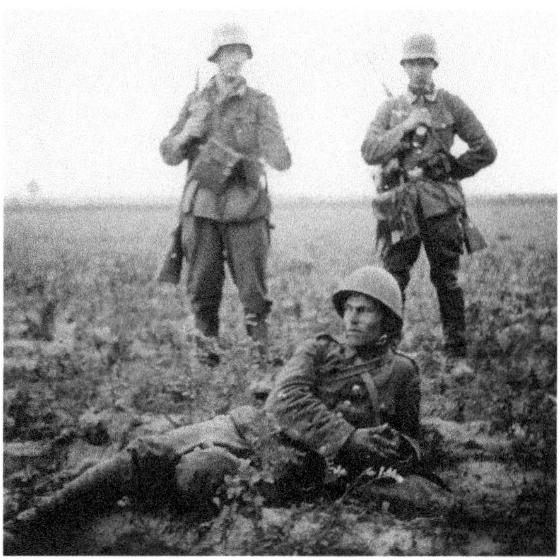

Trophy of the Polish Campaign, September 1939
Two NCOs stand guard over 'the first Polish prisoner', as stated by the handwritten notation on the reverse of this photo. Having taken a relatively relaxed pose, the prisoner ignores the camera.

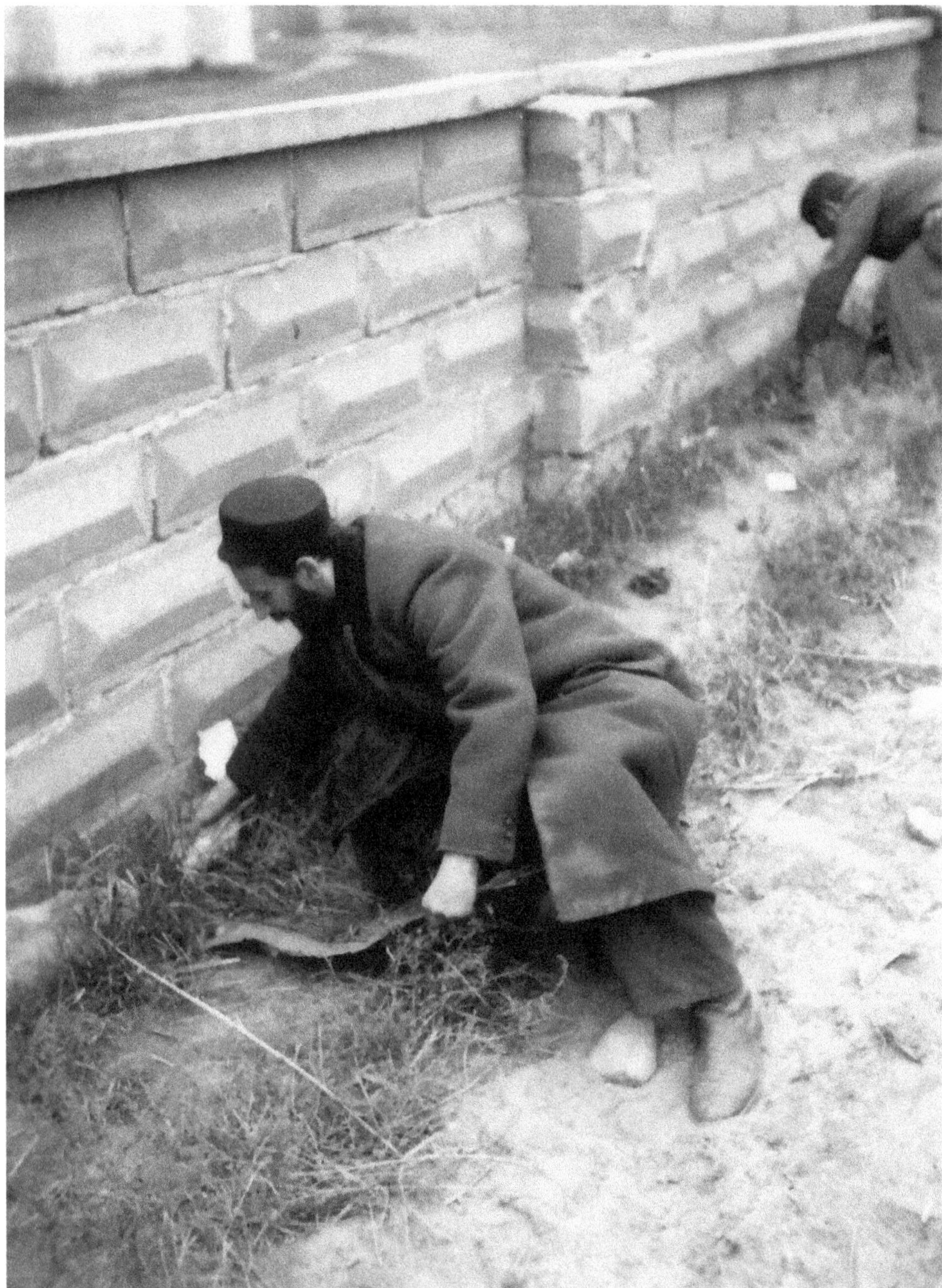

Poland – War Within a War
Appearing in a German soldier's photo album, the photo bears the original hand-penned captioning, 'Ein Polnische Jude'. Similar images were often mailed home to family and friends to justify the Nazi plan to 'rid Europe of the Jewish plague'. The extermination of the 11 million members of the Jewish population of Europe began with the mass murder of Poland's Jews, with some 3 million being sent to the Death Camps. The round-up and shootings began in the very first days of the German invasion.

Iconic Images

Several German designs became emblematic of the Third Reich and served to project technical superiority and overwhelming power, their photographic images repeatedly portrayed in both public and private communications.

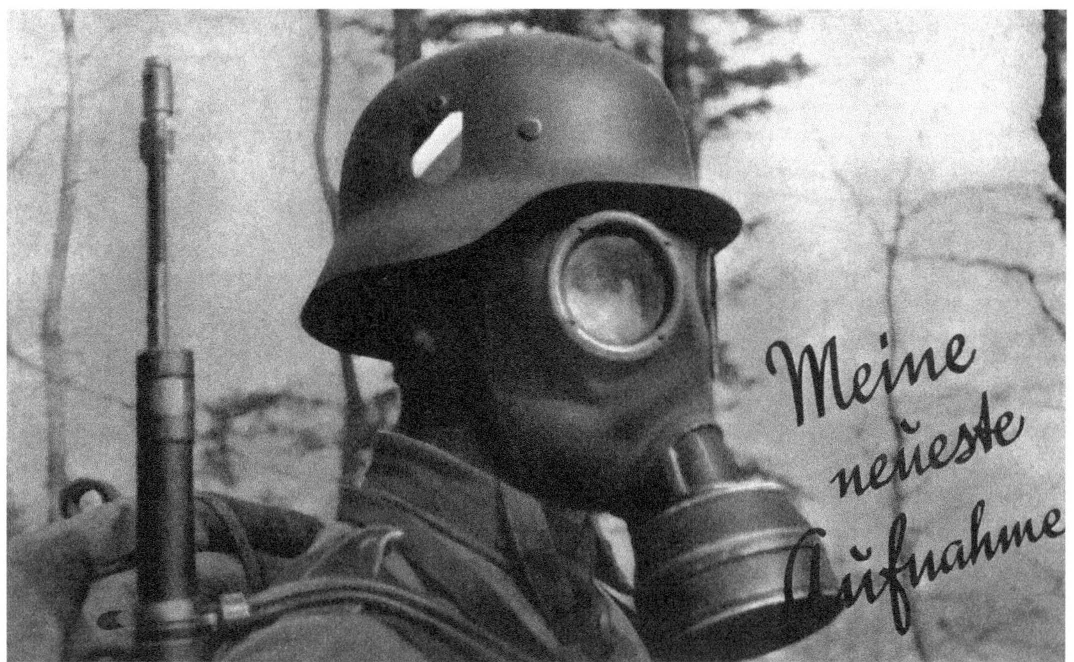

***Der Stahlhelm* – 'My Newest Look'**
This pre-war commercial photo postcard shows a Wehrmacht soldier wearing both the iconic German battle helmet and a gas mask. Joining the symbol of the swastika, perhaps no other image is as readily identifiable with the Third Reich as the *Stahlhelm*, or German military steel helmet. The distinctive design became an ominous icon of Nazi military efficiency and ruthlessness. The helmet still carries the pre-war national emblem decal, later replaced with the Nazi swastika. The gas mask is a vestige of the First World War, when poison gas was employed by both sides; the fear that it would be loosed again on the battlefield motivated the issuance of gas masks to all troops.

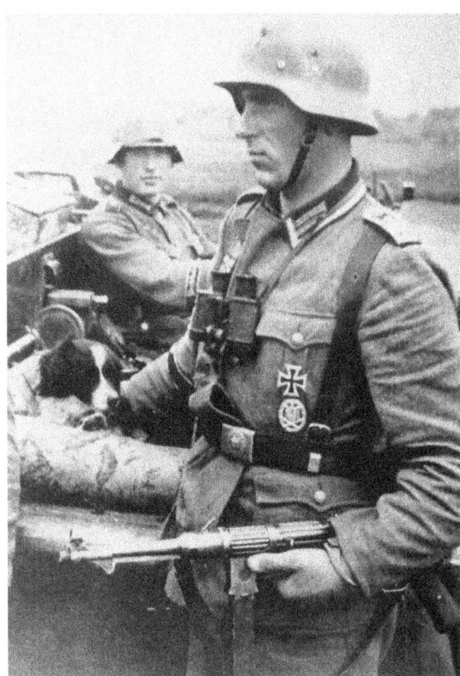

Poster Perfect
A Third Reich commercial postcard features the 'ideal Aryan soldier'. In one hand he carries his technologically advanced MP38/40 'Schmeisser' machine pistol, while the other hand caresses a puppy. The Iron Cross and the Infantry Assault badge attest to the NCO's combat experience, while the location is somewhere on the Eastern Front, where the Nazi 'total war' brought death to millions, both Russian and German.

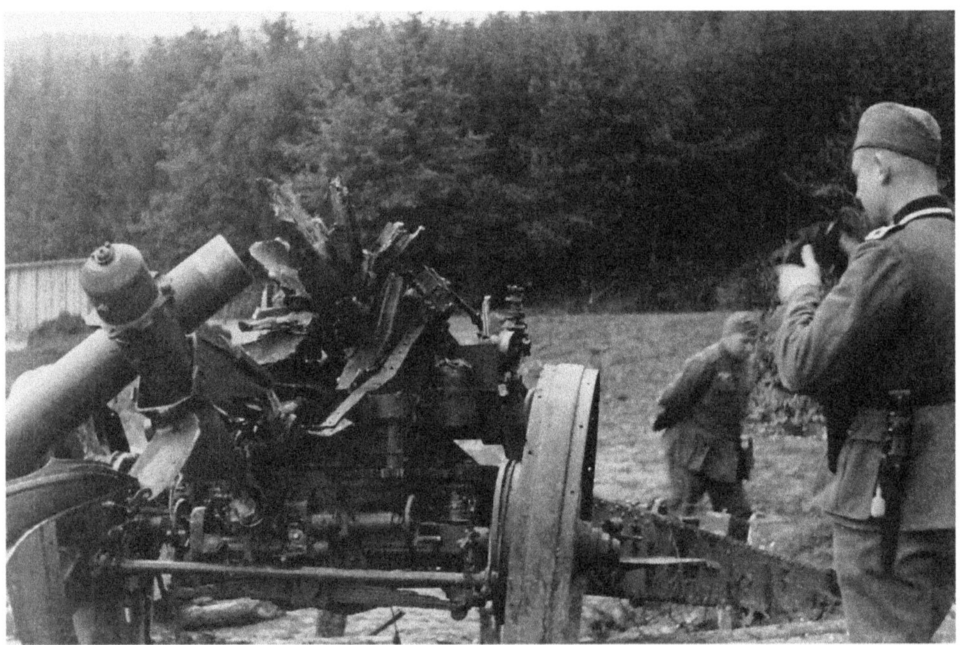

Twisted French Metal
A German Army NCO prepares to photograph a blasted French artillery piece. The fact that the barrel has been blasted apart while the rest of the carriage remains in place and intact indicates it may have been sabotaged by its own French gun crew to prevent it from falling into the hands of the enemy.

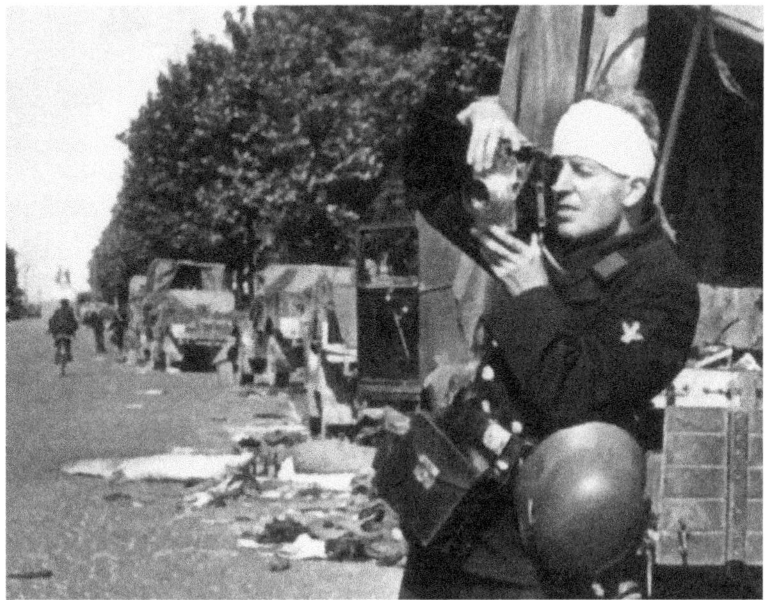

Paris Occupied, May 1940
A wounded German mechanised trooper with what appears to be a Voigtlander or Plaubel large format press camera.

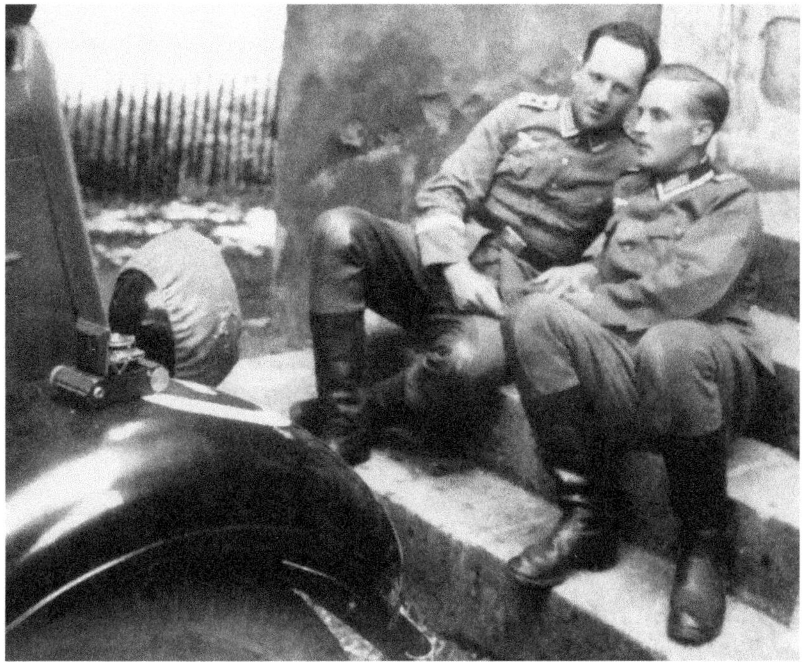

Camera in View
A pair of army NCOs relax on stone steps somewhere in France. A camera, possibly an Ikonta, is seen perched atop a military truck, its headlamp shrouded in a mandatory blackout cover.

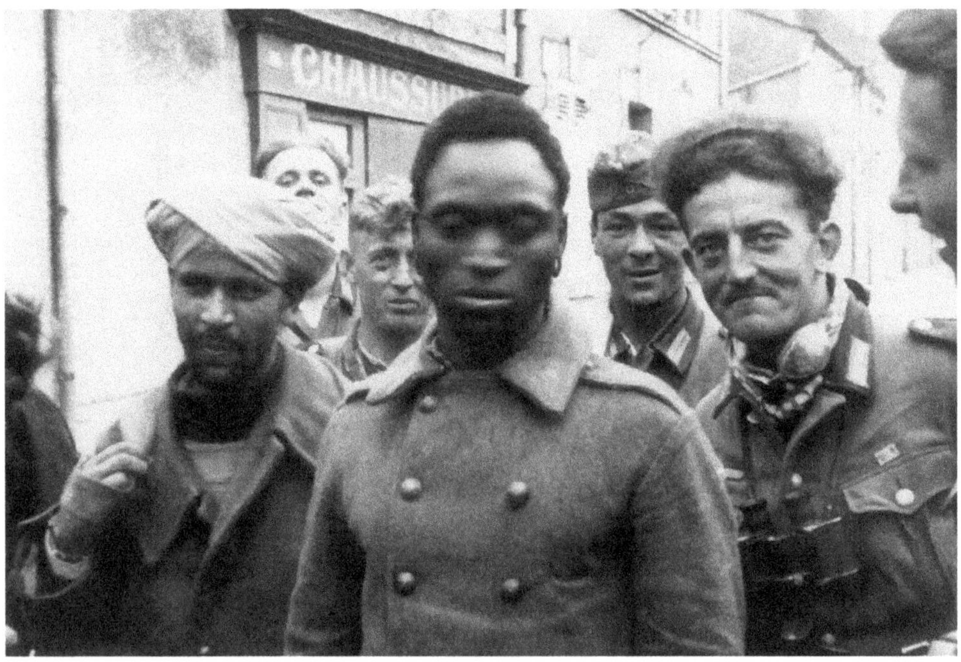

Souvenir Photo with the Exotics
Germans troops enjoy the plight of their French African Colonial prisoners, the soldiers recruited to fight far from home for their French masters. German troops who did not live in a major German city had never seen a black person. When meeting them on the battlefront they treated them as curiosities in some cases, but at other times such meetings had fatal consequences as the result of Nazi racist doctrines and anti-black propaganda.

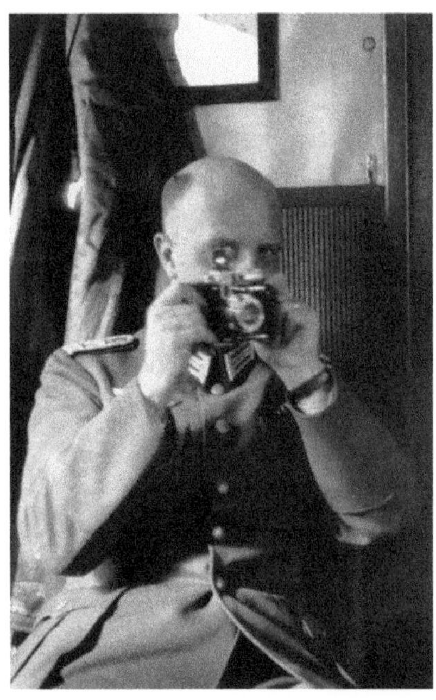

Through the Viewfinder
An army officer points what appears to be a Kodak Retina or a Zeiss Ikonta at his target.

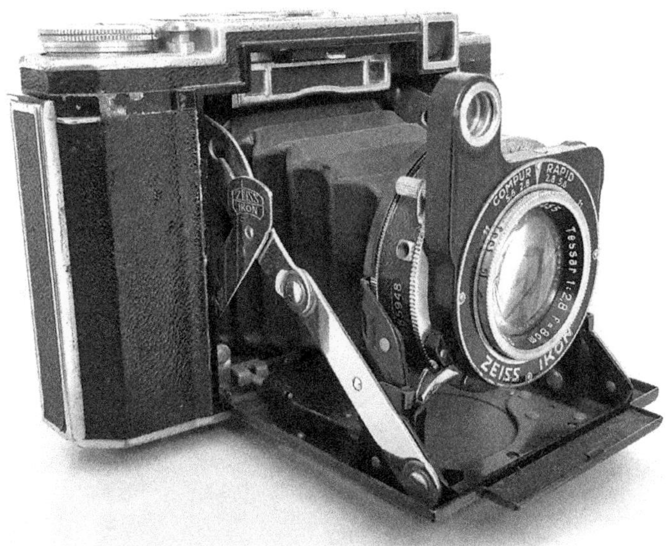

Carl Zeiss Super Ikonta B (530/16), *c.* 1934–37
The Super Ikonta first appeared in 1934 as the Model 530, featuring a Compur shutter and 75 mm lens, using 6x4.5 or 120 film format. The 1935-issued Model 532/16 featured the 80 mm F3.5 or F2.8 lens and the Compur Rapid lens, as seen here. The Super Ikonta (also known as the Super Ikomat) produced twelve exposures per roll and featured a coupled rangefinder, double exposure prevention and flash synchronisation.

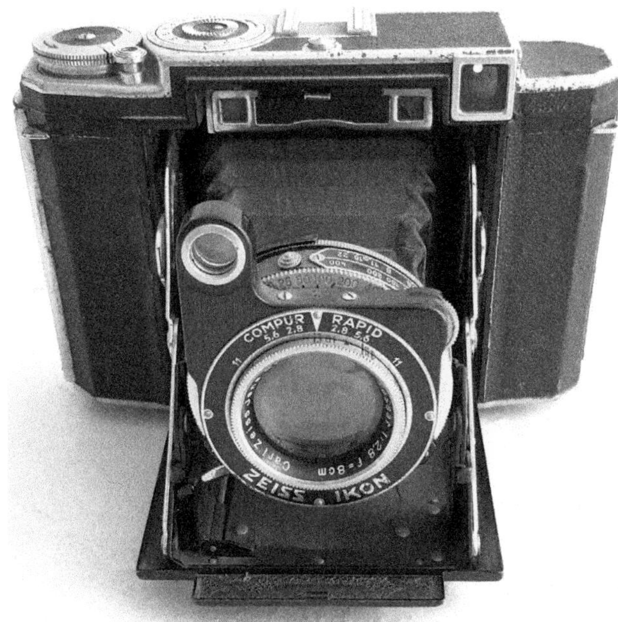

Expensive Quality
The Ikonta line was the top tier of Zeiss cameras. By 1939 and the first year of the war, the Ikonta was priced at approximately US $153.00, equal in 2017 to about $2,750.

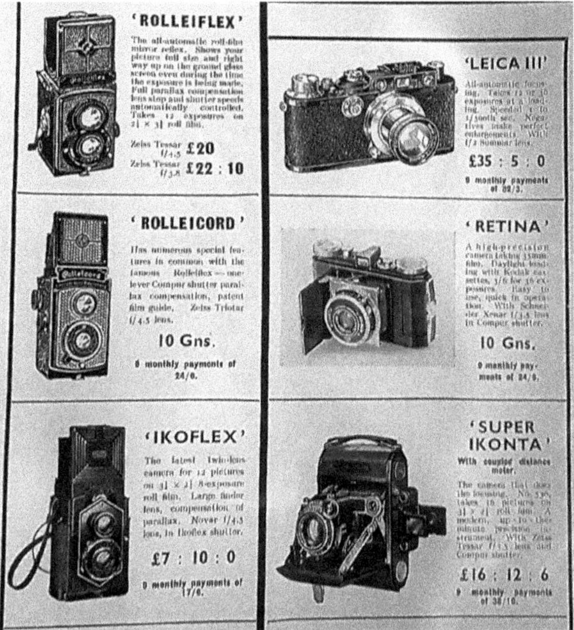

British Ad for German Cameras, 1933
The Leica III topped the price range with the Rolleiflex following. In 2017 the price of the Leica would equal about $675, but now as a highly sought after collectible it would fetch much more.

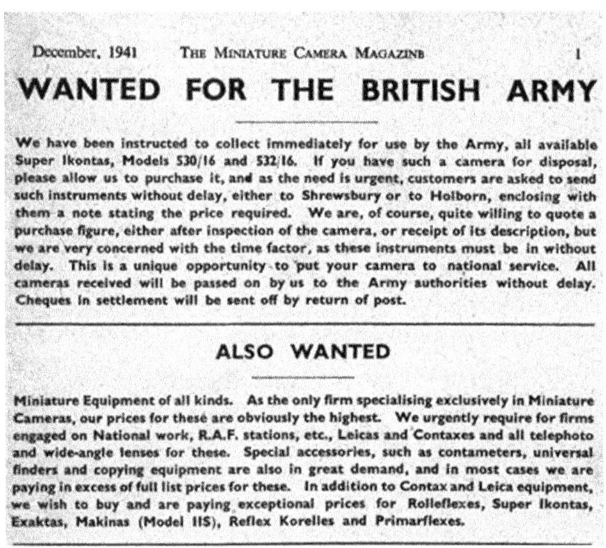

Cameras on the 'Wanted List', Christmas 1941
This announcement appeared in a wartime British publication and regarded the request for donations of much-needed high-quality German camera equipment to be used in the war effort. The term 'miniature' at the time referred to the relatively compact 35 mm cameras as compared to the earlier large press plate and more unwieldy cameras then in use. German brands in demand include Zeiss Super Ikonta, Leica, Contax, Rolleiflex, Exakta and Reflex Korelle.

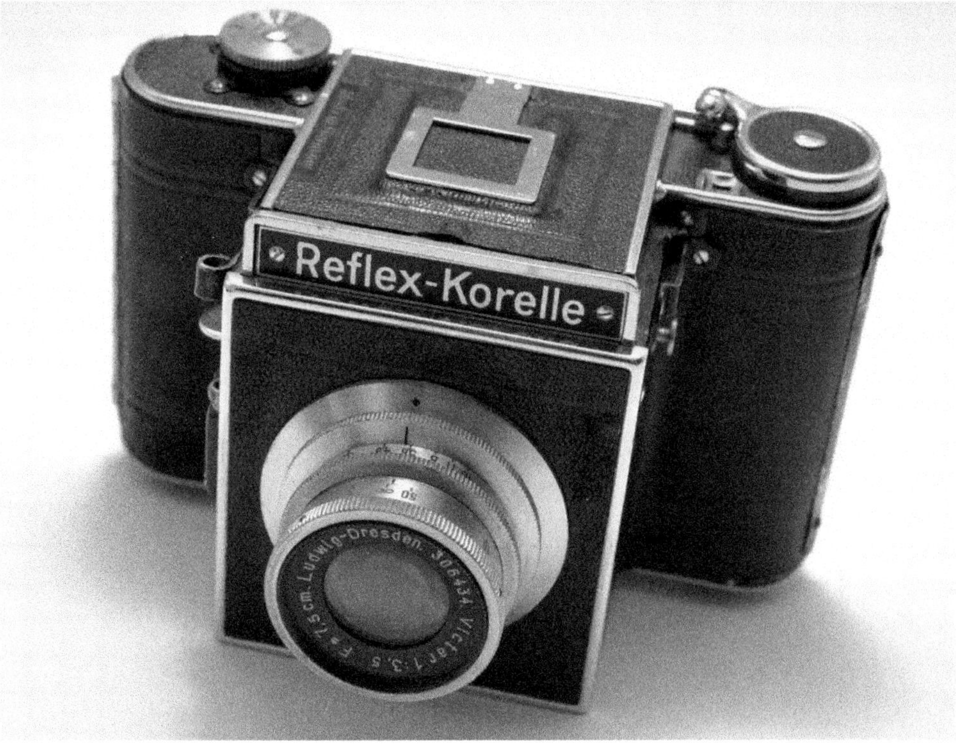

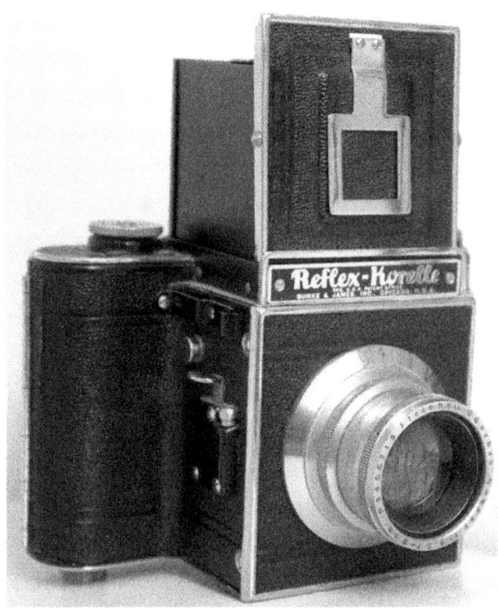

On the List – Milestone Camera: Korelle SLR
This Reflex-Korelle export model sold in Chicago was one of the first SLR designs. It featured a focal plane shutter with speeds of 1/25th to 1/500th of a second and film was 120 roll format or 6x6.

Korelle Innovator
In 1921 *Franz Kochmann Fabrik* of Dresden began producing high-quality, advanced professional and amateur cameras. Kochmann's most notable design was the Reflex-Korelle, first introduced in 1935. One of the most important and successful cameras of the 1930s and 1940s, it was also one of the first to feature interchangeable lenses.

With the Nazi Party's ascent to power, Franz Israel Kochmann and his family were forced to flee Germany, his company and extensive art collection seized. Even the company's name was obliterated and renamed Korellewerke KG in 1939 when taken over by G. H. Brandtman & Co. Prior to the outbreak of the war, the Reflex-Korelle was marketed in the United States through Burke & James Inc. of Chicago, having previously marketed the cameras for Kochmann.

Cameras Carried East

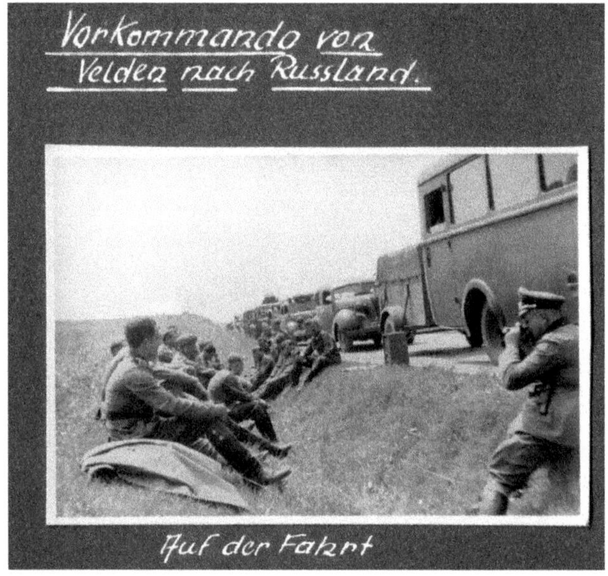

On the Way to the Invasion of Russia
An officer of a *Nachtrichten* (communications) detachment takes a rest stop to photo his comrades occupying a roadside ditch. Their ultimate destination in the summer of 1941 is the staging point for the 21 June invasion of the Soviet Union, the path first taking them through Poland. This photo was one of several contained in a photo album chronicling the expedition.

Opposite below: Dancing Cameraman – Latvia, 1941
German troops dance with the locals as a civilian stringed orchestra adds to the festivities. A lone cameraman stands in the midst (far left) of the moving bodies, his 35 mm camera firing away. In conjunction with the invasion of Soviet Russia, German forces occupied Latvia on 10 July 1941, the occupied area renamed Letland in the German parlance. Its Jewish and Roma populations were immediately targeted for elimination with mass shootings orchestrated by the *Einsatzgruppe A* along with often enthusiastic Latvian collaborators such as the Arjas Commando, its 1,500 volunteers responsible for some 26,000 Jewish murders. During the German occupation more than 70,000 Jewish men, women and children were killed, as well as over 2,000 Roma. Because of fractured allegiances and political motivations, Latvians fought with and against the Germans as well as for and against the Soviets.

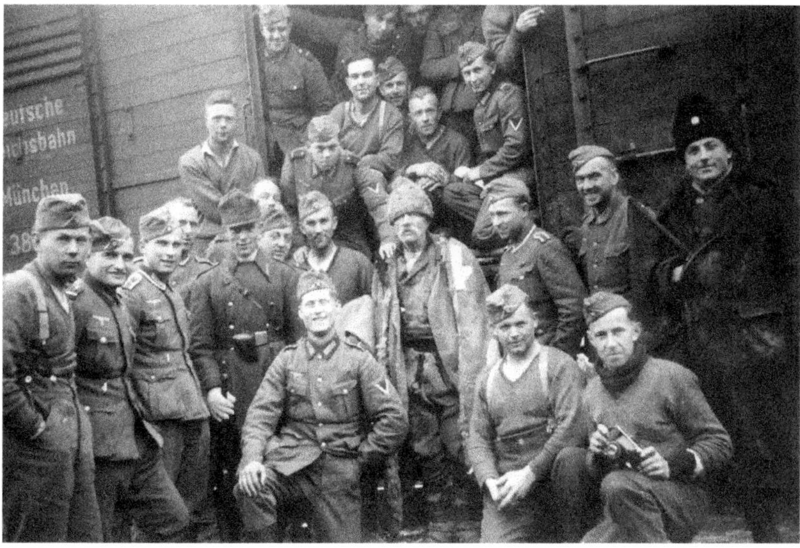

Souvenir Shot in Romania

A trainload of German Army infantry pose with an elderly Romanian civilian as centerpoint. They are joined by a Romanian soldier (left) while a Romanian special policeman in black (far right) assumes the classic 'Napoleon' stance with his hand inside his coat. In front of him is a German soldier holding a folding-strut camera.

When the German police mobile killing units set out to perform their operations, they found the Romanians had already murdered most of their fellow Jewish countrymen, including 150,000 by the Romanian Fourth Army. Romania was only second to Germany for the number of Jews killed by its military and civilians. During government-initiated 'ethnic cleansing and purification actions', members of the anti-Jewish right-wing *Esalon Operativ* attacked any and all Jews they could find, often using knives and crowbars. Even the Germans complained about their methods and their tendency to leave the corpses unburied.

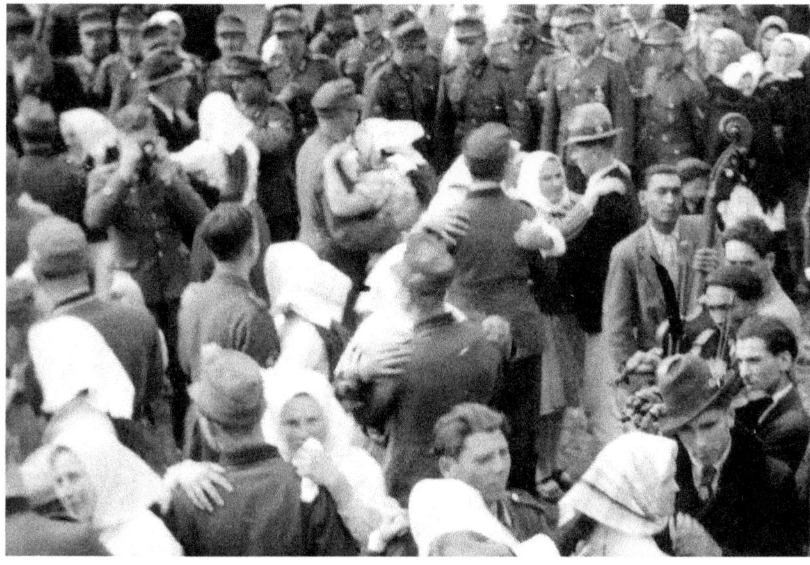

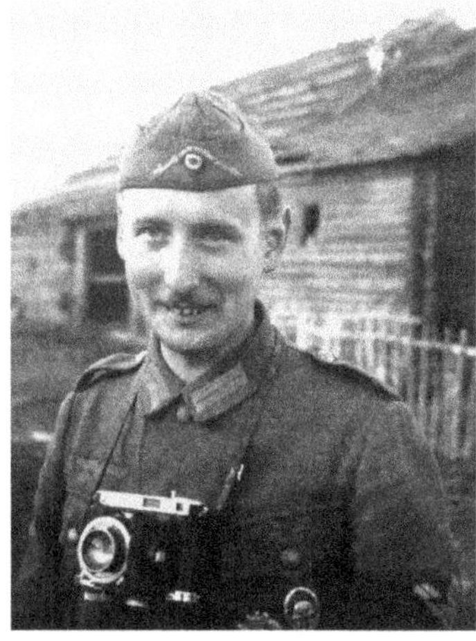

Russian Front Cameraman
An army corporal showing a wound badge has his own image captured while wearing a state-of-the-art large-format camera.

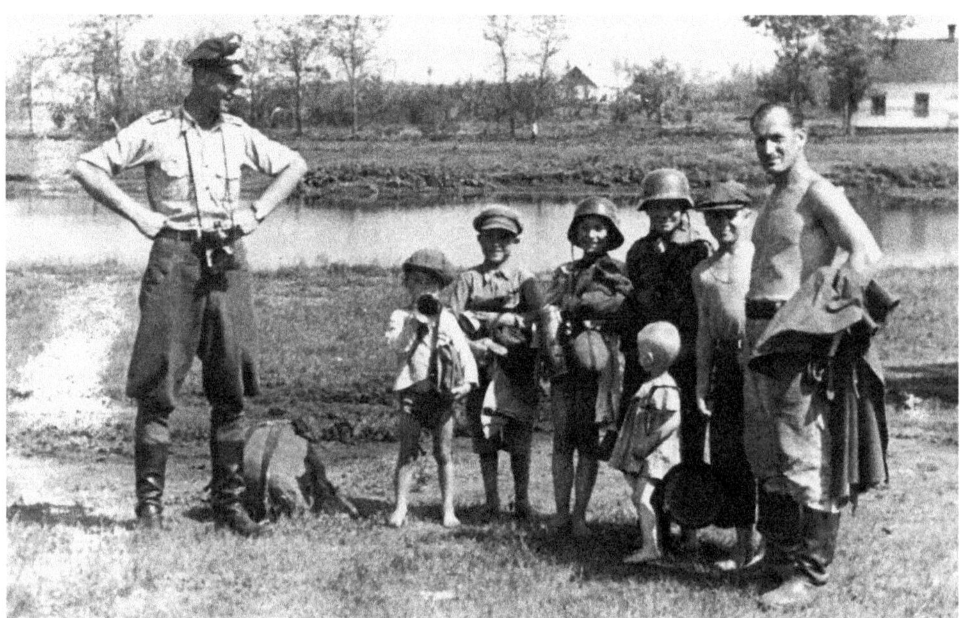

First Summer in Russia
Wearing his 35 mm camera, a Luftwaffe officer strikes a pose with a group of Russian children happily wearing German helmets, one blowing a bugle. Upon their arrival in the Ukraine, German troops were met with welcoming symbols of bread and salt, the civilians hoping they would be freed from Stalin's lethal tyranny that resulted in as many of 30 million deaths by starvation due to his draconian 'collectivisation' program as well as his deliberate efforts to eradicate Ukrainian nationalism. However, Nazi racial doctrines classified all 'Slavs' as *Untermensch* and planned for their enslavement or mass deaths by another 30 million to create *Lebensraum* for ethnic German resettlement. The mass murder of the area's Jewish population further contributed to the rise of resistance. While some Ukrainians joined in the killings, others formed guerilla groups to harass the Germans, some in coordination with the Red Army. Eventually some 10 million Russian military would die fighting the Nazis, with another 30 million civilians being killed during the occupation of Soviet territory.

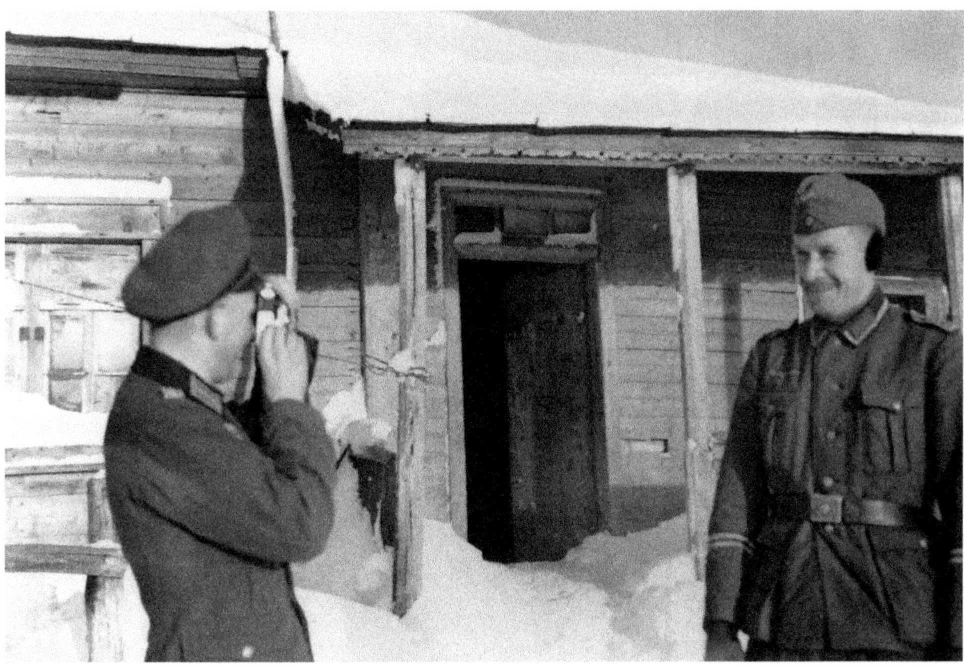

Earmuffs in Russia – First Winter

A 'Spiess' or top sergeant smiles for the camera while wearing his army-issue earmuffs, apparently the only winter gear available. When attacking the Soviet Union on 21 June 1941, the German High Command and Hitler were certain the Bolsheviks would 'collapse like a house of cards' in a matter of a few weeks. As a result of that fatal arrogance, German soldiers were not issued with winter gear, suffering greatly as a result, thousands freezing or suffering from frostbite.

Russian Mud

A soldier kneels on the ground as he extends the legs of his tripod-mounted plate camera, possibly a Deckrullo-Nettel, one of the most popular 'press' cameras of the 1930s. The infamous bi-annual *Rasputitsa* autumn rains and spring thaw turned the roads to a morass of mud that swallowed men and mechanised vehicles. Also known as 'General Mud', the harsh weather played a deciding factor in the devolution of the German invasion of the vast USSR.

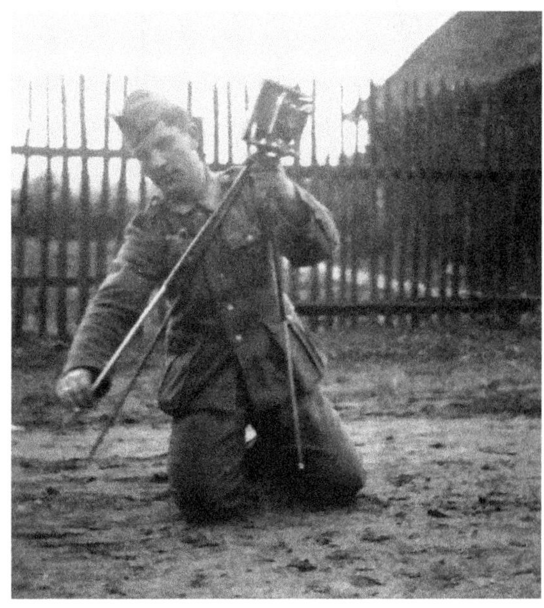

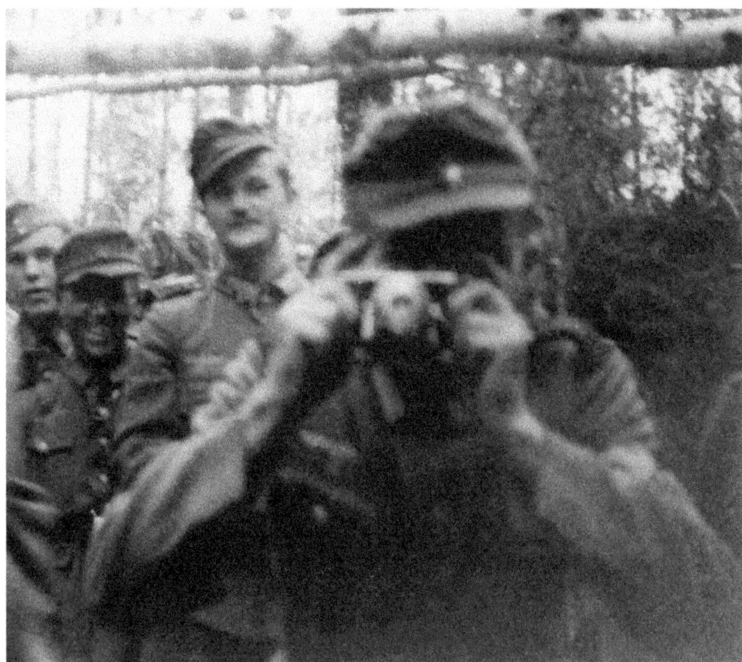

Fading Futures
Deep in a Russian birch forest, German troops still manage to smile for the camera.

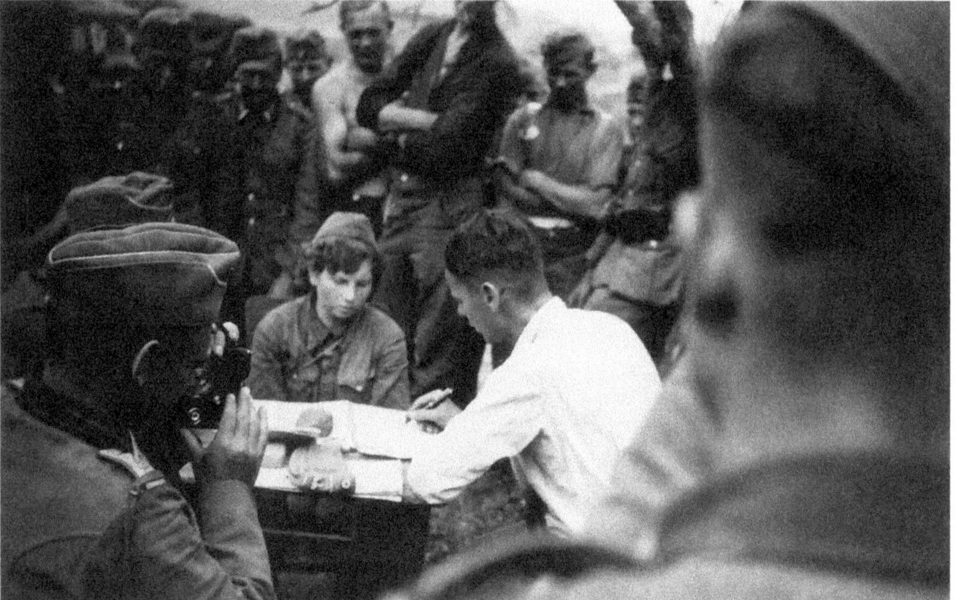

Still Camera on Movie Camera
A German movie camera, possibly a compact 16 mm Siemens, films the interrogation of a Red Army female soldier, as German soldiers gather around to view the 'oddity' of a woman soldier. Back home German housewives often erupted in anger when watching newsreels showing Red Army women in uniform and called for their summary execution. As a result of Hitler's Commissar Order, that was the fate for any Soviet political officer, man or woman.

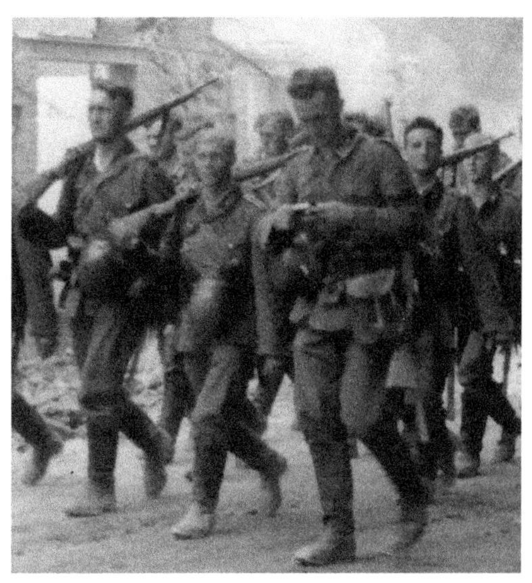

Marching in Step

While some have noticed the cameraman, battle-weary army troops make their way through the rubble of a Russian town as an NCO appears to adjust his camera. Of note are the varying sizes of the men, who all carry the standard issue Mauser rifle over their shoulders. The NCO also carries the standard document satchel in which records of the unit were kept.

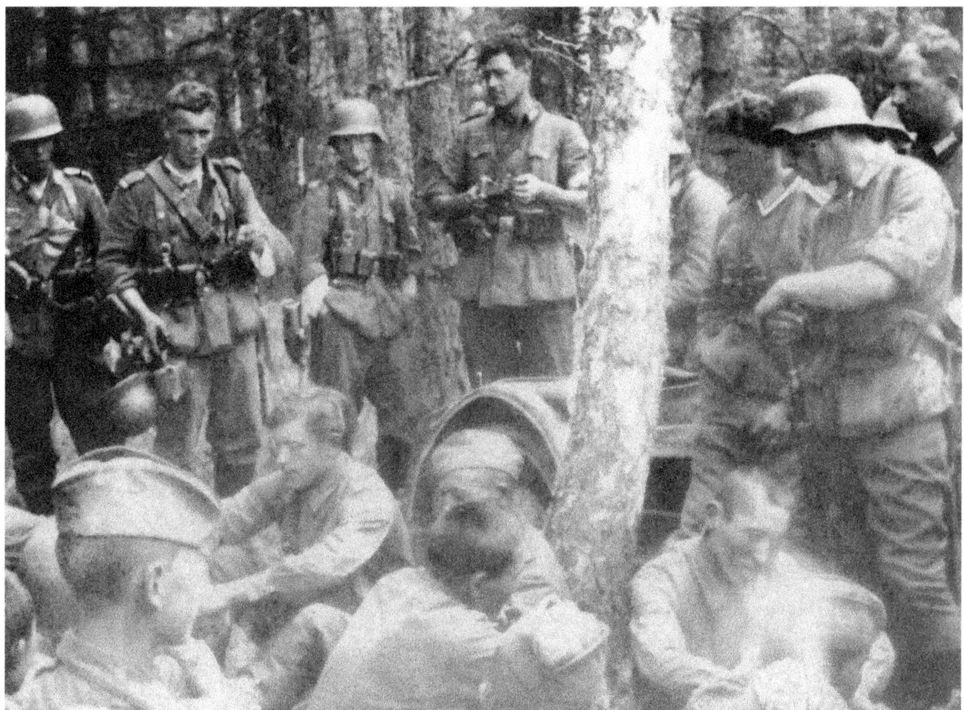

Focus of Attention – Death Hangs in the Balance for a Commissar

Compared to the short-cropped heads of the Russian Asiatic troops gathered around him, the photo suggests that the longer-haired Soviet soldier is either their commanding officer or a political commissar, or both. His German captors stare at him with a malevolent curiosity. The tallest of them (center) unfolds a camera while another unseen camera records the scene, perhaps the longest moment in the Russian officer's life – one very likely about to end violently as the result of Hitler's 'Commissar Order'.

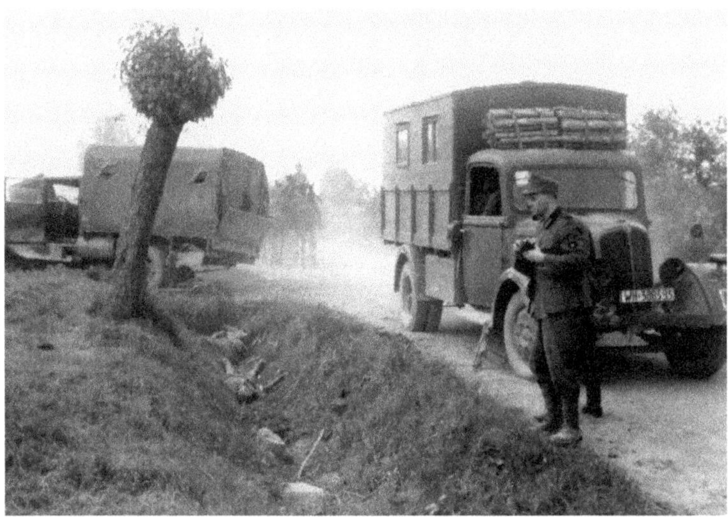

At the Edge
A private in the mountain troops ponders the dead lying in the roadside ditch, his camera poised. Barely seen standing alongside him is another soldier, one leg visible. The Wehrmacht communications truck behind them carries cords of wood either for fueling cooking fires or as traction when encountering muddy roads. In the background, horse-drawn wagons follow in the dust of the motorised vehicles.

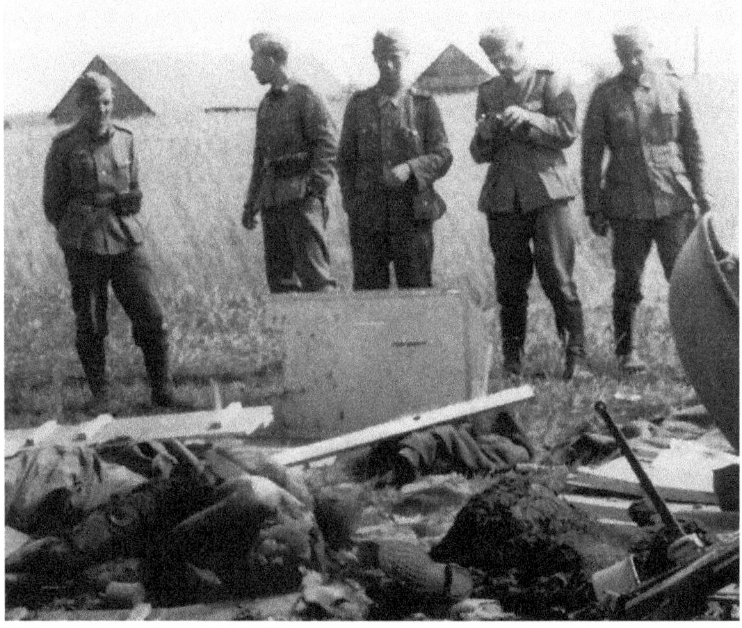

KIA on the Russian Front, Summer 1941
With a sundrenched wheat field in the background, a group of German privates and corporals have come upon the remains of a Russian unit. The burned and blackened bodies heaped at their feet elicit a variety of expressions, one soldier preparing his camera for a photo.

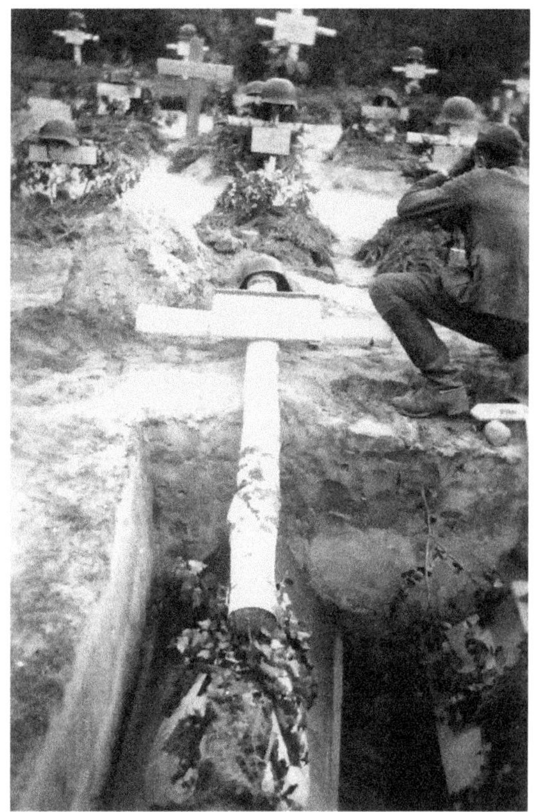

Fresh Grave in Russia
A German soldier crouches at the edge
of a newly dug grave as he photographs
one already occupied and marked with a
birchwood cross topped by a comrade's
helmet.

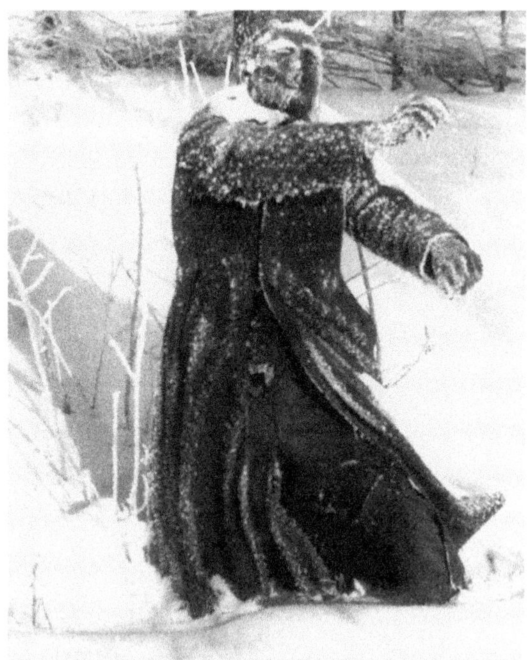

Souvenir from the Eastern Front
With temperatures dropping to -30°F,
there was an abundance of frozen
bodies both Russian and German. This
'walking dead' is unidentifiable and
may have been photographed as found
by a German camera or with the corpse
propped up in the snow for added effect.

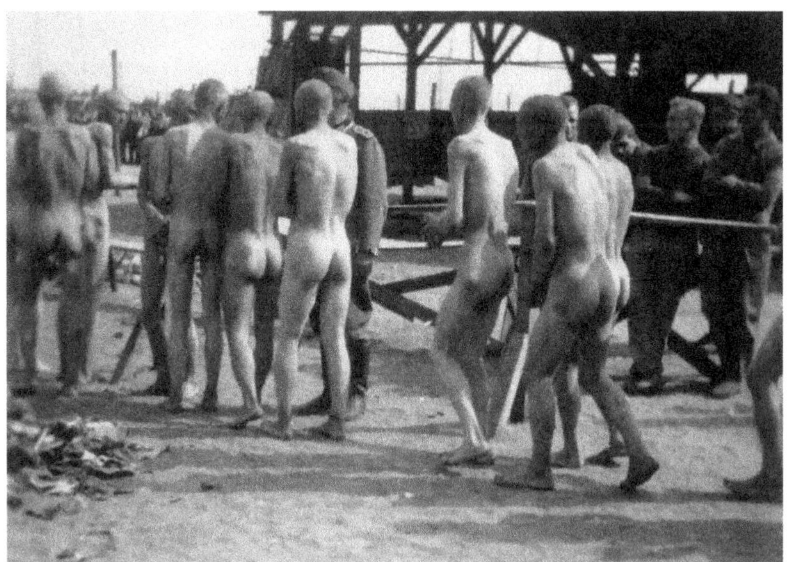

Crimes Self-Documented

German soldiers watch as Russian POWs are marched to whatever fate awaits them. Some 3 million were deliberately left to starve to death after their capture. The first Holocaust deniers were the Nazis themselves, who as the war turned against them sent special units to dig up the mass graves and grind the bones to dust. Because of the large number of such graves and the advance of the Red Army, many remained untouched, now obscured and lost by time. However, the photos taken by the Germans themselves would eventually serve to document and provide evidence of their crimes against humanity.

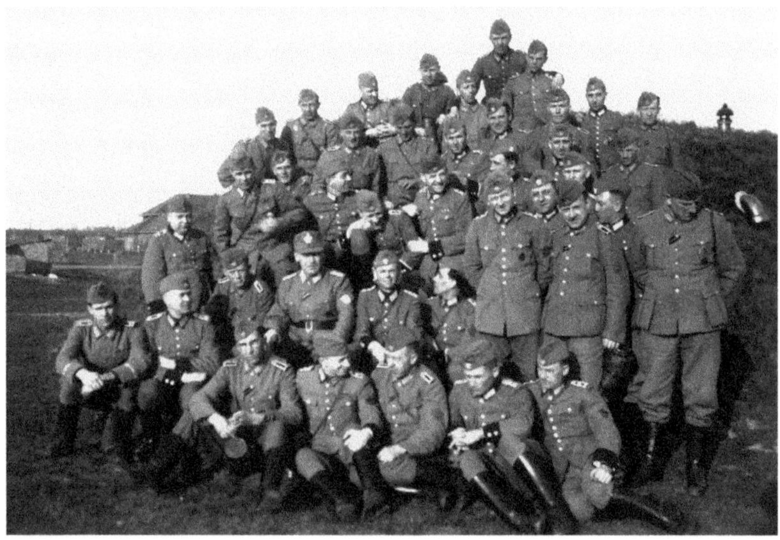

Mass Murderers Group Photo

Gathered for an informal group portrait with a munitions bunker as the backdrop, members of Police Battalion 322 display their medals and ribbons. The unit's own meticulous documentation of its activities on the Eastern Front records the murder of over 39,000 Jewish men, women and children.

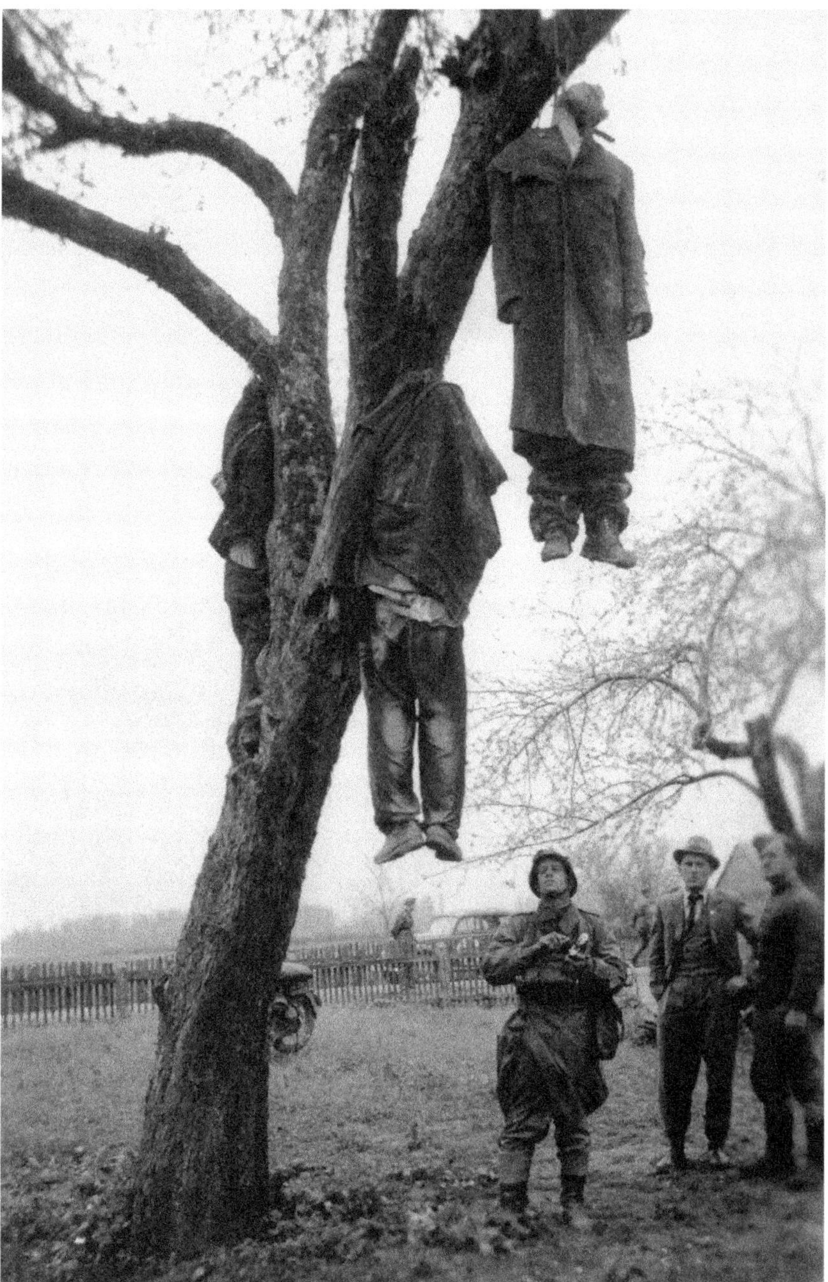

Camera at the Ready

A *Kradmelder* (cycle soldier) has stepped off his motorcycle to record the hanging of three men executed after being found 'guilty' of one of the many Nazi civil, military, political and racial 'crimes' punishable by death. While photos of mass executions were officially prohibited, individual soldiers often recorded the atrocities, many of the images coming back to literally and figuratively haunt the cameraman and the world. One must not forget that the doctrines promoted by the Third Reich were responsible for a war of aggression and genocide resulting in the deaths of an estimated 60 million men, women and children.

Moving Pictures: 8 mm, 16 mm and 35 mm Wartime Cameras

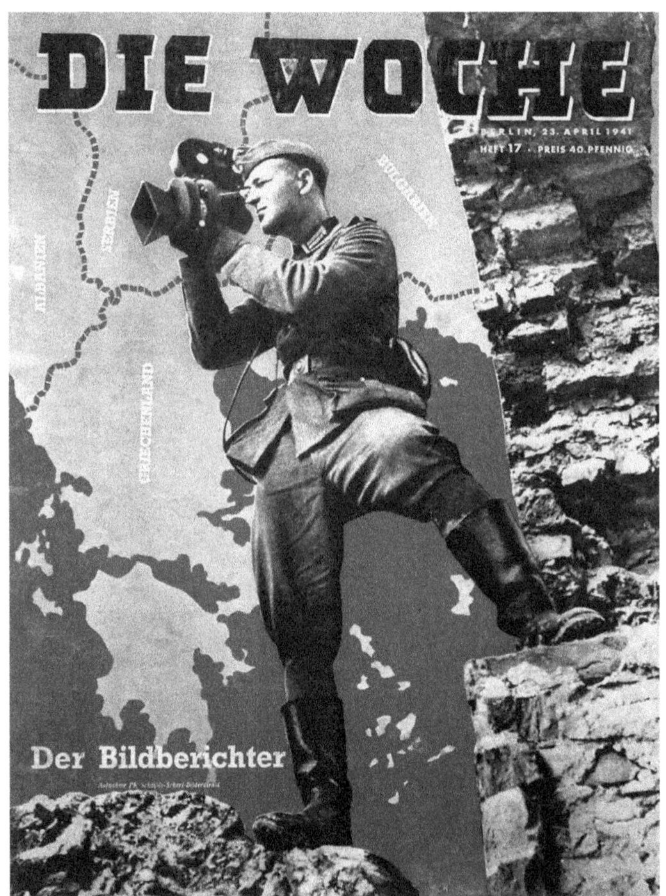

Foothold on the World
The cover of the 23 April 1941 issue of the weekly illustrated newsmagazine *Die Woche* features a story focusing on *Der Bilderichter*, or photojournalist. He is seen shouldering an Arriflex 35 mm movie camera with a 200-foot film magazine. The background illustration features a map of Greece, the country recently overrun by German forces – an unexpected intervention made necessary by Mussolini's military blunder when invading Italian troops were thrown back by the Greek defenders.

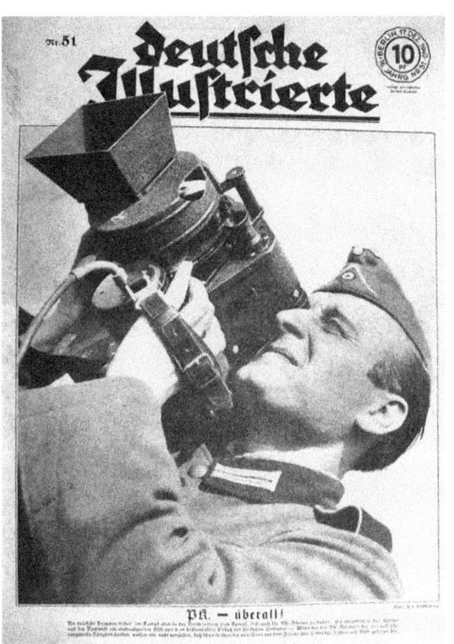

BR-Manner (*Bilderichter*)
'Photo-Documentarian'
A December 1940 issue of *Deutsche Illustrierte*
spotlights the important role and contributions of
the photojournalist, 'who records the bravery of
the German soldier and who also has sacrificed
his life for the Fatherland, Volk and the Fuhrer'.
A member of one of the many filmcrews
documenting the Third Reich, this soldier also
wields an Arriflex professional 35 mm movie
camera – the camera of choice for notorious Third
Reich filmmaker Leni Riefenstahl.

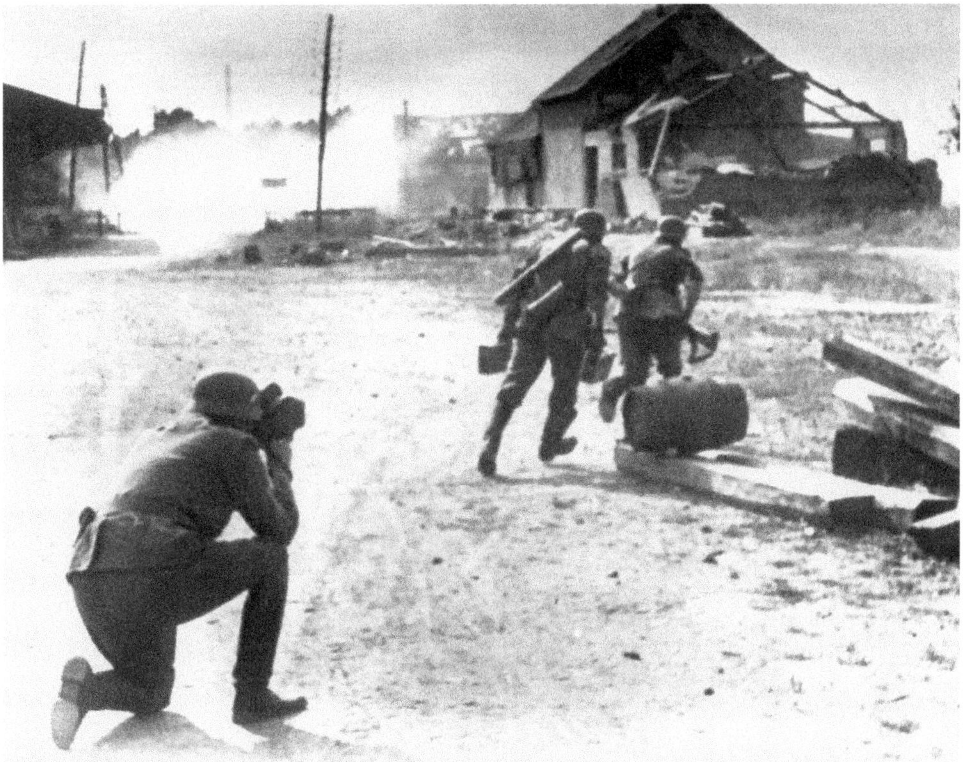

'Action on the Western Front' – Official Press Photo
A German machine-gun crew is seen rushing into battle while being filmed by a soldier armed
with a movie camera and sidearm.

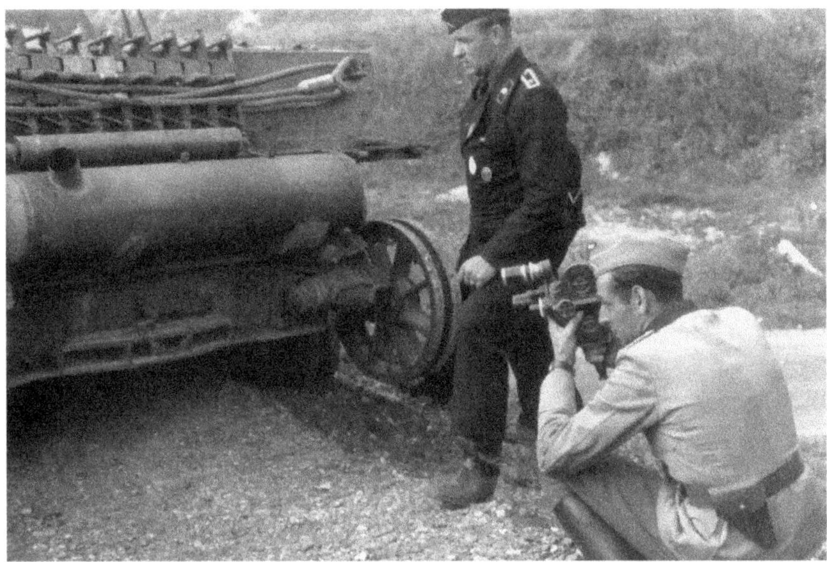

German Tank, American Camera

A member of a film unit operates an American-made Bell & Howell Filmo 16 mm camera to document some technical issue involving the rear section of what may be a captured enemy tank. The equally tank-tough Filmo was much valued by war correspondents on both sides. The cameraman likely carries a 7.62 caliber Mauser sidearm in his holster, a more compact weapon than the 9 mm Luger or its replacement, the Walther P-38. In 1927 Bell & Howell had introduced the world's first 16 mm turret camera, the Model C, which accommodated three lenses allowing for medium, wide-angle and telephoto filming.

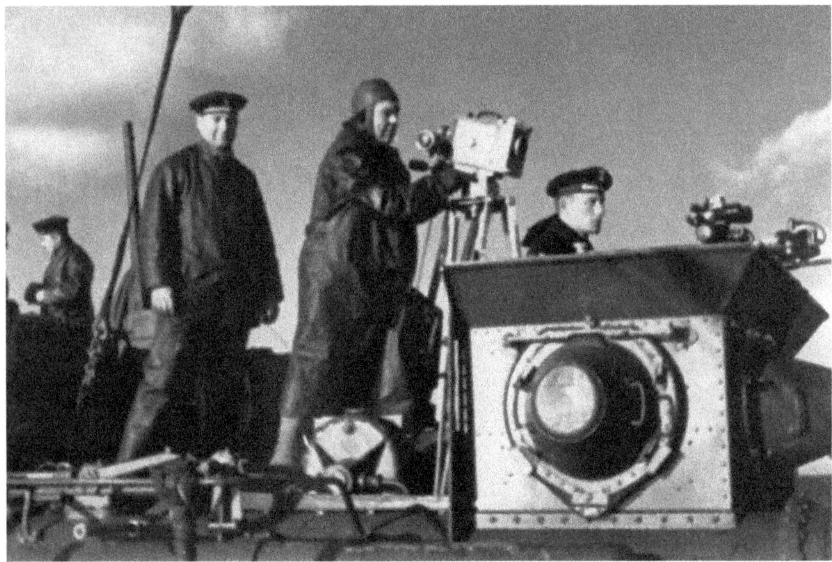

Air, Land or Sea

A film crew prepares to film the action on a *Kriegsmarine* warship, the cameraman dressed for protection from the elements, as is his specially housed camera.

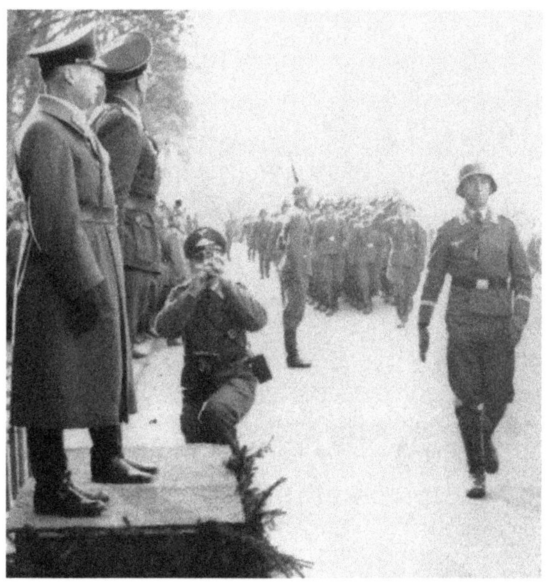

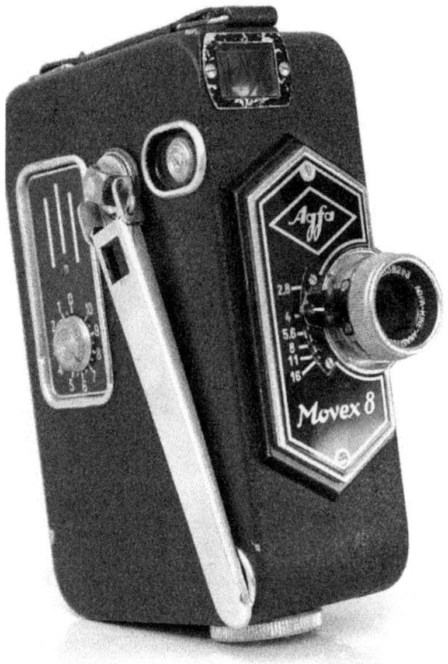

Above left: **Luftwaffe in Review**
A Luftwaffe solider wearing a sports badge crouches with his 8 mm movie camera aimed at the officers observing the troops passing in review, apparently flak or anti-aircraft crewmembers. Leading the marching group is an NCO, his 'cuff-titles' indicating a special group.

Above right: **Agfa 8 mm, 1937**
The Movex 8 mm cine camera was the first Single-8 mm movie camera to use a film cartridge. Equipped with an Agfa Kine Anastigmat F/2.8 12 mm lens of fixed focus and one running speed of 16 fps, its metal construction was covered in black crinkle paint and it was spring-wound by a long handle crank. Compact, measuring 4½ x 3½ x 1½ inches, when loaded with film it weighed approximately 2 lbs.

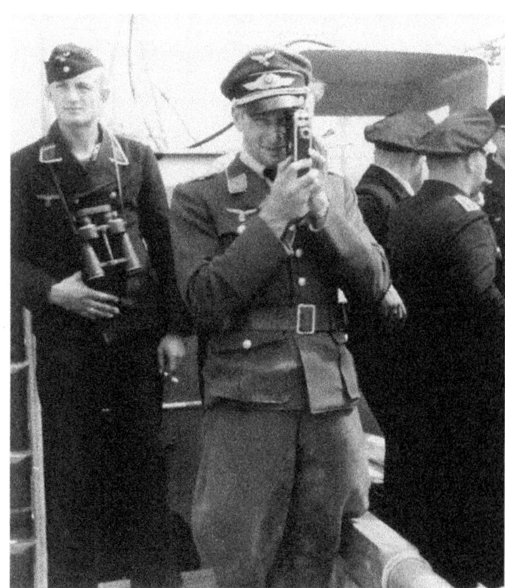

Mixed Company
A Luftwaffe lieutenant in the company of the *Kriegsmarine* films an event with an 8 mm camera.

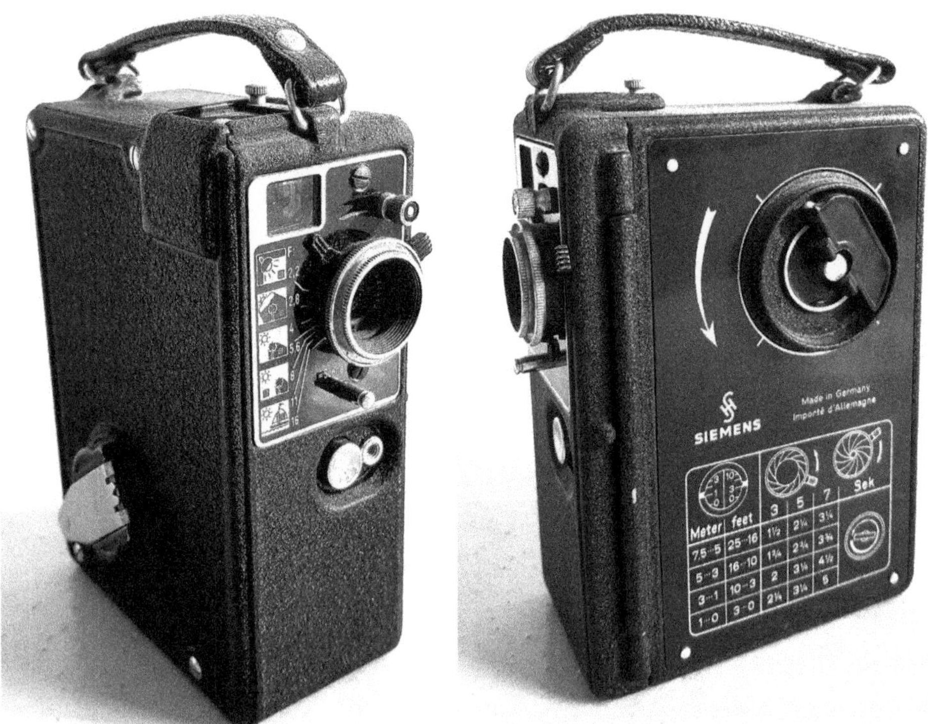

Above left: **Siemens 8R**
Another compact 8 mm movie camera of the era was the Siemens 8R, introduced in 1939.

Above right: **Instructions**
This very advanced-looking camera featured a Rodenstock Sironar F/1.2 10 mm lens and accepted an 8 mm film cartridge. This is an export model, thus the English and French language notations on the exposure guide.

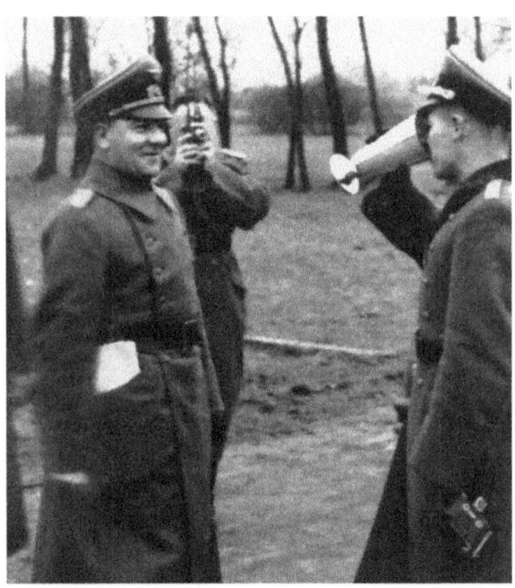

Special Toast
While the scene is filmed by a soldier using what appears to an Agfa or Bolex movie camera, a 35 mm still camera is visible in the hand of a soldier drinking from the ceremonial *Ehrenpokal der Luftwaffe* — the Goblet of Honor of the Luftwaffe. Hermann Goring, Reich minister of aviation and founder of the Gestapo, created the award in 1940 for Special Achievement in the Air War and it was given to pilots and air crew who had already earned the Iron Cross First Class. During the award ceremony, the goblet was traditionally filled with beer or a stronger drink. Cast from silver, some 15,000 were distributed before the war ended, with another 58,000 still slated for distribution.

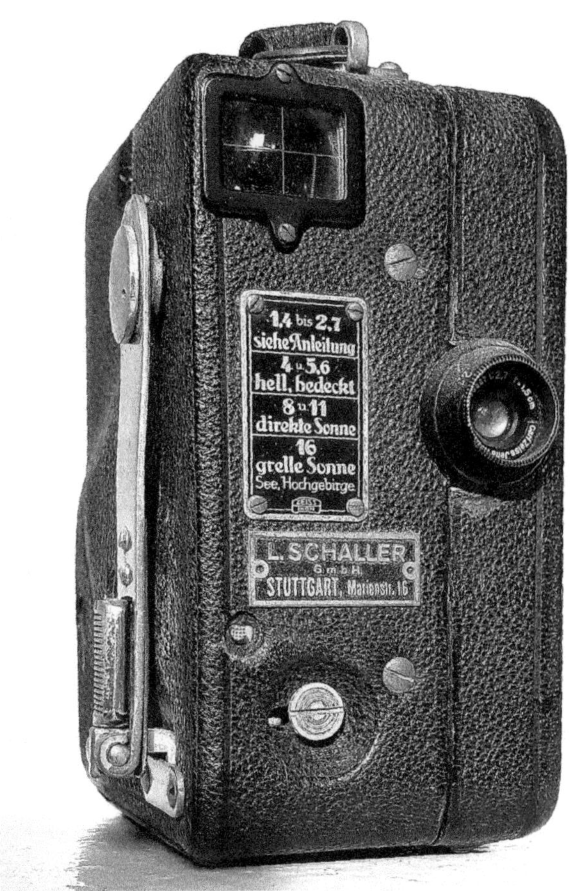

Kinamo S 10 16 mm, *c.* 1926–29
Featuring a Zeiss 15 mm Tessar F/2.7
lens, the compact movie camera is
wound by the chrome handle. Plaques
affixed to the face of the camera indicate
exposure settings for various lighting
conditions as well as the name of the
Stuttgart photography shop, L. Schaller,
which sold the camera.

**Waffen-SS Man Documenting History with
his 16 mm Kinamo**
An SS-*Sturmbahnfuhrer* (battalion commander)
aims his camera at an unseen target. His tunic
indicates his membership in a motorised
division and his lapel ribbon denotes the
awarding of the Iron Cross. The breast medal
is the German Cross (introduced 28 September
1941), an intermediary award following the
Iron Cross and prior to qualifying for the
vaunted Knight's Cross. He wears a wedding
ring on one hand and an SS Death's Head ring
on his other, as well as an expensive wristwatch.

The SS were Hitler's 'ideological' soldiers,
fanatically committed to Nazi doctrines
including the implementation of mass murder.
At the Nuremburg Tribunals they and armed
formations of the Waffen-SS were indicted
as a criminal organisation and charged with
numerous crimes against humanity.

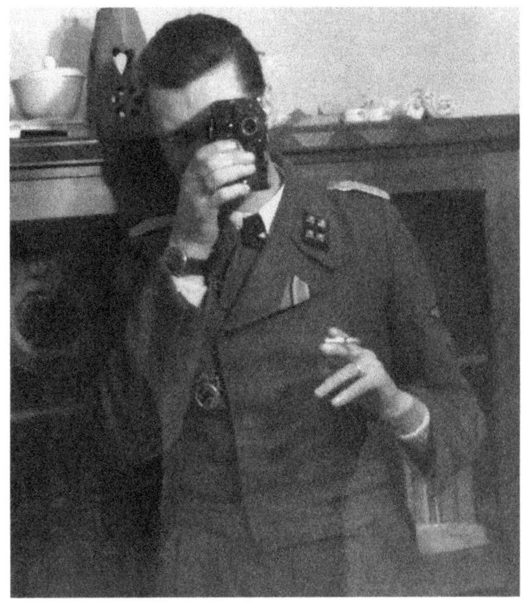

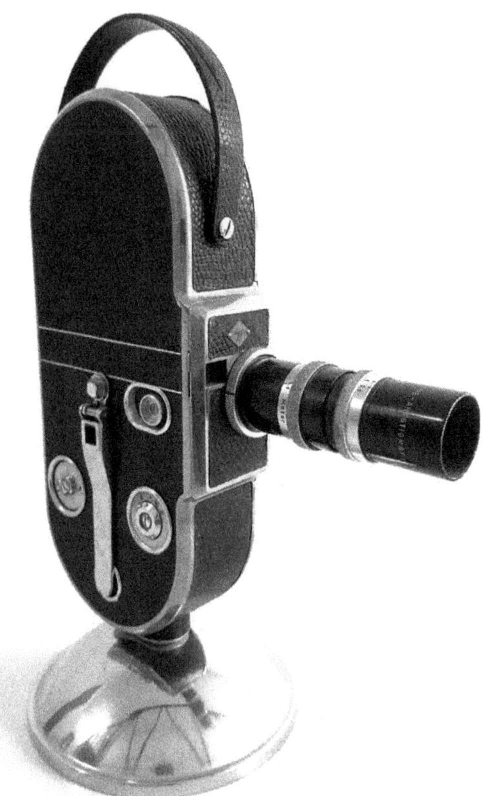

Agfa 16 mm Movex 30B, 1935
In addition to 8 mm movie cameras, larger 16 mm film format cameras were also available from Agfa, Bolex, Kodak, and Siemens. The Agfa 16 mm Movex 30B, produced in Dresden, was fashioned from die-cast aluminum with chrome fittings and an embossed leather covering. Carrying 100-foot spools of film, it was a popular camera with the German public as well as the military.

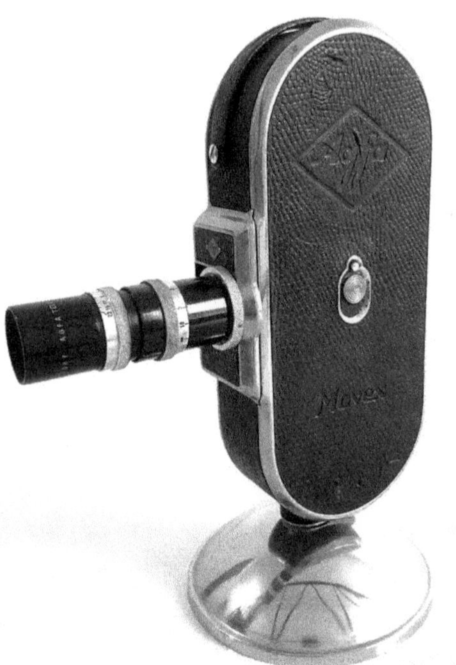

Telephoto Targeting
The standard general purpose lens was 20 mm but the camera also provided an integrated telephoto viewfinder for the use of additional lenses. In 1991, a ninety-minute documentary film titled *Mein Krieg* was released in Germany that contained amateur colour movie film footage shot by soldiers of the infantry, artillery and air force, both during training and their participation in the invasion of Russia. The unique footage was joined by interviews with the now elderly cameramen, almost all of whom expressed no sense of regret for the carnage in which they took an active part.

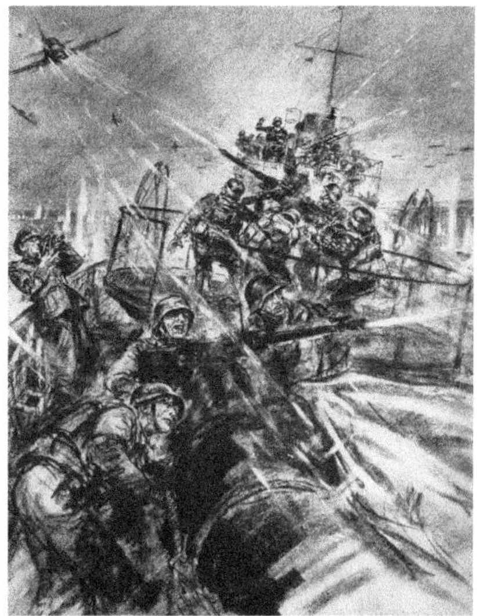

Cameraman Firing Away under Strafing
A newspaper illustration of a German warship under
attack by enemy aircraft depicts an officer (far left)
aiming his triple-lensed Swiss-made 16 mm Bolex as the
bullets fly.

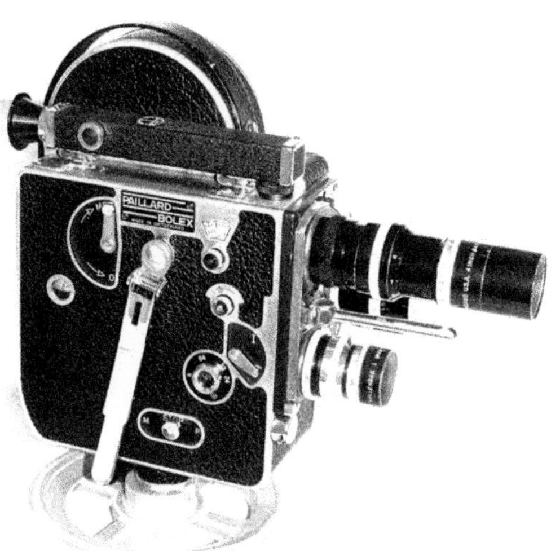

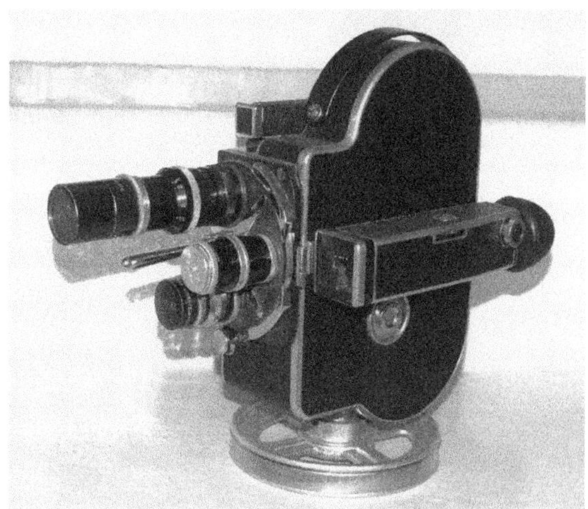

Above left: **Bolex 16 mm**
The history of Bolex is traceable to 1814 when E. Paillard & Co. was founded in Sainte-Croix,
Switzerland, by Möise Paillard from his small home workshop where he developed watch and
music box mechanisms. In 1920 Paillard opened a new facility in Yverdon, Switzerland, and
began producing Hermes typewriters. 1928 saw the appearance of the first 16 mm cine camera
bearing the Bolex name, the spring-wound or 'clockwork' design, single lens Auto-Cine A, the
camera designed by a Ukrainian engineer living in Geneva, one Jacques Bogopolsky.

Above right: **Triple Turret**
The new design was followed in 1929 with the Auto-Cine B camera, then a year later by the
Bolex Model C 16 mm projector. In 1930 Bogopolsky sold the Bolex company to Paillard, thus
forming Paillard-Bolex, the cine division of Paillard S. A., but he remained on staff for some five
years. The Bolex milestone year was 1935 with the introduction of now famous Paillard-Bolex
H-16 movie camera. The smaller 8 mm Bolex, the H-8, followed in 1938. Three years later, in
1941, as the war raged in Europe, sales to amateurs via mail order were available in the US.

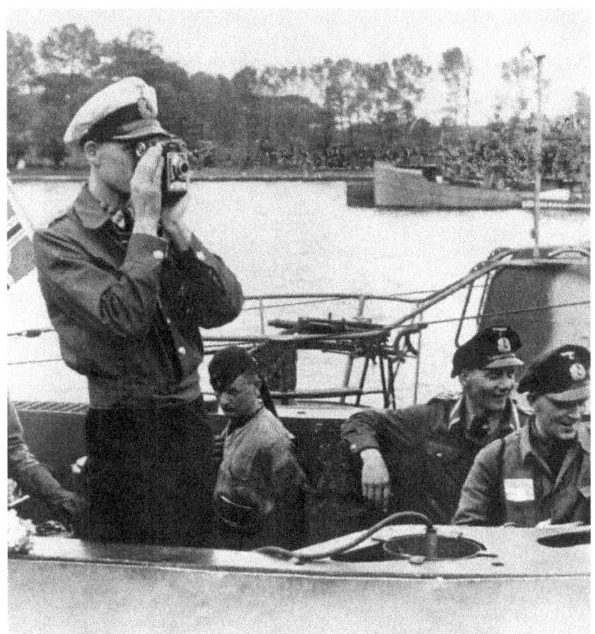

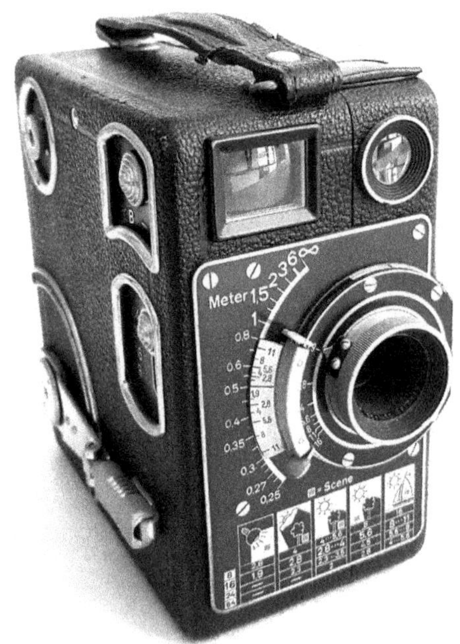

Above left: **U-Boat Commander with Siemens C Model 16 mm Movie Camera**
The original text accompanying this official Third Reich-era press release photo identifies the individual operating a Siemens 16 mm cine camera as *Kriegsmarine* submarine commander Reinhard Hardegen.

The translation of the photo caption reads: 'After a special message from the OKW (Supreme Wehrmacht Command) of 24 January 1942, German submarines, by their excursion in North American and Canadian waters, very near the enemy coast, torpedoed eighteen cargo ships totaling 125,000 BRT along with another escort. *Kapitanleutnant* Hardegen especially distinguished himself by alone sinking eight ships of 53,000 BRT, including three tankers off New York. Our picture shows *Kapitanleutnant* Hardegen with his film camera before setting sail on his mission.'

Not considered an ardent Nazi supporter, Hardegen was one of the small percentage of German submariners to survive the war (over 80 per cent were KIA). Held in captivity by the British authorities for a year before being released, he prospered in post-war Germany, running a successful oil company and serving in Bremen's parliament for over thirty-two years.

Above right: **Siemens 16 mm, 1933 – The Model Used by Hardegen**
Black leather and chrome beauties, Siemens cine cameras were the ultimate expression of quality and performance. Founded in 1847 as Telegraphen-Bauanstalt von Siemens & Halske by Ernst Werner von Siemens and Johann Georg Halske, Siemens was originally a Berlin electrical engineering company specialising in telegraph equipment. With affiliates in Britain and Russia, it prospered as the result of a patented electrical generator in 1867. During the 1930s Siemens also manufactured a limited number of their high-quality 8 mm and 16 mm amateur movie cameras.

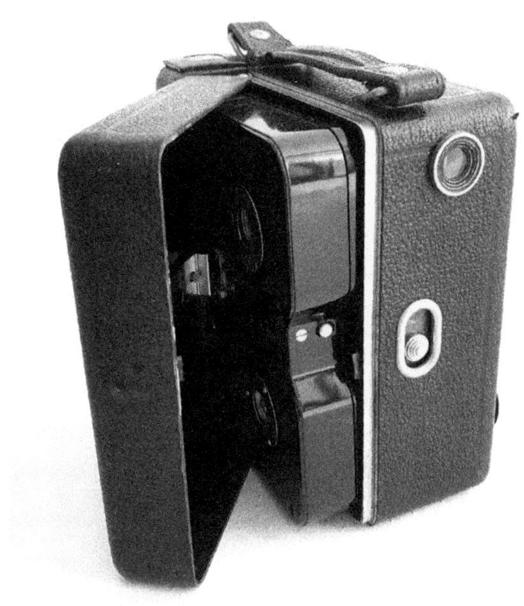

Modern Magazine Film Design
The Siemens accepted special 16 mm cartridges that eliminated light leakage problems.

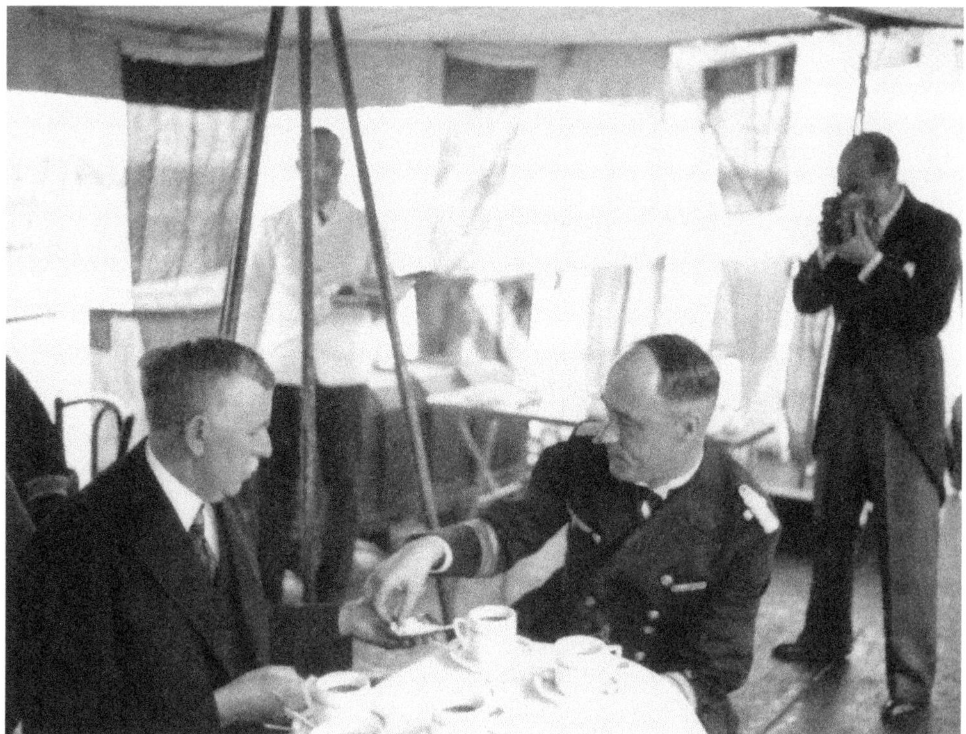

One Lump of Sugar
A high-ranking *Kriegsmarine* officer and a government representative enjoy their coffee while shipboard. A waiter stands in the background against the hanging sunshades while a formally attired cameraman films the event with what appears to be a Siemens 16 mm.

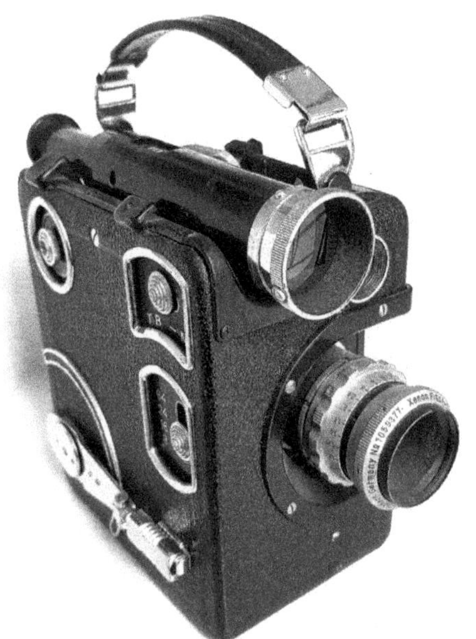

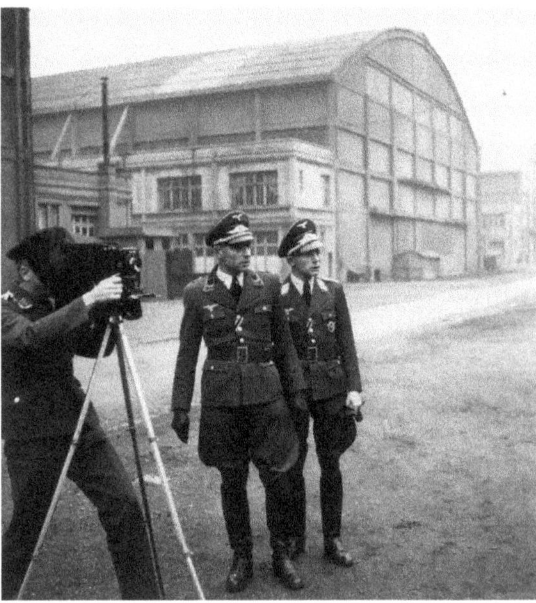

Above Left: **Siemens 16 mm, 1937 – Model FII**
Remarkably modern-looking, the camera is fitted with the optional adjustable telescoping
25–100 mm viewfinder to accommodate other lenses. In this case it carries a Schneider Xenon
25 mm F1.5 lens.

Above right: **Luftwaffe Officers and NCO Cameraman**
Both officers wear the ribbon for the Iron Cross Second Class in their uniforms' buttons, one
airman also showing the Air Crew Badge on his tunic. The object of the large press plate camera
is unknown as is the cause of the officers' concerned expressions.

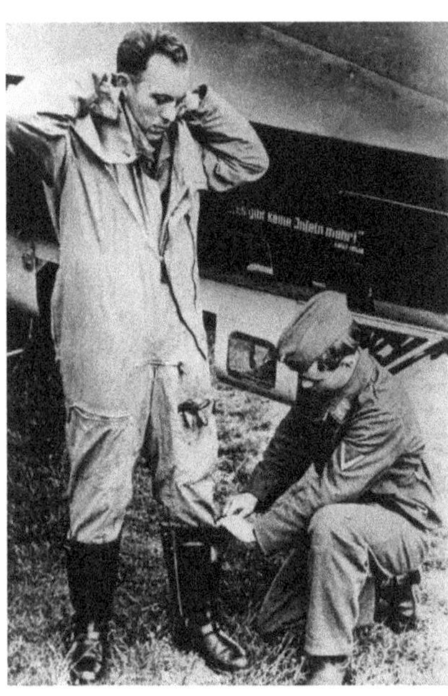

**Berlin Press Release Photo: Britain Still Afloat,
13 August 1940**
The image sourced from a Berlin newspaper shows a
pilot being prepared for a bombing run on England.
Inscribed on the fuselage are the words 'There are no
more islands', to which Adolf Hitler has signed his
name. Apparently he was also guilty of plagiarism or
was a fan of the poet since the line had appeared in
a recent poem by American writer Edna St Vincent
Millay.

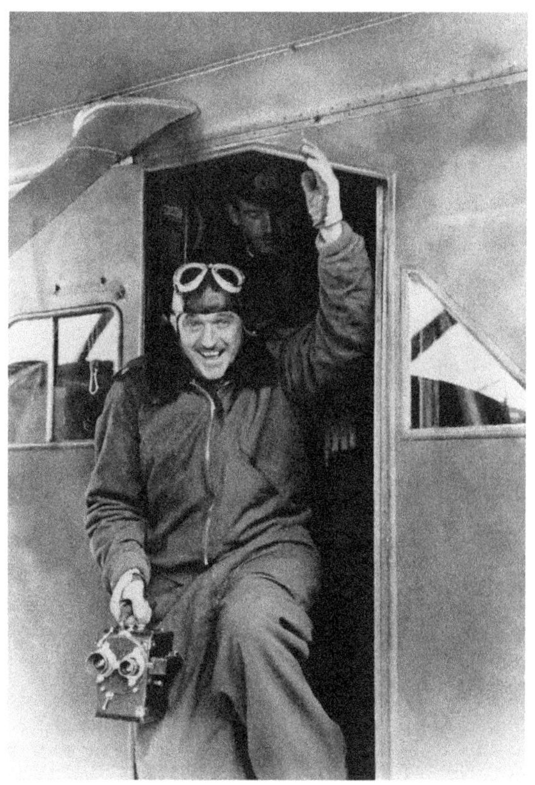

'Wieder Einmal Geschafft!' (Once More Accomplished!)

A German press photo dated 17 March 1941 spotlights an Italian airman (unnamed) carrying a large aerial photo-reconnaissance camera. The caption on the reverse reads: 'Italian fighters return from their successful enemy flight. The war correspondent with camera leaves the aircraft first and waves a joyful greeting to his comrades waiting on the ground.' While Hitler and Mussolini apparently shared a long friendship, the Italian leader often needed German rescue during several poorly planned campaigns and his troops were held in low regard by German forces. At one point Hitler ordered commandos to rescue Mussolini from captivity, but after Mussolini's overthrow and Italy's withdrawal from the war, Italian soldiers would be murdered in large numbers or enslaved by their former allies.

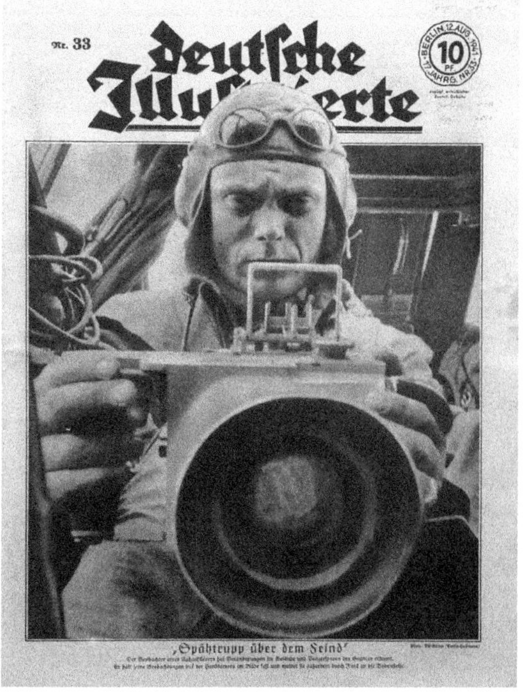

All-Seeing Luftwaffe Eye in the Sky

The cover image for the 12 August 1941 issue of the Berlin-published *German Illustrated* features a Luftwaffe airman with an aerial camera. In this month the German summer invasion of the Soviet Union swept forward, crushing whole Russian armies. At this point the Germans were occupying Estonia, the country renamed Ostland when assimilated into the Third Reich.

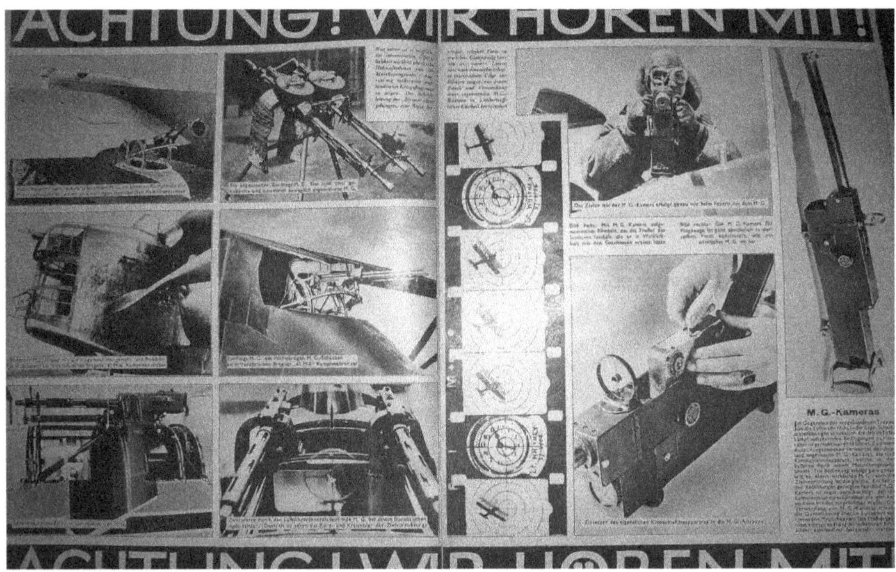

Attention! We are Monitoring!
Describing a variety of designs, a photo feature on aerial cameras and photo reconnaissance appeared in a September 1934 issue of a German Air Ministry journal.

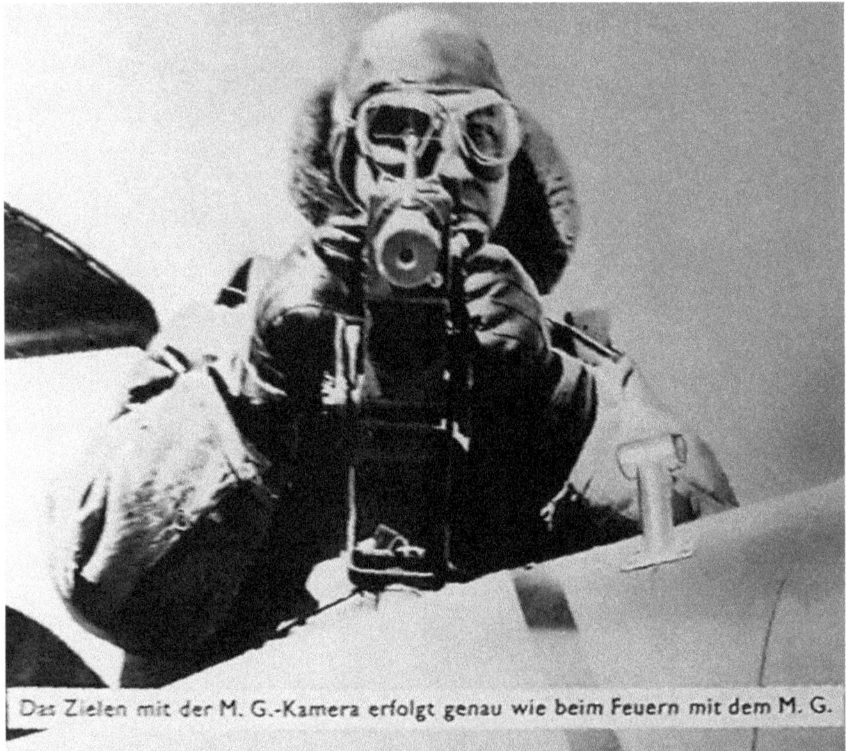

Cameras Fire with the Machine Gun

Photo Postscript

Addenda – Non-German Cameras/Non-German Cameramen

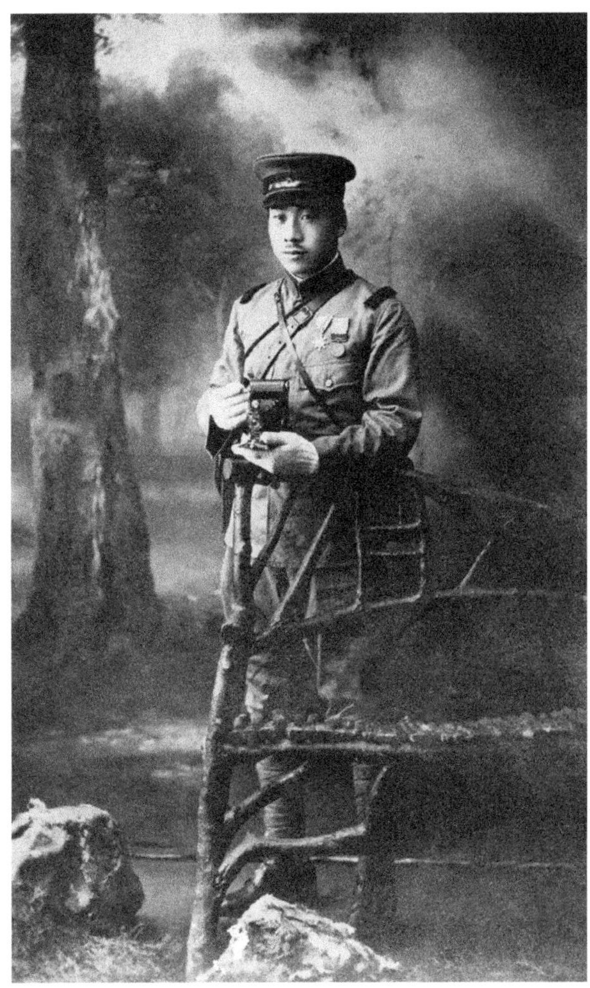

Early 1900s Studio Portrait –
Decorated Japanese Soldier Holds
his Prized Camera

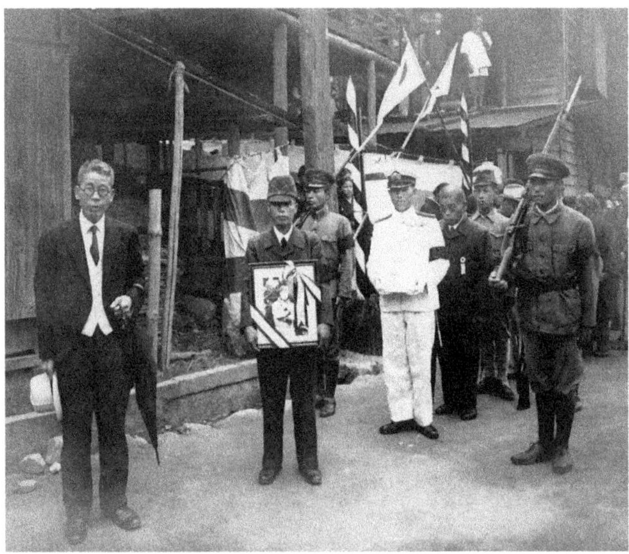

Funeral Procession with Photograph
A father clutching his prayer beads and an umbrella pauses during a funeral procession, his pilot son's photo presented to the camera. A naval officer carries the dead man's ashes in the traditional white box, hundreds of thousands of which would be returned to Japan during the war that had begun in 1931 with the attack on Manchuria. While the war with the United States would last three years and eight months, Japan was locked in warfare for fourteen years, during which some 1.7 million of its Imperial soldiers died, as did over 1 million Japanese civilians. Intense indoctrination had permeated both the military and civilian population, motivating them to sacrifice all for emperor and country. As the war ground on, Japan's cities incinerated, starvation ravaging the country and with surrender an unendurable disgrace avoidable only by suicide, the average Japanese became 'socialised with death' as the only outcome of the war until the atomic bomb convinced Emperor Hirohito to ask his countrymen to 'endure the unendurable' when announcing the end of the war and surrender.

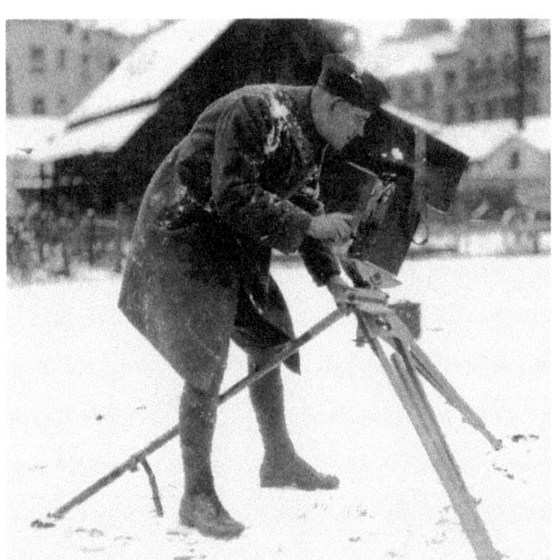

American Cameraman in Germany, Winter 1918
His Kodak mounted in the snow on a heavy-duty tripod, the US soldier is using a 'key' to hand-crank the movie camera sometime after the First World War ended with the defeat of Germany and its allies.

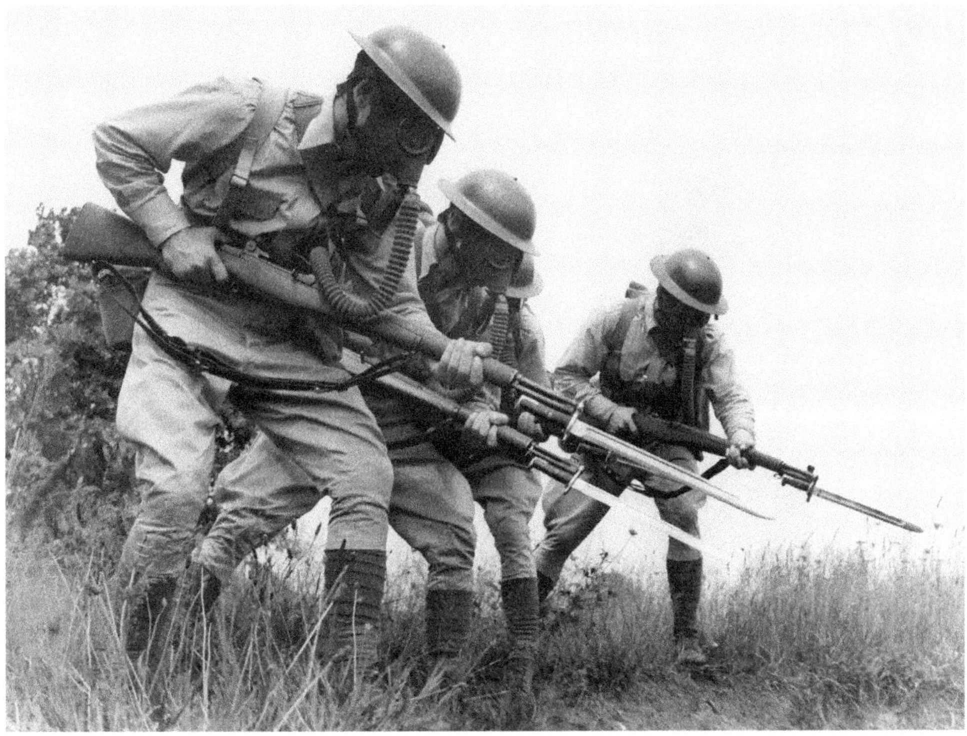

Another War – Milestone 'Mystery' Rifle, 15 July 1938
Pre-war, US newspapers published this dramatic image, introducing the public to the revolutionary new Garand M1 .30 caliber semi-automatic rifle, which was described as a 'shot a minute war winner'. The caption accompanying the photo further stated: 'Strategists say the gun will increase destruction power of the present army by five-fold.' The weapon lived up to its reputation and was later considered a deciding factor in the Second World War, with its eight shots per clip superior to the slower bolt-action, single-action German Mauser standard rifle. Some 5.4 million would be produced during the war at a cost of $1,250 each in 2017 dollars.

'Photography Forbidden Throughout the Premises'

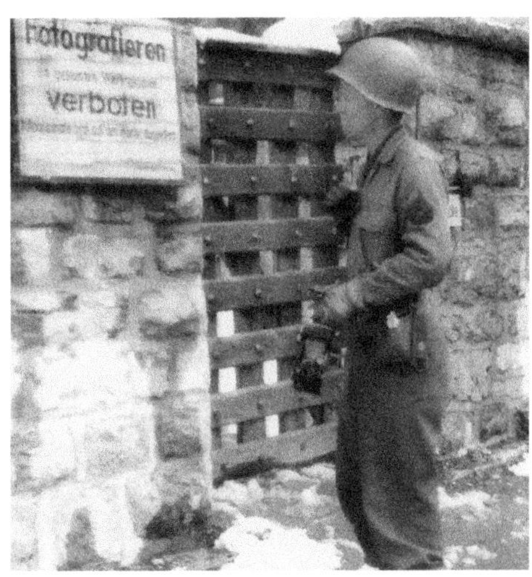

A US Army Tech corporal holding a Kodak folding camera ponders the warning of a sign attached to a wartime German installation. Three 'jerry cans' are visible, topped off by snow, indicating the time frame as the winter of 1944. On 11 September 1944 the first American troops crossed into Nazi Germany. While the milestone moment is in question, the generally accepted claim goes to members of a reconnaissance squadron of the 5th Armored Division (including one French officer) when they crossed the River Our near the hamlet of Gmuend. They met no resistance, although that would change drastically as the Allies fought their way into the Nazi heartland.

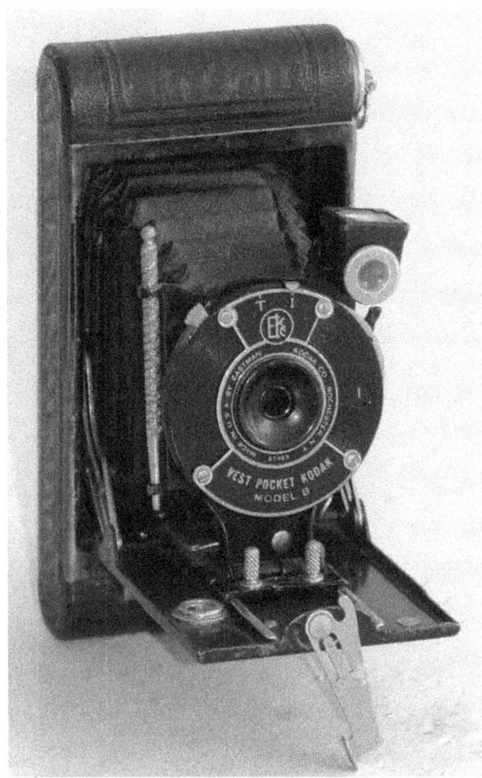

Kodak Vest Pocket Model B, 1926

Eastman Kodak introduced the first 'Autographic' Vest Pocket Kodak in 1915. As its film was the twenty-seventh in the various film formats developed, it was designated 127. The camera's original design was invented by American Harry Gaisman, from whom Kodak bought the rights for what was then an astounding $300,000. The camera was then redesigned to use Kodak autographic film, which could be marked with the metal stylus that came clipped to front of the camera, marking directly on the exposed negative through the back of the camera. As the First World War started and camera sales boomed, it was marketed as 'The Soldier's Kodak', the ad copy suggesting 'Make your own picture of the War'. By 1915 over 30,000 were sold in Britain alone.

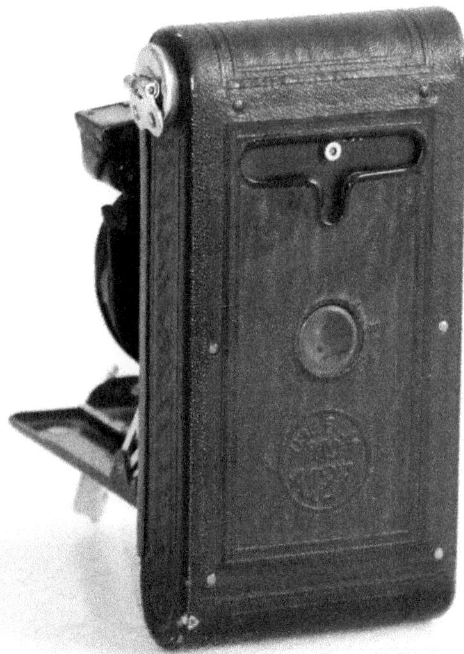

Notable Feature

The rear panel features a slide that lowers revealing a space to etch notes on the film, an early effort at photo dating. The center spot (red) is a window showing the number of exposures.

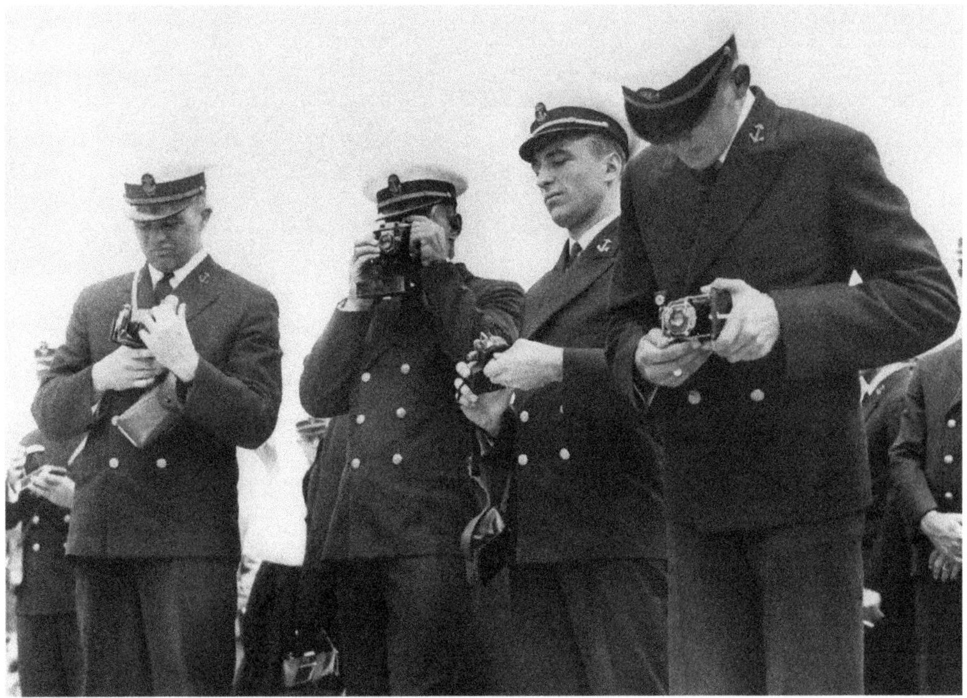

US Navy officers with Personal Cameras, 1940
Three of the sailors appear to be equipped with various Kodak cameras including a Vest Pocket while one (second from right) is winding his very compact Univex 8 mm cine camera. While war was raging in the Europe from 1939, America would not join the conflict until the end of 1941 after the Japanese attack on Pearl Harbor and the beginning of the Pacific War. Americans would first engage German troops in North Africa in November 1942 while the first combat forces landed in Europe during the Allied invasion of the Italian island of Sicily in July 1943, then again in June 1944 with the Allied invasion of Normandy.

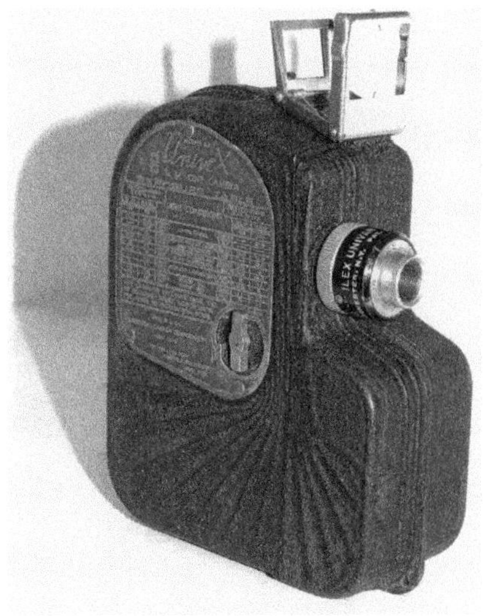

Univex Model A8 Cine Camera, *c.* 1936–39
Considered the smallest movie camera of its time, it measured 4⅛ inches high, 35⁵⁄₁₆ inches wide and 1½ inches thick. With its art deco styling, the Univex was a product of Universal Camera Corp. of New York.

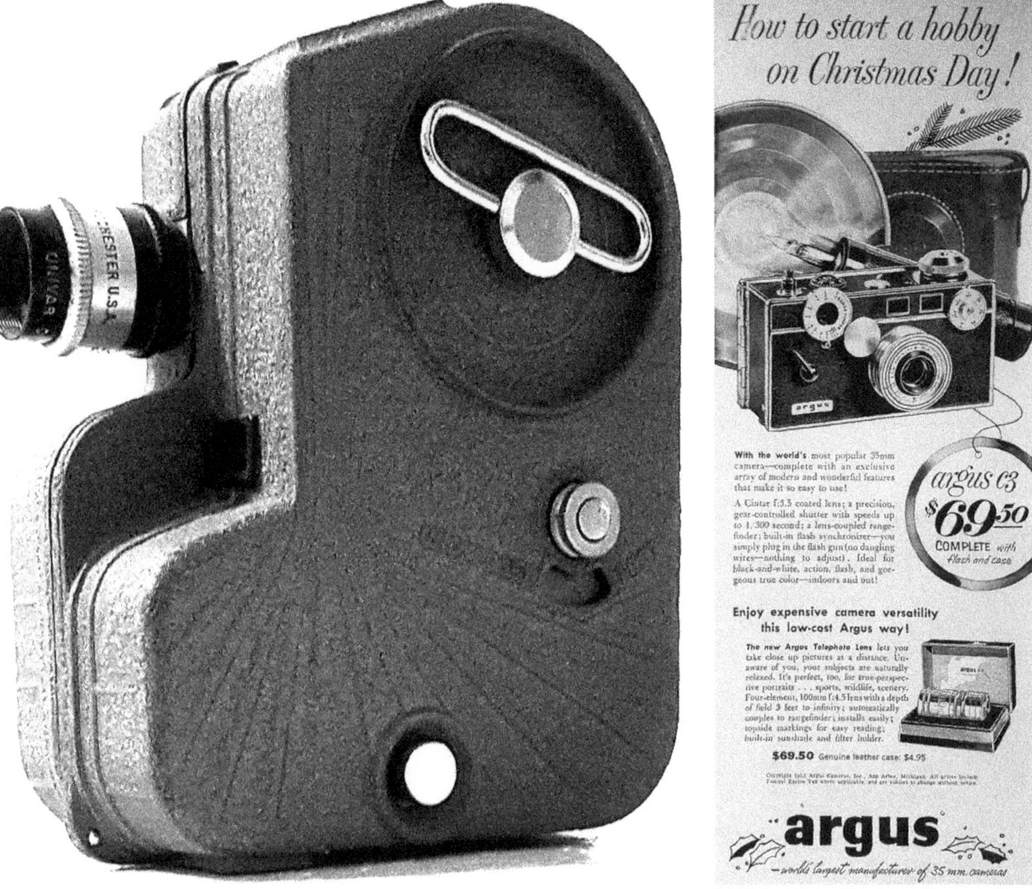

Above left: **Wind and Shoot**
While its motor was spring-wound, the body was tank-tough, made from zinc with internals of stainless steel, brass and aluminium. The Univex also featured the company's Universal F/5.6 lens while its simple viewfinder could be folded down as seen when not in use.

Above right: 'World's Most Popular 35 mm Camera'.

Opposite above: 'The Brick' – Argus C-3 Chronicles the War
First introduced in 1938, many of these simple, ruggedly designed and constructed 35 mm cameras went into service with American soldiers/photographers. Produced by the Argus camera company of Ann Arbor, Michigan, some 2 million cameras were sold during its twenty-seven-year manufacturing life. Best known of its users was Tony Vaccaro, who recorded his battlefield experience as a twenty-one-year-old member of the US Army Signal Corps serving with the 83rd Division in Europe (1944–45). It was decades later that he rediscovered the original negatives, as many as 8,000 having been originally taken and developed in his battle helmet 'developing tank'. An exhibition of the photos was recently shown, and also resulted in the production of a 2016 documentary film titled *Under Fire: The Untold Story of Pfc. Tony Vaccaro*. As of March 2018, Tony, who had post-war become a well-established fashion photographer, was still going strong and operating a gallery in Brooklyn, NY.

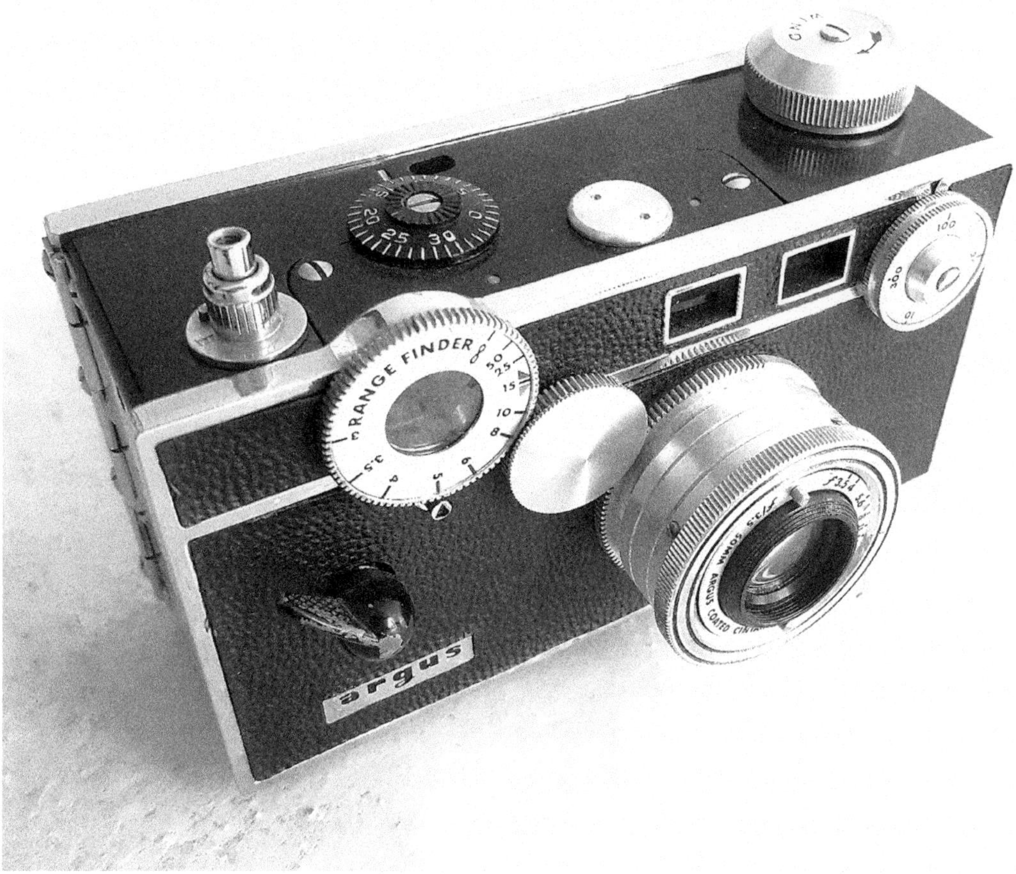

Kodak Medalist, 1941
Another Second World War era camera referred to as tank-tough was the Kodak Medalist, which some touted as the 'American Leica', in part due to its use of aluminum and steel, which were both in limited wartime supply. Credit for its design goes to Walter Dorwin Teague, a pioneering industrial designer of cameras, cars, radios, airplanes, Steinway pianos, glassware and military missiles for starters. In 1927 he began designing for Kodak, and later for Polaroid. Perhaps he chose the name Medalist because it deserved one.

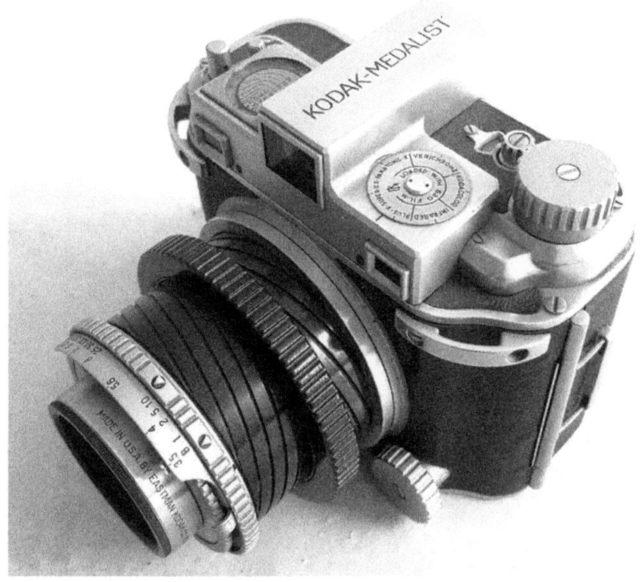

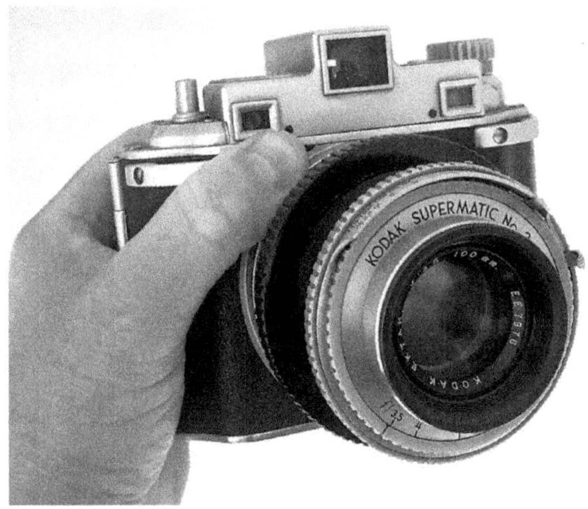

Kodak Ektar 100 mm F/3.5 Lens Captured the Action
Distinctive design elements of the relatively massive handheld camera included its helical focusing, allowing for sharp focus from infinity to 3 feet. Film types available included black and white, color and infrared. The Kodak Supermatic No. 2 refers to the Medalist's special shutter.

War Documentary Award Winner – DeVry Cameras

Appearing in an issue of the British *Illustrated Weekly*, the ad touts the accomplishments of the DeVry motion picture cameras in the filming of the *Desert Victory* documentary chronicling the British 8th Army's famous 1943 victory at El Alamein against General Erwin 'The Desert Fox' Rommel of the vaunted German *Afrika Korps*.

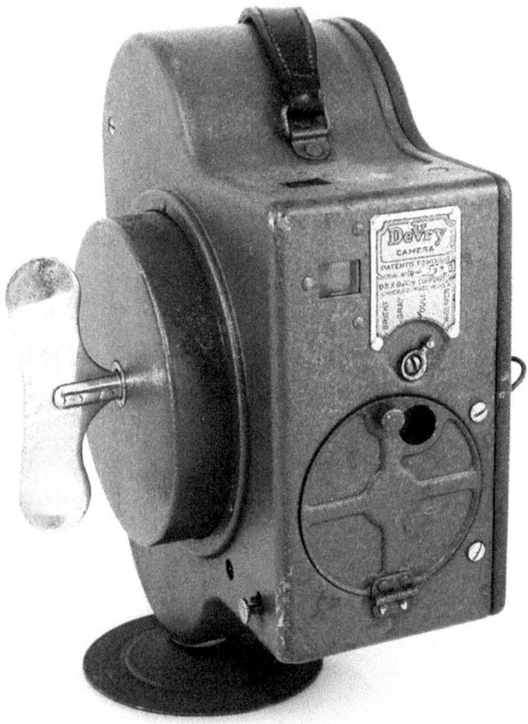

Ahead of its Time – DeVry Camera/ Projector
In 1928 the QRS Music Company of Chicago, makers of radios, tubes and speakers, ventured into the new home movie market. A year later the company merged with the DeVry Camera Corporation, resulting in this hand-cranked 16 mm combination movie camera and projector. Designated the QRS-Model B, it soon carried the DeVry logo. A flick of the switch converted it from a movie camera to a projector, but the company soon dropped the camera component and sold it as only the projector version.

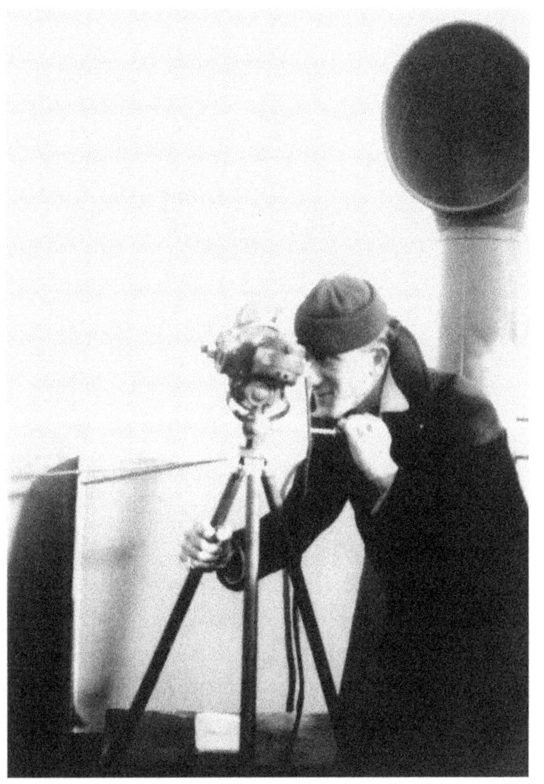

US Sailor with Bell & Howell Filmo 16 mm
The camera has been fitted with the optional electric motor drive, allowing for continuously filming without needing to hand-wind the camera. Second World War era B&H ad copy read: 'Filmo motion picture equipment is in the thick of the fight on all fronts of this global war. It is cutting many hours off training time. It is providing priceless hours of essential relaxation. It is saving countless lives by making it possible for American armed forces to learn the right way-without having to learn the hard way!'.

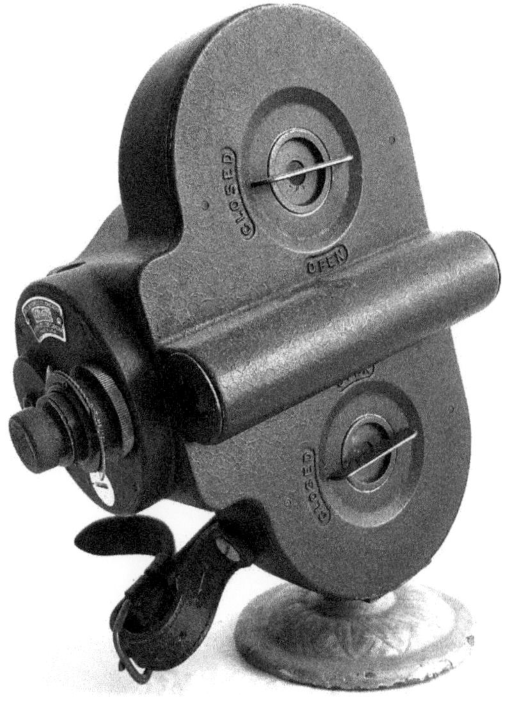

B&W Filmo – 1930s
The early model came standard with Hobson Cooke 1-inch F/3.5 lens. Twin handles unlock the panel to reveal the film reservoir. The external tube shape houses the camera's viewfinder.

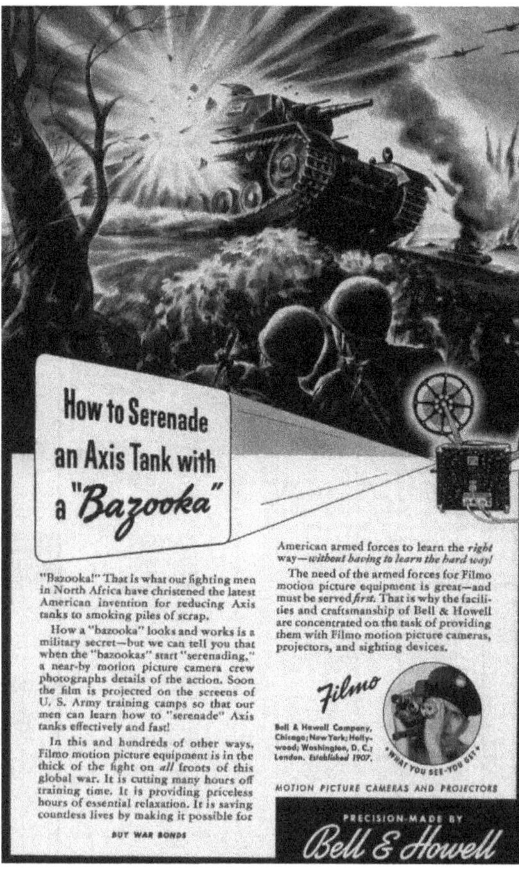

1943 Magazine Ad – Bazookas and Bell & Howell
While the B&H ad describes the devastating new weapon in the US arsenal, it does not actually show it, but rather what appears to be a flamethrower team, the canister just visible. The ad's principal focus is extolling the virtues of the Bell & Howell Filmo movie camera as a military training aid.

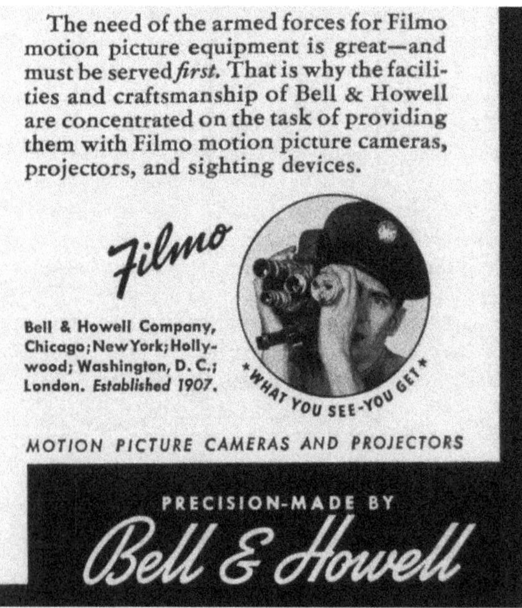

Serving the War Effort
'"Bazooka!" That is what our fighting men in North Africa have christened the latest American invention for reducing Axis tanks to smoking piles of scrap. How a "bazooka" looks and works is a military secret-but we can tell you that when the "bazookas" start "serenading", a nearby motion picture camera crew photographs details of the action. Soon the film is projected on the screens of US Army training camps so that our men can learn how to "serenade" Axis tanks effectively and fast!'

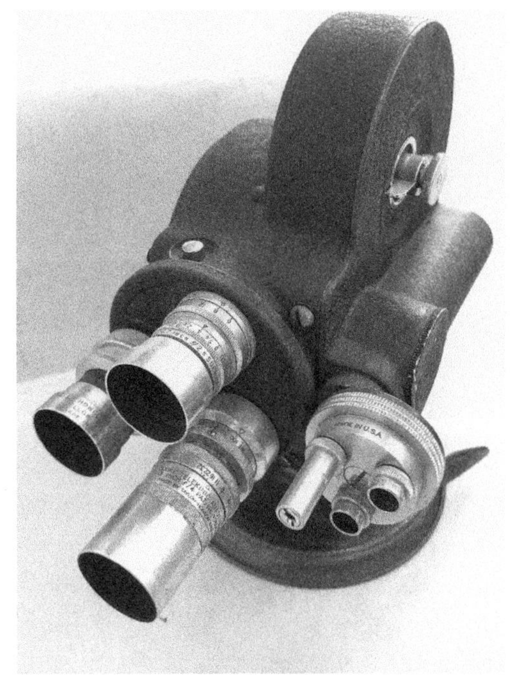

Bell & Howell 16 mm Filmo D Cine Camera – Turret Lenses

As tough as a US Sherman or even a Russian T34 tank, the Second World War era Filmo was a heavy, combat-hardened movie camera that was very popular with war correspondents. The newer model featured triple turret-mounted normal, wide-angle and telephoto lenses as well as side-by-side integrated viewfinders. Twin keys unlocked the compartment for inserting a 50-foot film cassette, while later models could be adapted to 100-foot magazines. An attached leather hand strap offered some support while a longer shoulder strap was also included.

Triple Turret Turning Point: America's Milestone Military Camera

The Filmo cameras were sold with a life-time guarantee – perhaps not factoring in world wars and their use in aerial reconnaissance through flak-filled skies.

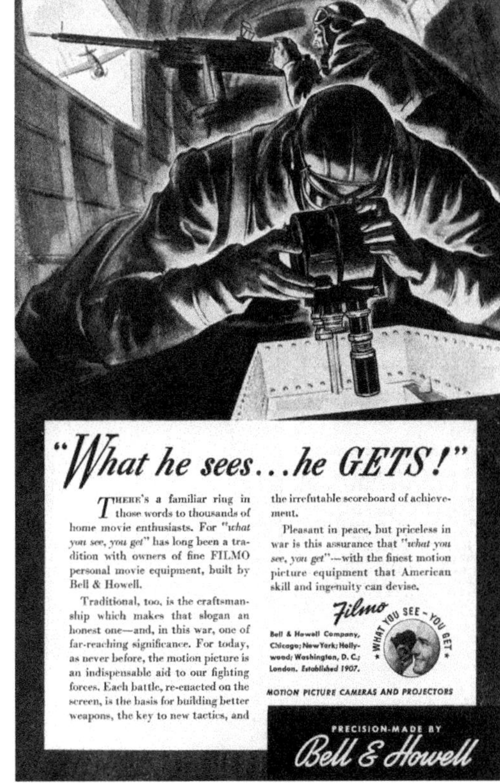

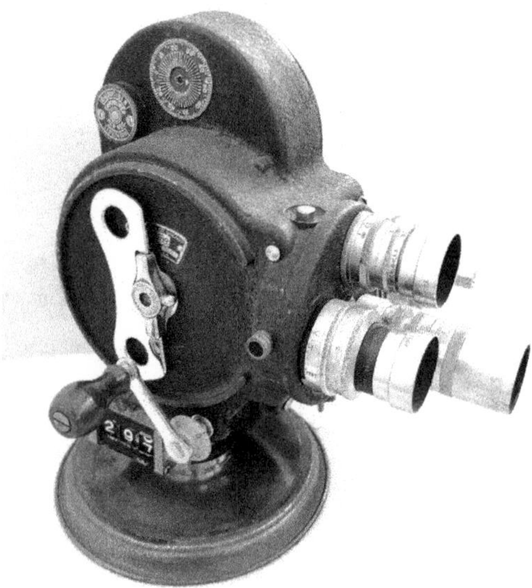

Optional Film Counter
The B&H Filmo offered a host of accessories, including electric motor drive and larger capacity film attachments. While early models required manual alignment of viewfinders with lens choices, later editions featured an 'automatic' integration of finder and lens via a cogged wheel interface. This version also features an additional footage counter and auxiliary fast-action crank.

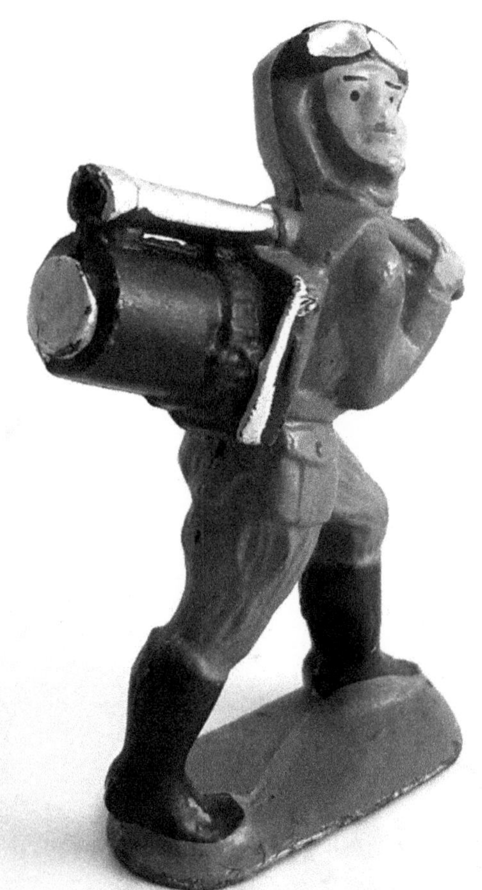

'Camera Carrier' – Manoil Catalog #115
This rare vintage figure of a military aviator is depicted carrying a large aerial photo-reconnaissance camera. Among the US toy soldier manufacturers, the Manoil company was described as 'the most realistic, the most vivid and the most jaunty'. Founded in 1927 by brothers Jack and Maurice Manoil and Canadian designer-sculptor Walter Baetz, by 1940 the Brooklyn-based company was producing an amazing 80,000 toys of various kinds on a daily basis.

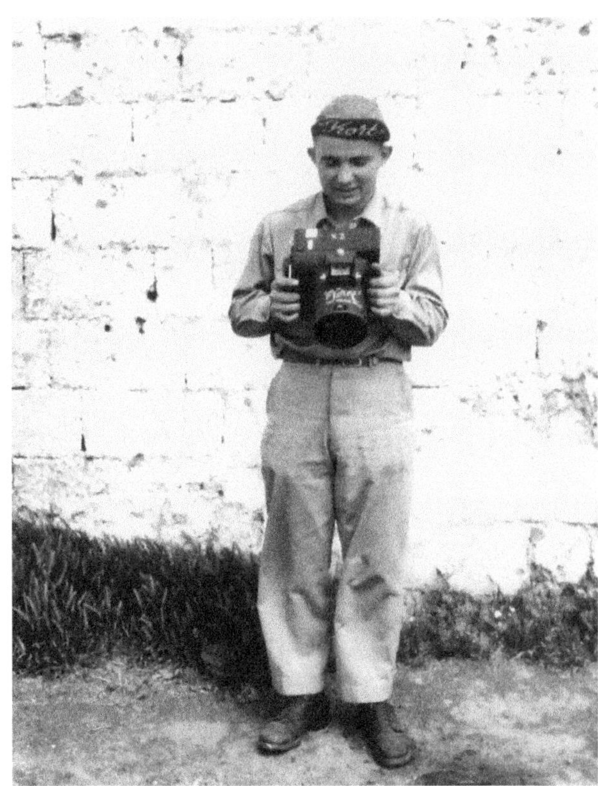

Second World War US Cameraman Kort with K20 Aerial Camera

Folmer Graflex K-20 Aircraft Aerial US Navy Camera
The K-20 aerial camera was designed by the Fairchild Camera & Instrument Company to US Government specifications. Completely manual in operation with no electrical connections, it was exceptionally reliable. Approximately 15,000 were also manufactured under license for military contract by the Folmer Graflex Corporation in Rochester, NY, between 1941 and 1945. Most US and other Allied air force and navy bombers were equipped with them.

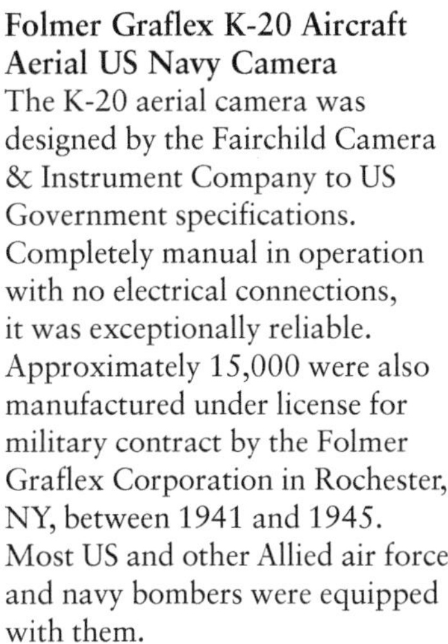

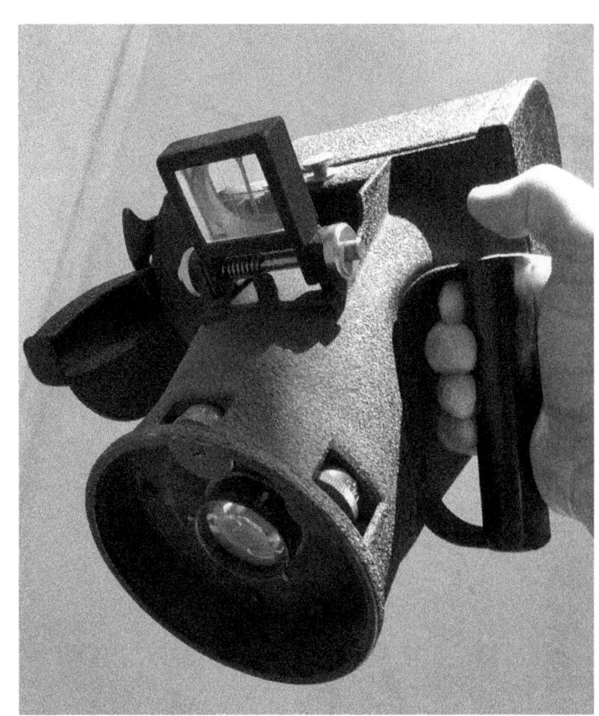

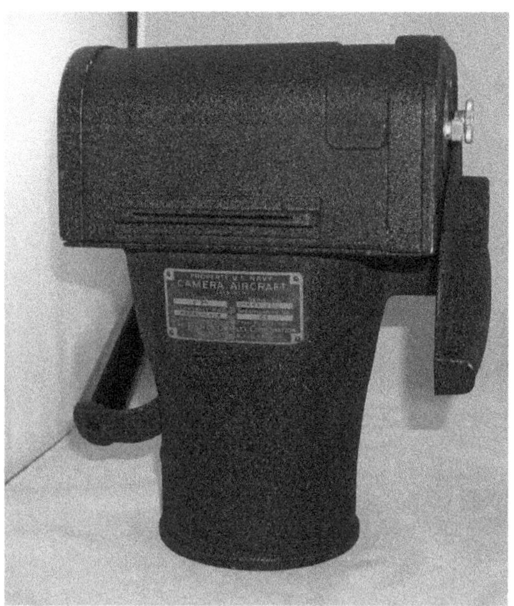

As Rugged as the Planes that Carried Them into Battle
A K-20 was aboard the *Enola Gay* A-Bomb aircraft, operated by its tail gunner where it captured the iconic image of the mushroom cloud rising over Hiroshima. The K-20 can take a 5.25x20-foot film roll of special roll film providing dozens of high-resolution 4x5-inch negatives. Made by Kodak, Ilex or Bausch & Lomb, the non-interchangeable lens was a 6⅜-inch F/4.5, incorporating an adjustable diaphragm.

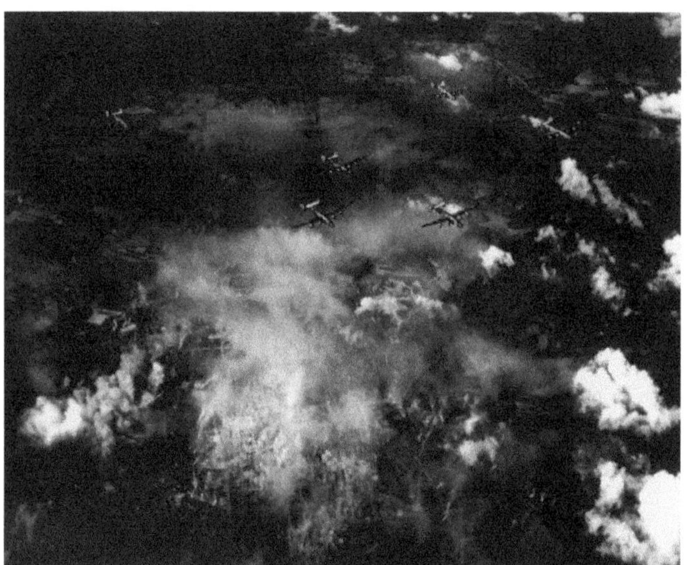

Original Bombing Run Photo, 1944 – Auschwitz Untouched
US Flying Fortresses pass over Auschwitz concentration camp as documented by a photo taken by the aforementioned aerial photographer Kort. No bombs were ever dropped on the site despite the fact that the Allies were well aware of the industrialised mass murder in progress. Official explanations included that more strategic military targets had priority. More cynical observers suggested the Allies counted on the Germans tying up their train system in their fanatical efforts to continue the exterminations even at the expense of wartime rail transport needs – and they were correct. Post-war, survivors of Auschwitz testified they had prayed for the bombs to fall on them, and in addition had managed to send messages to the West begging for bombs to fall to stop the carnage, but to no avail.

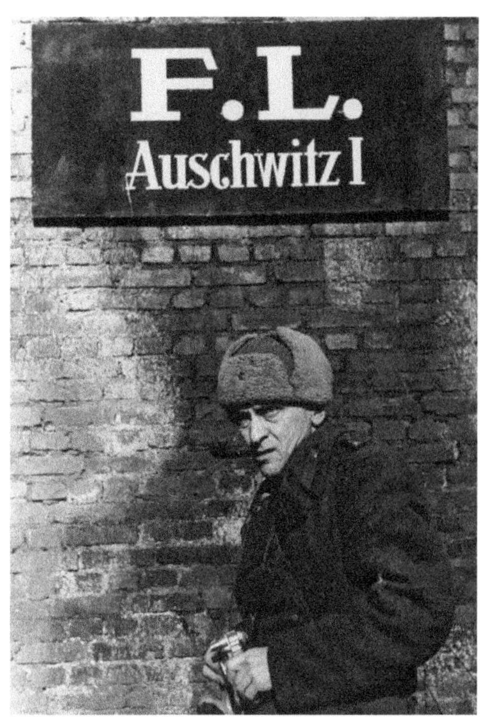

Ground-Level with Auschwitz

A Russian Army war correspondent poses at the infamous camp, his camera apparently a German Leica. Soviet forces liberated many of the concentration camps as they fought westward through Eastern Europe on their way to Nazi Germany. Auschwitz-Birkenau, located in Poland, was composed of both a Death Camp and sections focused on slave labor and processing the mountain of belongings taken from the prisoners as they arrived by train. Within moments, they would be forced into gas chambers.

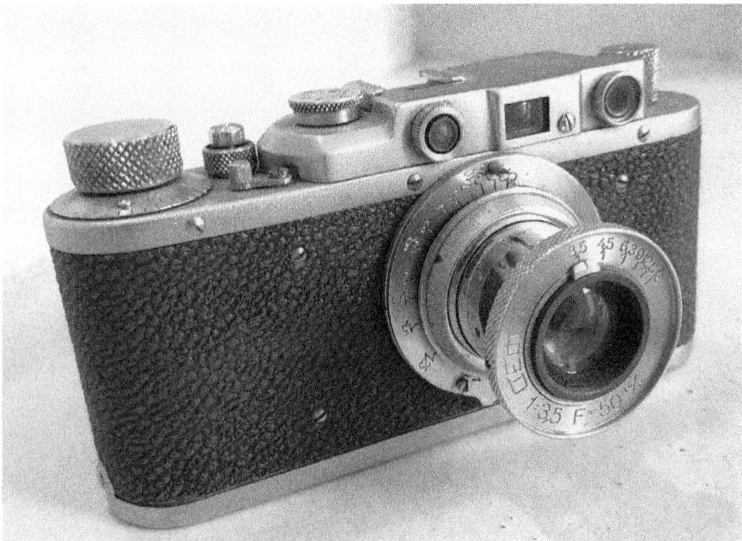

Russian Leica 'Clone'

At first glance the FED/Zorki can be mistaken for the classic 1930s German 35 mm, but closer inspection reveals Russian Cyrillic lettering. Its inscription indicates it was made at a Russian secret police factory for use by its agents. The cloning of these Leica copies began in 1934. The 'FED' designation is derived from the initials of Felix Edmundovich Dzerzhinsky, the founder of the Soviet secret police. The FED-1 (*c.* 1934–55) was the earliest successful Leica II(D) copy, and the only one achieving any measure of success before the Second World War.

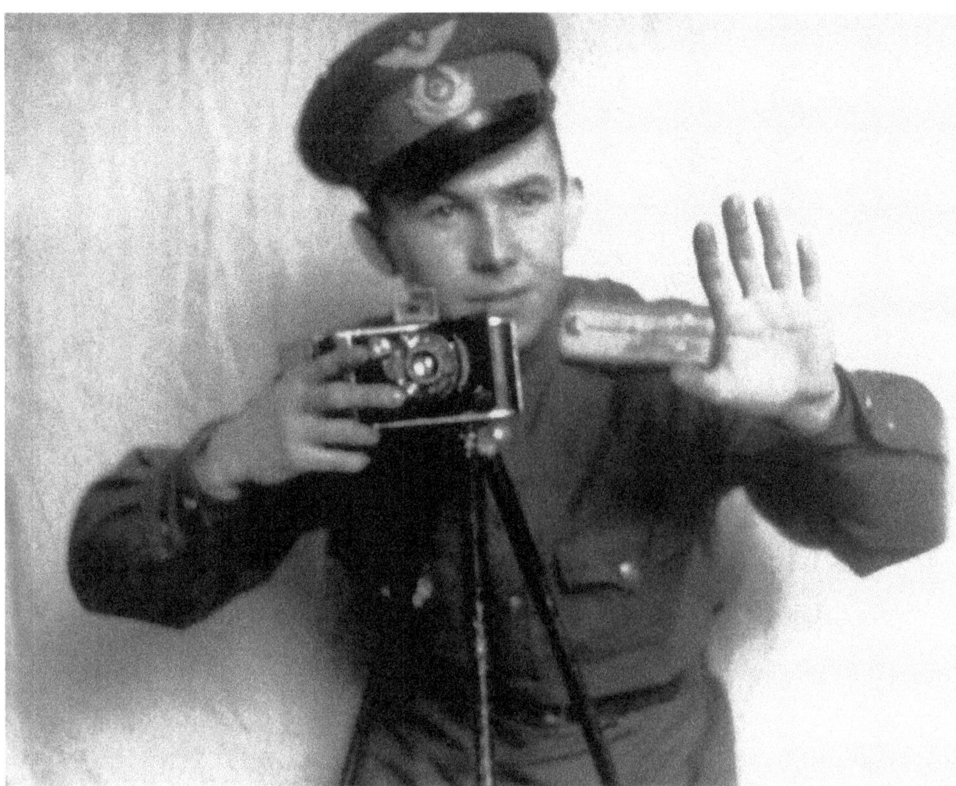

Red Army Photographer Self-Portrait
The photographer relies on an older strut-folding camera. His uniform shoulder boards indicate he is a member of the military secret police. Unlike German troops, regular Red Army soldiers were not allowed to use cameras without permission.